DISPOSSESSION AND THE ENVIRONMENT

LEONARD HASTINGS SCHOFF MEMORIAL LECTURES

University Seminars
Leonard Hastings Schoff Memorial Lectures

The University Seminars at Columbia University sponsor an annual series of lectures, with the support of the Leonard Hastings Schoff and Suzanne Levick Schoff Memorial Fund. A member of the Columbia faculty is invited to deliver before a general audience three lectures on a topic of his or her choosing. Columbia University Press publishes the lectures.

Charles Larmore, *The Romantic Legacy*   1996
Saskia Sassen, *Losing Control? Sovereignty in the Age of Globalization*   1996
David Cannadine, *The Rise and Fall of Class in Britain*   1999
Ira Katznelson, *Desolation and Enlightenment: Political Knowledge After Total War, Totalitarianism, and the Holocaust*   2003
Lisa Anderson, *Pursuing Truth, Exercising Power: Social Science and Public Policy in the Twenty-First Century*   2003
Partha Chatterjee, *The Politics of the Governed: Reflections on Popular Politics in Most of the World*   2004
David Rosand, *The Invention of Painting in America*   2004
George Rupp, *Globalization Challenged: Conviction, Conflict, Community*   2006
Lesley A. Sharp, *Bodies, Commodities, and Biotechnologies: Death, Mourning, and Scientific Desire in the Realm of Human Organ Transfer*   2007
Robert W. Hanning, *Serious Play: Desire and Authority in the Poetry of Ovid, Chaucer, and Ariosto*   2010
Boris Gasparov, *Beyond Pure Reason: Ferdinand de Saussure's Philosophy of Language and Its Early Romantic Antecedents*   2012
Douglas A. Chalmers, *Reforming Democracies: Six Facts About Politics That Demand a New Agenda*   2013
Philip Kitcher, *Deaths in Venice: The Cases of Gustav von Aschenbach*   2013
Robert L. Belknap, *Plots*   2016

DISPOSSESSION AND THE ENVIRONMENT

Rhetoric and Inequality in Papua New Guinea

Paige West

Columbia University Press ᨒ New York

Columbia University Press
Publishers Since 1893
New York   Chichester, West Sussex

cup.columbia.edu

An earlier version of chapter 1 was published as "'Such A Site for Play,
This Edge': Surfing, Tourism and Modernist Fantasy in Papua New Guinea"
in *Global Sport in the Pacific*, ed. Fa'anofo Lisaclaire Uperesa and Tom Mountjoy.
Special issue of *The Contemporary Pacific* 26, no. 2 (2014). Reprinted with
permission of the University of Hawaii.

"The Blackest Crow" (trad.) as performed by Laurie Lewis © 2002 Spruce
and Maple Music, from the album Birdsong.

Library of Congress Cataloging-in-Publication Data
Names: West, Paige, 1969- author.
Title: Dispossession and the environment : rhetoric and inequality in Papua
    New Guinea / Paige West.
Description: New York : Columbia University Press, [2016] | Series: Leonard
    Hastings Schoff lectures | Includes bibliographical references and index.
Identifiers: LCCN 2016008164| ISBN 9780231178785 (cloth : acid-free paper) |
    ISBN 9780231178792 (pbk. : acid-free paper) | ISBN 9780231541923 (e-book)
Subjects: LCSH: Ethnology—Papua New Guinea. | Indigenous
    peoples—Ecology—Papua New Guinea. | Indigenous peoples—
    Papua New Guinea—Social conditions. | Papua New Guinea—
    Social conditions. | Papua New Guinea—Environmental conditions.
Classification: LCC DU740.42 .W643 2016 | DDC 305.8009953–dc23
LC record available at https://lccn.loc.gov/2016008164

Cover design: Rebecca Lown
Cover image: Photograph by J.C. Salyer

For Liam Tiso Irunei, Solomon Aini, Vincentia Aini,
Jasmine Aini, and Jeremiah Aini, who all call me aunty
and in doing so make me want to make a better world.

Contents

Acknowledgments

The essays in this book are based on research conducted in Papua New Guinea between 1997 and 2015. My biggest debt is to the Gimi-speaking people, with whom I have worked continuously during this time, and the people living in New Ireland Province, with whom I have worked since 2007. I can't ever give back what these people have given me—they have given me my life, for my life is fully intertwined with my work as a professor and a scholar of Papua New Guinea. And I am a tenured, full professor of anthropology because I have published books and papers, given talks and seminars, concerned with the lives of these people in Papua New Guinea. Thank you, to all of you.

I also want to thank my colleagues at the Papua New Guinea Institute of Biological Research and Ailan Awareness. I especially want to thank my friends—people who have become more like family than anything else—Miriam Supuma, John Aini, Banak Gamui, Anna Koki, Onika Okena, Kamena Yoriene, Sisera Kamena, Muse Opiang, Enock Kale, Katayo Sagata, Debra Wright, and Andrew Mack. Miriam Supuma and John Aini are the sister and brother I never really had before, and that means everything to me. I am grateful as well to all of our students over the years and all of the researchers who have come in and out of the offices of these two amazing organizations. Paul Igag, one of the co-founders of PNG

IBR, who passed away recently, was an inspiration. Finally, in Papua New Guinea, I want to thank Mal Smith, Jim Robbins, Kevin Smith, Shaun and Shannon Keene, Ian Tong, Hugh Walton, Dani and Adam Smith, and Karyn Allen and Peter van den Heuvel.

Professionally I have too many wonderful colleagues and students to list everyone to whom I owe a debt of gratitude. Jerry Jacka, Jamon Halvaksz, Joshua Bell, and David Lipset all make my thinking about Papua New Guinea better and sharper. Additionally, through their friendship they provide a haven in the often-strange labyrinth that is professionalized anthropology. Fa'anofo Lisaclaire Uperesa, Adriana Garriga-López, Danielle DiNovelli-Lang, Ariela Zycherman, Elizabeth Nichols, Leo R. Douglas, Georgian Cullman, Jessica Barnes, Ann Iwashita, Scott Freeman, Nina Alnes Haslie, Arthur Laurent, and Patrick Nason, all former or current PhD students, have made me a better more careful thinker through our work together. Dorothy L. Hodgson has been my mentor since 2005, when she took me on as a graduate student. She has also been a friend, a colleague, and an endless source of advice and support. I thank her with all of my head and heart. I also want to thank Danielle Dinovelli-Lang, Jerry Jacka, Molly Doane, Joshua Bell, Andy Bickford, and G. S. Quid for their wonderful readings of this book in its manuscript form, the book is so much better because of their careful comments. At Barnard and Columbia, in the department of anthropology I want to thank my colleagues and friends for encouraging me to be a careful scholar and for the past decade and a half of lively conversations and hilarious interactions. I can't list them all here but I can say that I love and respect each of them and that I think the BC/CU anthropology world is extraordinary. Thanks also to Josephine Kovacs for her editorial help on this project.

These essays were presented in various forms as lectures at: Columbia University (the Leonard Hastings Schoff Memorial Lectures), the University of Goroka (Papua New Guinea), Duke University's Marine Laboratory, the American Museum of Natural History, the Field Museum, the National Museum of Natural History at the Smithsonian, the University of Minnesota, Bergen University (Norway), Aarhus University (Denmark), the Australian National University, the University of Texas at San Antonio, Yale University, the University of Toronto, the National Museum of Natural History (Paris), Temple University, Wesleyan University, the University of California, Santa Barbara, the University of Hawai'i, Manoa, and New York University. I thank all of these institutions for the invitation to share my work with some of their faculty and students and everyone who came to the lectures and gave me valuable feedback. I want to especially thank David Hajdu and Alisa Solomon from the Columbia University School of Journalism. For the past decade I have been giving a series of guest lectures in their Arts and Culture MA program required seminar. Those lectures have allowed me to think about the issues presented in this book over the course of a long period of time with a group of wonderful students and colleagues.

At Columbia, I also want to thank the directors and staff of The University Seminars at Columbia University: Robert Pollack, Alice Newton, Pamela Guardia, Summer Hart, and Gessy Alvarez-Lazauskas. Robert Pollack, in particular, has been a wonderful friend and mentor and although I know it will embarrass him, I want to be like Bob when I grow up. He is a scholar and a thinker and a leader in so many ways. At Columbia University Press I would like to thank Anne Routon, Miriam Grossman, and Glenn Perkins for their extraordinary editorial support

The research in Papua New Guinea on which many of these essays are based been funded by The Wenner-Gren Foundation, The Christensen Fund, Barnard College, Columbia University's Institute for Social and Economic Research and Policy (ISERP), National Geographic, and the Columbia University Center for Environmental Resource Conservation (CERC). I thank all of these institutions for funding my work. Additionally, I want to thank the National Research Institute of Papua New Guinea for vetting my projects and sponsoring me for a research visa for many years now. Georgia Kaipu deserves special thanks for helping so many of us do good work in her country.

As always, Patricia Henry West and J. C. Salyer deserve more thanks than I am able to articulate. My mother's trip to Papua New Guinea with me in 2007 was the beginning of her retired life as a bit of a traveler. She spent a month living with me in the Gimi-world and came to see why her child goes so far away every year. Her constant support of my choices and her utterly ridiculous sense of humor give me endless reserves of strength. J. C., my husband, is the best person I know. This book, and all of my work, benefits from discussions we have and insights he brings. Whether it is sitting in a café in Port Moresby, Papua New Guinea or sitting at the bar at Winnie's in New York City, he listens to me and thinks with me, and makes me a better person through his very being.

I wrote this book on land that belongs to Lenape people, a Native American group that numbered at least 15,000 in the mid-sixteenth century. My office building is about 805 meters from what was probably a seasonal encampment and about 400 meters from what was probably a trail that had been used for hundreds and hundreds of years by 1609, the date of the maps I'm drawing on for this. Lenape would have hunted spotted turtle, white-tailed deer, eastern gray squirrel, wood duck, and snapping turtles nearby. They would have gathered blackberry, serviceberry, chokeberry, Carolina Rose and Jack in the Pulpit in the coastal oak hickory forest that covered this landscape. And they may have seen beavers, eastern cottontails, muskrats, four species of bats, wolves, otters, bobcats, minks, mountain lions, grey fox, and black bears as they brought this landscape into being through their lives and labors. What happened to the Lenape between 1524 and today was, and is, dispossession. Given that the topic of this book is dispossession, it would be the worst of wrongs not to acknowledge the Lenape people who lived and loved this land for thousands of years before colonial contact, and their descendants who were forced to move west into what is now Ohio in 1758 and then, from there, to what is now Oklahoma in the 1860s, and their many descendants who are living today. I hope that my work with indigenous peoples in New Guinea, in some small way, honors Lenape peoples and their ongoing struggle with accumulation by dispossession.

For these chapters, I draw material from three previously published papers: " 'Such a Site for Play, This Edge': Surfing, Tourism, and Modernist Fantasy in Papua New Guinea," in *Global Sport in the Pacific*, ed. Fa'anofo Lisaclaire Uperesa and Tom Mountjoy, special issue of *Contemporary Pacific* 26.2(2014):411-432. "Scientific Tourism: Imagining, Experiencing, and Portraying Environment and Society in Papua New Guinea," *Current Anthropology* 49.4(2008):597–626; "Translation, Value, and Space: Theorizing an Ethnographic and Engaged Environmental Anthropology," *American Anthropologist* 107.4(2005):632–642. I wish to thank the journals for permission to reprint portions of those essays here.

Chapters 1, 2, and 4 were taken from the Leonard Hastings Schoff Memorial Lectures I delivered in 2013.

The maps in this book were drawn by Vin Dang and are the property of the author. The photographs in this book are provided by J. C. Salyer.

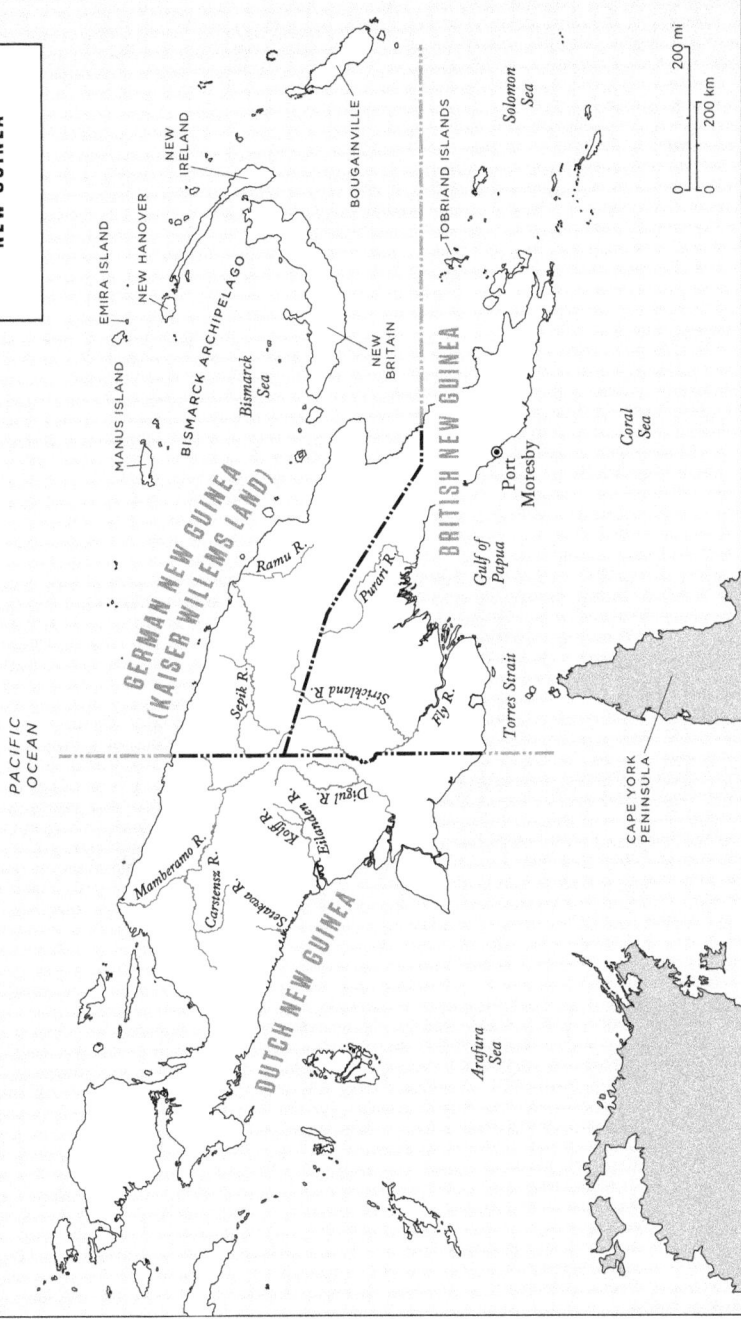

EARLY COLONIAL
BOUNDARIES OF
NEW GUINEA

PACIFIC
OCEAN

MANUS ISLAND

EMIRA ISLAND

NEW HANOVER

NEW
IRELAND

BISMARCK ARCHIPELAGO

Bismarck
Sea

NEW
BRITAIN

BOUGAINVILLE

Solomon
Sea

TOBRIAND ISLANDS

GERMAN NEW GUINEA
(KAISER WILLEMS LAND)

Ramu R.

Sepik R.

Purari R.

BRITISH NEW GUINEA

Port
Moresby

Gulf of
Papua

Coral
Sea

Strickland R.

Fly R.

Torres Strait

CAPE YORK
PENINSULA

Mamberamo R.

Carstensz R.

Setakwa R.

Eilanden R.

Kolff R.

Digul R.

DUTCH NEW GUINEA

Arafura
Sea

200 mi

200 km

0

DISPOSSESSION AND THE ENVIRONMENT

Introduction

This is a book about some of the ways inequalities are produced, lived, and reinforced in today's globalized world. In it I argue that there are deeply socially embedded rhetorics of representation that underlie all uneven development and that if we examine the various representational strategies we see every day, we can begin to develop a more robust understanding of the ideological work underpinning the differential economic climates that capital needs for its constant regeneration. Throughout, I attempt to show how representational strategies with regard to the social forms that have been called "nature" and "culture" are complex acts of dispossession and carefully crafted accumulation strategies as well as ideologically grounded attempts to persuade and motivate. It is a book of ethnographic essays, three of which were presented as the Leonard Hastings Schoff Memorial Lectures at Columbia University in the fall of 2013. The essays are based on my engagement with New Guinea, a place anthropologists have made famous and that has given anthropology some of its most enduring topics.

The island of New Guinea sits within the global region that has come to be known as "the Pacific." The Pacific Islands cover about 10,000 square kilometers of land and the Pacific Ocean covers approximately 165,250,000 square kilometers of water, making the combined area over one-third of the earth's surface. Even though the Pacific has risen to the center of foreign policy agendas of Western nations today (Clinton 2011; Petri et al. 2012), historically, the area has often fallen to the bottom of most European "hierarchies of knowledge" in terms of assumed political, economic, and social importance (Teaiwa 2006) and has been continually articulated through various colonial-era frames such as smallness, remoteness, and insularity by politicians and policy makers (Hau'ofa 1994). These ideas, combined with colonial-era racial science, resulted in the geographic containers "Melanesia," "Micronesia," and "Polynesia"— the "dark islands," the "small islands," and the "many islands," respectively (D'Urville 2003; see also Tcherkezoff 2003). The island of New Guinea is located in what is referred to as Melanesia.[1]

Humans have lived on New Guinea, the second largest island in the world, which sits directly to the north of the Australian continent, and its associated smaller islands for between 30,000 and 50,000 years, and the high mountain ranges that make up the central spine of the island, called "the Highlands," are the site of early and independent agricultural origins approximately 10,000 years ago (Bourke 2009). Although the mention of New Guinea often evokes images of a place cut off from the rest of the world, the island has a deep history of trade and connection with other areas. By the eighth century, much of the coast of Western New Guinea was enmeshed in Malay trading networks that moved bird of paradise plumes all the way to China and India.[2] By the twelfth century this same coast was part of the spice trade, which drew the Portuguese, Spanish, English, and Dutch to the region. By the early part of the sixteenth century various European powers were claiming to have discovered the island, with Spanish explorer Íñigo Ortíz de Retes bestowing the island with the name it is now known by in 1545. By the 1880s, as fashions in Europe began to demand more bird of paradise feathers for women's hats, the interior of New Guinea became part of an extensive trade network in animals and animal products (Swadling 1996). The colonial period began in earnest in terms of the alienation of land, labor, and natural resources on the island when the Dutch claimed the western half of the island in 1828; between then and 1975, the Dutch, Germans, British, and Australians all held parts of the island as colonial possessions (Waiko 2007; see also Moore 2003: chap. 5).

New Guinea boasts an extraordinary diversity of animals, plants, and ecosystems that has lured scientists who wish to discover, describe, possess, and conserve them since the early nineteenth century (Frodin 2007). At 786,000 kilometers square, it is less than one-half of one percent of the earth's surface, but it contains an estimated 10 percent of the total species on earth. Many of these species are endemic, found only on New Guinea. Terrestrially, New Guinea has montane rain forests, sub-alpine grasslands, mangrove forests, lowland rain forests, freshwater swamp forests, savannas, grasslands, and one of the world's last remaining tropical glaciers.

Today the island is split in half by an international border. The western half has been a settler colony for Indonesia since 1961 (Kirksey 2012). The eastern half of the island, the independent nation of Papua New Guinea, which established its sovereignty and achieved independence from Australia on September 16, 1975, is the focus of the essays in this book. Today Papua New Guinea is a parliamentary democracy with an elected national parliament and, through that parliament, a prime minister. It is a Commonwealth nation, meaning that it is part of an association of fifty-four countries that were part of the British colonial empire. The country is slightly bigger than California, with between seven and ten million residents who speak 850 different languages, making it the most linguistically diverse nation on earth. That diversity, which maps onto extraordinary social or ethnic diversity, has drawn anthropologists to the area for almost 150 years (Lederman 1998; Soukup 2010; Sillitoe 1998).

In *Imagining the Other: The Representations of the Papua New Guinea Subject*, Regis Tove Stella, a literary scholar from Bougainville, Papua New Guinea, writes about colonial representations of nature and culture in what is now Papua New Guinea. He shows us that the twinning of representational practices concerned with "the native" and "the jungle" has a deep history across Oceania and that when deployed by agents of colonial power, practices intertwine to set the conditions of possibility for seeing citizens, subjects, and space.[3] The representations of nature that Stella excavates from the colonial documents assume a world that is alluring and repulsive, romantic and dangerous; a world that is waiting to be discovered by intrepid white explorers. That world is desirable as a site for both discovery and self-discovery, yet it is nevertheless also a site where "white savagery" is prone to emerge unless measures that separate the explorer from the jungle and its natives are taken (Stella 2007:48–50). The fantasy jungle world written in colonial documents is home to savage primitives who are both childlike and overtly sexual; people who are exotic and dangerous, yet ridiculous in their unsophisticated lack of modern understandings (Stella 2007). Throughout his work Stella shows how these images structure colonial practice and the creation, and enforcement, of colonial law. He also demonstrates that these images presuppose and underpin the creation of the colonial economy and the means

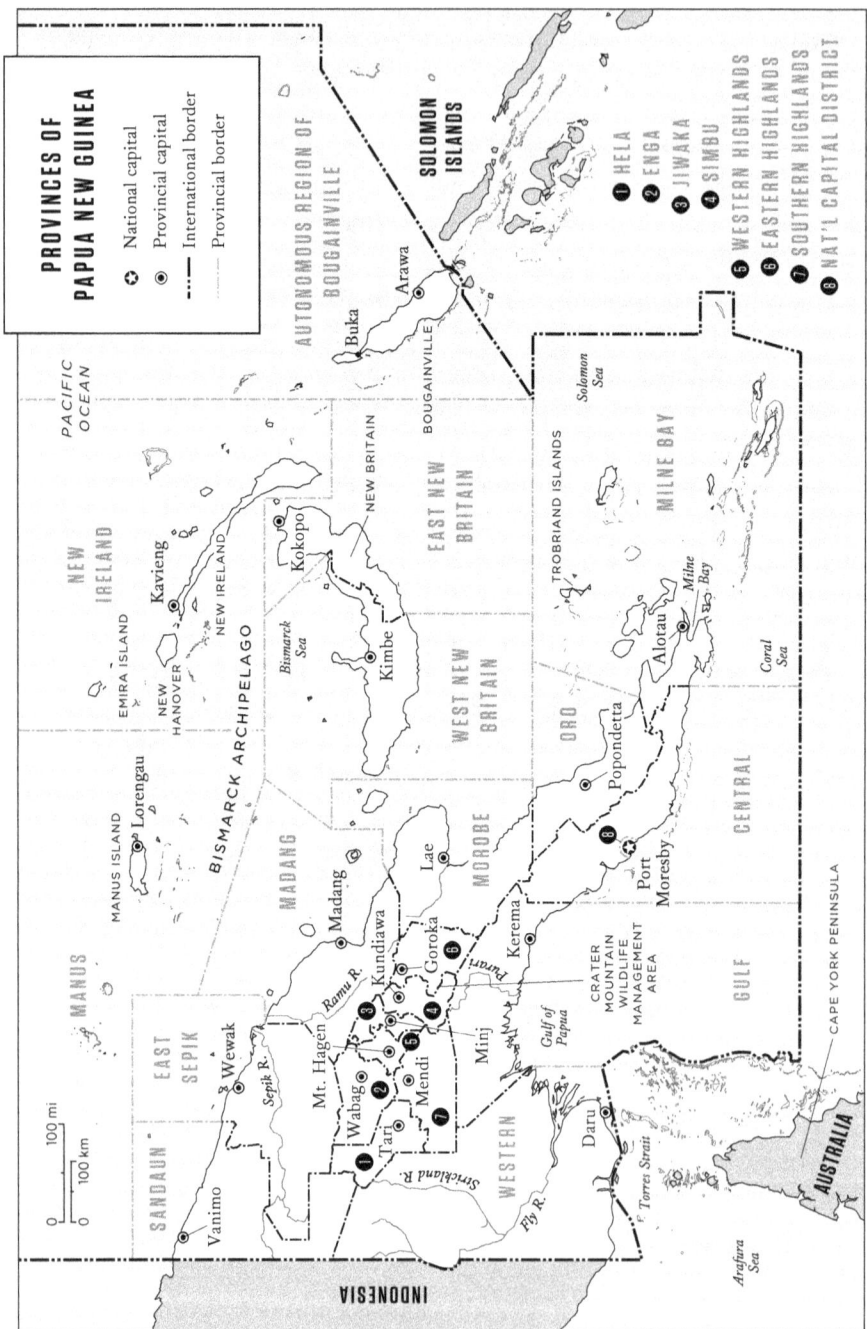

FIGURE 0.1 Papua New Guinea.

to access it. The colonial government affords and restricts access to the economy and to other state-connected forms of support for inhabitants, written into the record through the documents Stella analyzes. He brilliantly links these representational practices to the cultural milieu of their day—the tail end of the "scientific" acceptance of ideas about classical social evolution—that nineteenth-century social theory generated from Europe and taken global that assumed that all societies moved through a particular progression of lineal stages—each after the next increasingly complex—toward "Western Culture" as a pinnacle of progress.[4]

The twinned image of savage nature and savage native that derives from this nineteenth-century episteme endures today in the representational practices and rhetorical strategies that surround Papua New Guinea. All of these images—what Stella, following Stuart Hall (1997), calls "representations" and what I have come to think of and call "representational rhetorics"—are grounded in a particular European-American-Australian ideology of autochthonous peoples, places, and times. Autochthonous refers to what is formed or originating in the place and time where it is assumed to still be located. I use the term "autochthonous" here and not "indigenous" because I am trying to mark the externality of this ideology and the fact that it conjoins so-called nature and so-called culture in ways that assume that indigenous peoples who do not fit within this ideology should no longer be afforded the possibility of sovereignty over their land, labor, bodies, representational practices, or futures.

What I mean by ideology is a set of both conscious and unconscious ideas that are meant to be normative, that have an internal logic tied to a particular historical genealogy, that are meant to persuade, that guide people's actions and help them see and understand the world, and that serve as a logic and means by which people justify their actions. I also see ideologies as sets of conventions that represent the desired material relationships of those with power. Ideology blurs and makes invisible both the violence and the structural conditions that keep some people in power and others disempowered (Marx and Engels 2001:64). It does not, however, create a false understanding of the world; rather, it sets the conditions for our actual experience of and, more importantly because it is actually accessible for understanding, our narration of the world around us (Althusser 2001:108). In addition to its relationship to language and narration, ideology is made present through our material social practices (Althusser 2001:114). Finally, we constitute others as particular kinds of subjects—in part—through ideology (Althusser 2001:116).

The term "sovereignty" refers to the ability to control, and have autonomy over, one's life in whatever manifestation the society of which a person is part articulates what the fundamental parts of "life" are. While sovereignty is often taken to mean jurisdiction, rule, power, and domination as these forces are tied to a state, nation, or governing body, following contemporary scholars of indigenous worlds, I take an expanded view of sovereignty when it comes to Papua New Guineans (Barker 2005; Mihesuah and Wilson 2004; Simpson 2014; Trask 1987, 1993, 1994; Warrior 1992). In Papua New Guinea political sovereignty and material sovereignty are deeply interwoven with the ongoing dispossession of "intellectual sovereignty" (Warrior 1994), "representational sovereignty" (Raheja 2013), and "rhetorical sovereignty" (Lyons 2000). So in what follows "sovereignty" means control over meaning, representations, the future, ideas, and the creation of social worlds and social reproduction, as well as political control and material manifestations of control. This expanded notion of sovereignty comes from the work of indigenous scholars, and I attempt to build on it.

These chapters demonstrate how representational rhetorics that are grounded in this European-American-Australian ideology of autochthonous peoples, places, and times result in the denial of multiple forms of sovereignty and are linked to material dispossession and accumulation. They show that this ideology has created the conditions of possibility for seeing and narrating and ordering the peoples of Papua New Guinea so that they seemingly cannot be thought of outside of it. Specific rhetorics are used to perpetuate ongoing racial disenfranchisement and oppression in postcolonial Papua New Guinea. These are much more pernicious and dangerous than we often imagine. They are more than just "discourse."[5]

Discourses, following Michel Foucault, are the material and linguistic infrastructures through which knowledge, power relations, and subjectivities are produced over time (Foucault 1975). They constitute the conditions of possibility for being, thinking, and acting, as well as the epistemological systems and processes that interpenetrate them (Foucault 1970; see also Weedon 1987:108). For Foucault, the episteme, or the accumulation of structures that lay under the production of knowledge, is grounded in a particular time and place and is unconscious and singular (Foucault 1970). In *The Order of Things* he writes, "in any given culture and at any given moment, there is always only one episteme that defines the conditions of possibility of all knowledge, whether expressed in a theory or silently invested in a practice" (Foucault 1970:168).

Part of my argument in this book is that we have never had an "episte-mological rupture"—a moment during which the unconscious nature of the episteme at play is destroyed and new modes of knowing that create new conditions of possibility for seeing, understanding, and thinking are possible—in the epistemic worlds that surround people from Papua New Guinea and places in Papua New Guinea as they are configured by others (see Bachelard 1986 and Althusser 2001). A second part of my argument is that the deployment of these representational strategies today are rhe-torical in nature, they are meant to persuade, to motivate, to influence thought and action; that they are not ever fully unconscious. Foucault argued that "truth" comes through epistemic process and that it brings about power (Foucault 1980). I argue that economic and social power brings about the "truth" that is endlessly rhetorically produced and rein-forced concerning the nature and culture of Papua New Guinea and that that power is directly connected to ongoing accumulation, ongoing dis-possession, and uneven development (Said 1978; Smith 1984). Discourse is always thought be between ideology and practice. I use the term "rheto-ric" in these chapters because I am documenting a strategy in or of dis-course that is talk and image and more. It is directed at bringing about a particular world; it is consciously meant to entrench and strengthen white supremacy and capitalism. Three examples of what I mean by "rep-resentational rhetorics" will make my argument clearer.

Lunch with the Prime Minister

In December 2004, Sir Michael Somare, who was at the time the prime minister of Papua New Guinea,[6] visited my university in New York to give the commencement address at the business school's winter graduation. I was invited to the luncheon afterward. The luncheon guests included former deans of the business school, department heads, econom-ics faculty, Papua New Guineans working in New York and Washington, people from the Papua New Guinea mission to the United Nations, the Papua New Guinea embassy to the United States, and the prime minis-ter's staff. A few faculty and recent business school graduates were also thrown into the mix. As one of the only Americans there who had actually been to Papua New Guinea, I was seated at his table for lunch.

The guests at the table included a historian, an economist, several peo-ple from the Papua New Guinea department of planning, and me. During lunch the prime minister, who is undeniably a statesman—impeccably dressed, eloquent, gentlemanly, and seemingly genuinely interested in everyone he meets—asked the historian, the economist, and myself about our research, our experience at the university, and our families. He started with me, and we had a rather long talk about environmental conservation in his country, the politics of Western critiques of locally generated conservation politics, and coffee production as a form of ecologically sustainable development—all topics that I was writing about at the time. He then moved to the historian and finally the economist. When asked about his research, the economist steered the conversation away from himself and toward the topics of cannibalism and crocodiles.

The economist had recently seen an episode of *The Crocodile Hunter* on TV, and the show mentioned the island of New Guinea, cannibalism, and the Sepik River, on the banks of which the prime minister had grown up. Sir Michael Somare was good-natured about the line of questioning. He "played along"—so to speak—when the economist asked him question after question about cannibalism in New Guinea, about the "remoteness" of the island, the "impenetrable jungles," and if there were places where natives had still never seen Westerners. The prime minister, throughout maintaining his posture of dignity and respect for others, talked about how old men from his village told stories about eating people during times of war, about playing on the banks of the Sepik, and "wrestling crocodiles" as a young man. He moved with alacrity between the role of elder statesman and architect of his country's constitution and that of tolerant storyteller as he listened to this man who knew nothing about his country, a country he helped to found, establish, and build, go on and on.

Conradian Journeys

A Papua New Guinean acquaintance of mine, whom I will call Max, delights in particular sorts of international visitors. He loves to talk to visitors—tourists, journalists, missionaries, aid workers—who fantasize about his country as an exotic, magical place full of primitive Stone Age–like savages. Max was born in Goroka, educated in missionary-run schools, was a member of the national parliament in the 1980s, and owns a successful coffee-related business. He is elderly, eloquent, charming, and loves both playing golf at the Goroka Golf Club and telling people that he is a cannibal. The scene is usually something like this:

Max is at the bar at the Aero Club, the Goroka Yacht Club, or the Bird of Paradise Hotel, and he or one of his friends has overheard some international visitor regaling someone with a story about how exotic their trip was or how they know that there are still cannibals "out there somewhere" just waiting to be found. Max slyly joins the conversation, introducing himself as "a real live cannibal." He then spins a yarn of Conradian proportions, which usually includes warfare, sorcery, colonialism, gold mining, deep dark forests, or World War II and culminates in him declaring that he ate someone—a clan enemy, a colonial officer, a gold prospector, or a Japanese soldier.

Along the way, during the trip down the dark river of imagination, Max has relieved the rapt international visitor of South Pacific Lager for himself and all of his friends. After one particularly rousing version of this tale, told to a American journalism student visiting Papua New Guinea for the first time, I asked Max why he derives joy from what I consider to be troubling, at the very least, and racist depictions, in many senses, of Papua New Guineans. Max said, "Have you seen the movie *Cannibal Tours*? They want us to be primitive—right out of the Stone Age—I give them what they want, and they go home and talk about it for the rest of their lives."

Bourgeois Books

In a 2013 piece in *New York* magazine, Elizabeth Wurtzel, an American journalist in her mid-forties, a Harvard College and Yale Law graduate who attended elite private schools in Manhattan as a child and developed a taste for heroin in her late twenties, which she chronicles in one of her two memoirs, writes about her "failed" life in New York City:

> I never wanted to be a millionaire or a billionaire or anything at all like that, because the happiest thing would be doing what I love. Which is how it turned out, and so it goes with talented and thoughtful people who move to places like New York and L.A. and Chicago and Austin and wherever else you take your wits these days. It isn't just creative types, also public-interest lawyers and public-intellectual academics and political thinkers—collectively, the professional class. In a city, these are the people who make the place vital and fun. They work hard but still have time to try a no reservations restaurant on the Lower East Side or check out the small boutiques in Nolita and

help interesting young designers get off to a start. Mostly, they make six-figure incomes and somehow manage. And they are happy for the privilege. But these are people who soon won't exist anymore. Soon New York will be nothing but a metropolis of the very rich and those who serve them—and the lucky and desperate still hanging on. All of the fun jobs are disappearing. If great talent did not require infrastructure to nurture it, Norman Mailer and Martin Scorsese would as likely exist in Papua New Guinea, or, for that matter, Norway. But the arts have thrived, and great work has supported itself without the benefit of government subsidy, because this country was founded with an intellectual-property system and a free press that understood that creativity and capitalism are happy partners. (Wurtzel 2013:46)

Wurtzel recast a more pithy version of the same sentiment in her 2014 book *Creatocracy*: "If human genius could thrive without a system to support it, Hollywood and Silicon Valley would be located in Papua New Guinea" (Creator 2014). Both of these recent quotes seem also connected to other seemingly-off-the-cuff mentions of Papua New Guinea by Wurtzel in other publications:

The honest truth is that when two people connect—I mean really connect—it is damn near impossible to keep them apart. In spite of infinite obstacles, ultimately it will become apparent that the powers that be have conspired to bring them together, and no other outcome could be possible. I have friends who are living happily ever after (for now anyway) with people they'd met when they were married to someone else or living somewhere else or in some way completely unavailable. The long and complicated sorties of how they got together—how they kept in touch through marriages and divorces and a tour of duty in Brazil or an assignment in Papua New Guinea—are small and petty and meager compared to the largess of love. (Wurtzel 2001:75)

There are other things that other women need to do: they need to have lesbian affairs; they need to drop out of medical school and become investment bankers; they need to fly with the Air Force in Iraq or work for the Peace Corps in Papua New Guinea; they need to sleep with their brothers-in-law; they need to—heaven help us— sleep with their brothers; they need to live in New Orleans for five

months, in Krakow for three months and in Bangkok for two years.
(Wurtzel 1999:393)

My economist colleague at Columbia University takes lunch with the
prime minister as a cue to articulate his understanding of Papua New
Guinea as a remote jungle full of cannibals where there might still be
lurking men and women who had "never seen a white man" before. My
friend Max, having met hundreds of young Euro-American-Australian
visitors, draws on the rhetorical images that have been articulated to
him over the years and mirrors them back to visitors as a way of mock-
ing them publically. Wurtzel uses Papua New Guinea to index the opposite of all that she holds dear. It stands as the negative to her bourgeois
sense of what matters in the world. Art, literature, creativity, intellectual
pursuits—these are all the opposite of the negative space that is Papua
New Guinea. These things are the "natural" and the "cosmopolitan" and
are opposed to Papua New Guinea, which sits outside of culture and
the natural order. It also indexes the opposite of the organization, infrastructure, and reasonable governance that she imagines resulted in the
flourishing of the arts in places like New York, Austin, Los Angeles, and
Chicago. It stands for all that is without state-sponsored order, talent, and
creativity. Papua New Guinea embodies the opposite of her fantasy of
humanity and human existence that she sees as the pinnacle of societal
evolution: New York City in the 1990s. In the earlier quotes she simply
uses it to index the furthest other—a place that is unimaginably remote.

How do these actors, these representers, all participate in the same
rhetorical community where Papua New Guinea comes to index a particular set of ideas about nature and culture? It is my contention that it is not
enough to be irritated by these three situations—the conceit of the economist, the naiveté of the journalist, and the bourgeois white privilege of
Wurtzel—rather, we must understand what material effects these forms
of rhetorical representation have in the world and how these material
effects reinforce structural inequality. Papua New Guineans have complex
relationships with these forms of rhetoric.

Accumulation and Dispossession

The essays in this book derive from my work as an anthropologist, my collaborations with my Papua New Guinean colleagues, my

learning from the work of other scholars, my listening in various social settings in the country, and experiences, over almost twenty years, of spending time with my Papua New Guinean friends. In all of these forms and areas, I have watched my research participants, my colleagues, my friends, and complete strangers endure multiple forms of dispossession. Many of these forms of dispossession start with the kinds of representational rhetorics that you see in the three examples above. Yet we must understand these kinds of rhetorics as the discursive beginnings of structures of dispossession.

In everyday terms, dispossession is often defined as putting people out of possession or occupancy, or taking something away from them that they own. It is also commonly used to refer specifically to taking away people's land or homes. Embedded in that notion is a secondary aspect of the idea of "dispossession": for something to be taken away, somebody has to do the taking. Dispossession and accumulative strategies that drive it can only be understood if we start with Karl Marx's analyses of "primitive accumulation" or "original accumulation" in *Capital* and then move to Rosa Luxemburg's work to correct Marx in *The Accumulation of Capital*.[7]

Marx wanted to understand and demonstrate the process by which wealth and power came to be concentrated in the hands of a few and how this concentration of wealth and power was directly tied to the increasing misery of most other people (Marx 1975: chap. 25). The transformation of human labor power into a commodity and the privatization of property were the central elements in his analysis of this process. Part of his project was to, as we would say today, "denaturalize" the idea of "haves" and "have-nots" being a natural part of social life. He argued that the forms of inequality that we perceive between people are not the result of anything natural but rather that they are historically produced.[8]

Connected to this, Marx also wanted to denaturalize a set of assumptions about human nature that he traces back to John Locke and Adam Smith's imaginings of the transition from precapitalist social relations to capitalist social relations. He argues that Smith saw "two sorts of people": one set, "the diligent, intelligent and above all frugal elite," and the other set, "lazy rascals, spending their substance, and more, in riotous living." The first kind of people accumulated money and power, leaving the second kind with "nothing to sell except their own skins." Smith, Marx contends, assumed that this "original sin" was the beginning of inequality between people, "the poverty of the great majority" and "the wealth of the few" that somehow increases "although they have long ceased to work" (Marx 1975:873).

To counter Smith's dualism, Marx recounts a different version of history whereby "conquest, enslavement, robbery, murder" and brute force "play the greatest part . . . in the creation of laborers . . . and the process . . . that clears the way for the capitalist system" (Marx 1975:845). He calls this process "original" or "primitive" accumulation and claims that as people are dispossessed of their means of production they necessarily become poor laborers tied to the very people who dispossessed them of their lands in order to make enough money to live and reproduce their families over time (Marx 1975: chap. 26). He temporalizes this process, observing that "the so-called primitive accumulation, therefore, is nothing else than the historical process of divorcing the producer from the means of production. It appears as primitive, because it forms the prehistoric stage of capital and of the mode of production corresponding with it" (Marx 1975:847).

As a part of his analysis of this original accumulation, Marx also attempts to trace out how means of production in precapitalist societies were transformed or "converted" into private property (Harvey 2005:128). He acknowledges that some of the early capital in the system was derived from merchant profits but, famously, contends that "the conversion of means of production accumulated under pre capitalist modes of production to capital" was the result of violent dispossessions.[9]

These two aspects of Marx's work form the basis for all analysis of capitalist accumulation and dispossession since. For Marx, primitive accumulation is at its foundation "about the violent dispossession of a whole class of people from control over the means of production, at first through illegal acts, but ultimately, as in the enclosure legislation in Britain, through actions of the state" (Harvey 2005:293). This violent dispossession happens through brute force, legal and illegal acts, and the perpetuation of the ideas of freedom and liberty as they were derived from Adam Smith's work. Marx shows that freedom and liberty are fictional ideas that are also, when framed in market-related terms, seductive ideas. David Harvey reads Marx's focus on freedom in this way: "Laborers are free only in the double sense of being able to sell their labor power to whomsoever they chose at the same time as they have to sell that labor power in order to live because they have been freed and liberated from any and all control over the means of production" (Harvey 2005:290). Marx wants to understand and demonstrate how this kind of freedom was secured and seeks his answer by asking how labor and land became commodities.

In his discussion of the expropriation of agricultural populations and the end of feudalism in *Capital*, Marx argues that once land is taken and transformed (turned into pasture in the examples he uses) community dissolves and people are forced to move to cities in order to enter into a wage-labor system in order to support their families and reproduce society. Money becomes social power as it dissolves communities, but communities do not dissolve easily. The peasantry is dispossessed of their land through the creation of laws. Here Marx also shows the formation of a bourgeoisie that consists of several kinds of capitalist landowners, merchants, finance capitalists, and manufacturing capitalists, contending that together they "conquered the field for capitalistic agriculture, made the soil part and parcel of capital, and created for the town industries the necessary supply of a 'free' and outlawed proletariat" (Marx 1975:805).

The agricultural populations who do not move to cities to sell their labor become seen by the capitalists and the state, which is now part and parcel to the deployment of capitalist laws, as criminals. They are cast as outlaws and thieves if they neither work their own lands nor work in manufacturing. They are remade in social terms as aberrant, lazy, and outside of the natural order of things (Marx 1975: chap. 28). Physically, they are made unable to support themselves and reproduce society as free labor, people who can subsist by their own agricultural labor on their own lands. Food becomes a commodity, and when people cannot grow their food or trade their food for other commodities, other artisanal markets begin to disappear. At the same time all of land and nature becomes commoditized and monetized as capital comes to circulate both through nature and human bodies (Smith 1984; Harvey 2005:197). The environment and people come to be seen as having value and worth only if they are generating surplus capital for the capitalists. They are devalued if they are perceived as outside the system or on the edge of the system looking in. Yet in this moment they are also conjoined—nature and culture, perceived as outside of capital, are melded into one. This perspective sets the conditions for understanding non-European worlds for hundreds of years after industralization.

At some point, dispossession begins to have its own logic that, after annihilating feudalism and paving the way for the development of industrial agriculture and manufacturing, results in a new social form. Laborers are no longer working for themselves, capitalists are exploiting many people at once, and land only has value as a commodity.

This expropriation is accomplished by the action of the immanent laws of capitalistic production itself, by the centralization of capital. One capitalist always kills many. Hand in hand with this centralization, or this expropriation of many capitalists by few, develop, on an ever-extending scale, the cooperative form of the labour process, the conscious technical application of science, the methodical cultivation of the soil, the transformation of the instruments of labour into instruments of labour only usable in common, the economizing of all means of production by their use as means of production of combined, socialized labour, the entanglement of all peoples in the net of the world market, and with this, the international character of the capitalistic regime. (Marx 1975:809)

In *The Accumulation of Capital* (1913), Rosa Luxemburg makes two interrelated arguments. The first addresses what she sees as a logical flaw in Marx's analysis of expanded reproduction with regard to surplus value. She contends that Marx fails to acknowledge that capitalism needs outside sources of raw materials and outside sinks for surplus commodities in order to expand. Because of this she argues that a capitalist system cannot exist alone, or in what Michael Perelman (2000) calls a "pure system," but rather that it can only exist in conjunction with precapitalist systems. Luxemburg's second argument is that while capitalism emerged and flourished in connection to these precapitalist systems—indeed, that its existence is due to them—that in the end capitalist states and businesses will destroy all other systems of production. She bases these two arguments on empirical materials, both historical and contemporary, concerned with the relationship between capitalist and noncapitalist economic systems. Much of Luxemburg's evidence comes from the relations between nation-states and colonies, places that can have areas inside and outside of capitalist relations of production simultaneously. The key to her arguments is that while the systems exist alongside each other for a period of time, capitalism, because of its need to constantly expand, will destroy all other systems. It will do this through force, power, and murder, all things that Marx highlighted, *and* through propaganda, something that Luxemburg brings into focus clearly only at the end of her book (Luxemburg 2003:467).

For her first argument, Luxemburg focuses on Marx's analysis of surplus value. She acknowledges that surplus value emerges when the value produced by a worker is greater than the value of her labor power. This value is located in the commodity and that commodity has to be sold if the surplus value is to be realized as money. Once sold, the capitalist uses that money to invest in new labor power and new means of production. For Marx, it is the money derived from surplus value that keeps capitalism flowing and growing. Surplus value allows the system to reproduce itself. Luxemburg perceives this as a closed system that ultimately will not allow for expanded reproduction.

For the system to reproduce itself, Marx argues, there must be within the system total demand for all commodities produced. That demand comes from capitalists (who need to constantly replace used-up means of production and buy extra means of production to expand, as well as goods for consumption and social reproduction), from workers (who spend their wages on consumption goods), and from nonproductive laborers like lawyers and clergy (who spend their wages on consumption goods). Marx traces all of this back to the capitalists because they pay the workers and the nonproductive labor. Everything flows from the capitalists in the form of payment for labor and flows back to the capitalists in terms of people spending their wages.

Luxemburg sees this closed system model as unable to account for the need for surplus capital, the capital that the capitalists (and others) amass over time. She maintains that amassing capital is the key to expanding the system. Initially this could mean adding more workers. When capitalists add more workers there are more commodities to be sold, more money is made, and workers compete for jobs so wages can be lowered, so there is money to be amassed. But eventually all that money has to go back into the system to keep it going. In order to sustain themselves, Luxemburg argues, capitalist systems must expand through imperialism, and she uses her discussion of imperialism as the basis for her second correction to Marx.

Luxemburg defines imperialism as "the political expression of the accumulation of capital in its competitive struggle for what remains still open of the non-capitalist environment" and claims that while imperialism prolongs capitalist expansion, it is also the source of capitalism's demise:

> Still the largest part of the world in terms of geography, this remaining field for the expansion of capital is yet insignificant as against the high level of development already attained by the productive forces of capital; witness the immense masses of capital accumulated in the old countries which seek an outlet for their surplus

product and strive to capitalise their surplus value, and the rapid
change-over to capitalism of the pre-capitalist civilisations. On the
international stage, then, capital must take appropriate measures.
With the high development of the capitalist countries and their
increasingly severe competition in acquiring non-capitalist areas,
imperialism grows in lawlessness and violence, both in aggression
against the non-capitalist world and in ever more serious conflicts
among the competing capitalist countries. But the more violently,
ruthlessly and thoroughly imperialism brings about the decline of
non-capitalist civilisations, the more rapidly it cuts the very ground
from under the feet of capitalist accumulation. Though imperialism
is the historical method for prolonging the career of capitalism, it
is also a sure means of bringing it to a swift conclusion. This is not
to say that capitalist development must be actually driven to this extreme: the mere tendency towards imperialism of itself takes forms
which make the final phase of capitalism a period of catastrophe.
(Luxemburg 2003:446)

In the long run, capitalist and noncapitalist systems do not, and cannot, live together—Luxemburg sees noncapitalist systems as fixed, inflex-
ible, and static and capital as relentlessly stalking the earth for the fodder
for growth. That fodder is a combination of land, labor, natural resources,
and new consumers. Her observation expands Marx's idea of primitive
accumulation tremendously. For Marx, accumulation was always about
labor and labor alone. Land was a benefit of dispossession, but the dispossession was intended to create more labor. Luxemburg identifies other
primary goals of capitalist dispossession:

Since capitalist production can develop fully only with complete access to all territories and climes, it can no more confine itself to the
natural resources and productive forces of the temperate zone than
it can manage with white labour alone. Capital needs other races
to exploit territories where the white man cannot work. It must be
able to mobilise world labour power without restriction in order to
utilise all productive forces of the globe—up to the limits imposed
by a system of producing surplus value. This labour power, however, is in most cases rigidly bound by the traditional pre-capitalist
organisation of production. It must first be "set free" in order to be
enrolled in the active army of capital. The emancipation of labour

power from primitive social conditions and its absorption by the capitalist wage system is one of the indispensable historical bases of capitalism. (Luxemburg 2003:362)

Like all teleological Marxists, Luxemburg relies on a simplistic sense of historical progression in her tracing out of how capitalist imperialism emerges: "We must distinguish three phases: the struggle of capital against natural economy, the struggle against commodity economy, and the competitive struggle of capital on the international stage for the remaining conditions of accumulation" (Luxemburg 2003:368). But instead of just seeing "natural economies" as sites for dispossession and primitive accumulation, she also perceives them as sites for the introduction of commodity economies and sites for the consumption of commodities to create surplus value. Capitalism has to dispossess to continue to grow, and it has to create consumers and the desire for commodities and set up a seeming social and political barrier between workers and rural dwellers so that politically these two sections cannot form an alliance to fight their dispossession. Workers are made to feel like their industries and interests are different from those of people living in rural places (Luxemburg 2003:369–371). She shows clearly that there always need to be new "sink" areas for capital: areas that are seen as empty or prior to capital, that can be transformed by capital investment, and that can provide flows back to the "source" areas.

Finally, Luxemburg argues that capital and capitalists can do things abroad that they could never do in Europe, which provides a new kind of flexibility that allows for things besides labor to become the focus of dispossession and for new, and extreme, forms of violence that are unbounded by law or that even work to create new laws. Abroad, capitalism can be violent. It can kill; it can do anything it wants. It is unbounded by law, it creates laws, it taxes such that people can't say no to the system, it steals land, and it creates (through propaganda) a false history, a false world.

David Harvey argues that Marx and Luxemburg are writing about a process that can be happening anywhere at any time. What they describe is not a particular unilinear historical progression; rather, we can see their arguments about primitive accumulation as a case analysis of a more general principle. Harvey argues that to talk about it as "primitive" or "original" accumulation embeds the idea that this sort of accumulation is over and that we (and capital) have moved on. "Accumulation by

dispossession" is another way of saying primitive accumulation or original accumulation without these temporal assumptions.[10]

"Countertopographies": New York–New Guinea

It may seem strange to move from Rosa Luxemburg's brilliant
analysis of how imperialism and colonization are elaborated forms of the
accumulation and dispossession that Marx wrote about to New York City
as a way to understand New Guinea. However, this jump allows me to connect some seemingly disparate ideas that are crucial for our understanding
of accumulation and dispossession in Papua New Guinea today *and* dispossession as a process more broadly. Luxemburg theorized a geographic
fix—what David Harvey calls a "spatial fix"—for surplus capital, and in
doing so she extended Marx's theories to explain how capitalism can seem
like a closed system yet constantly pulls in new land, labor, and natural
resources in order to keep itself going. Shifting the scene from turn-of-the-
century theory to modern New York City also helps us understand how it
can be that Luxemburg was wrong about capitalism eventually erasing all
other modes of living, modes of being, and modes of production. This is
important because Papua New Guinea is one of the global sites that has
been used, over and over again, to show, contrary to many classic social
theories that hold that the expansion of capitalism and its social forms
causes the full displacement or erasure of other social forms, that other
social forms endure alongside and interpenetrate through capitalist modes
of being. In other words, capitalism does not necessarily erase indigenous
ways of knowing, seeing, narrating, and being-in-the-world. Other social
forms endure over time and often rework capital into new structures and
processes based on these prior forms.[11] Nevertheless, capitalism always
needs new sites for sinking, or investing, surplus.

In order to understand dispossessions in Papua New Guinea, I take
a cue from Cindi Katz's *Growing Up Global*, in which she theorizes
global capitalism's avenues of dispossession as they connect to the lives
of children by moving back and forth between New York City's Harlem
neighborhood and a rural village in Sudan (Katz 2004). In the book she
asks, how do children learn about and make knowledge about, or understand, their environments, and how does this process change over time
as communities intersect in new ways with multiple forms of capital? To
answer these questions she develops what she calls a "countertopography,"

a method of reading two places alongside and against each other to discover how the processes unfolding in each place are linked and how they construct new, global realities. Katz sees children in both of her sites, one ravaged by structural adjustments and one by deindustrialization, becoming different kinds of subjects because of these global interlinked processes. Children are engaged in new modes of being because of the intersections of these global processes in their day-to-day lives, and these new modes of being are making different kinds of persons.

Katz also theorizes a counterperspective to the taken-for-granted notion of "time-space compression," the idea that technology has elided distances across space and through time in ways that allow for a speeding up of various social, economic, and political processes (Harvey 1990). Katz sees what she calls "time-space expansion" in Sudan and Harlem. She argues that because of structural adjustments and failed development projects in Sudan and the defunding of public schools and public spaces in Harlem, people have to reach farther and farther outside of traditional terrains to continue social reproduction.[12] People engage in expanded zones for their sociomaterial production and reproduction, and they understand that these new pressures are due to processes they associate with global centers of power. People also develop what she calls "rural cosmopolitanism" whereby their desires are produced by and articulated through categories that are derived from their knowledge that the world is big and that they are most certainly not in the center of it but that people who are have more than they do (Katz 2004:225–231). In other words, in addition to there being new terrains for social reproduction, there is a spreading of the ideological terrain that people use to understand and define themselves and through which they articulate their desires.

There are moments when the circulation of capital itself becomes reworked and when places become narrated, cast, and valued in new or different ways so that this reworking can benefit some people (Smith 1979:24). The circulation of capital, as Luxemburg noted, is key to its continued vigor. While she thought that it would eventually overtake all other systems and modes of being trying to erase new venues for its investment, the geographer Neil Smith, in his work on urban gentrification and uneven geographical development, teaches us that capital investment, and the people who accumulate based on its investment, can find "frontiers" over and over again.[13]

In his early work and his landmark book on gentrification, *The New Urban Frontier*, Smith proposes a theory of urban social change, through

processes of accumulation and dispossession, that focuses on production. Earlier theories of urban change had focused mostly on the desires
of consumers, or "gentrifiers," in understanding how and why poor urban
neighborhoods came to attract wealthy investors in the 1980s. They basically argued that young people who grew up in the 1960s and 1970s developed a kind of aesthetic around both the look of their neighborhoods and
the politics of suburbanization that drove them to inner cities. Theorists
assumed that liberal or progressive college graduates wanted to move
away from the disembodied apolitical feel of suburban America, which
drove them to invest in urban areas. Smith argued that gentrification was
a process that brought together an ongoing restructuring of the capitalist
economy with what Henri Lefebvre had called "the production of space"
(Lefebvre 1991). A key part of Smith's argument was that production and
the needs of capital investors, including both public and private investors,
were driving gentrification and that the desires of consumers were actually only the social manifestation of these larger processes. He proposed
a "the rent gap theory" of gentrification to round out the analysis.

The rent gap theory is as follows: In the 1960s and 1970s cities
expanded outward so that capitalists could take advantage of inexpensive land on the outskirts of urban areas, land previously used in other
ways—such as farmland or public natural spaces. Because of this investment outside cities, the prices of property in urban centers fell and state
services tapered off so that they could be refocused on the growing suburbs. With the decline in state services, people who could move did, but
people who could not move were left to the mercy of landlords who saw
no reason to keep property structures healthy since the economic value
of the property had gone down. Through this process, land and other
property become devalued and rent becomes inexpensive (Smith means
"rent" as in paying rent for an apartment and "rent" as in the cost to buy
property or land). He proposes that there is a "rent gap" between the
price of urban property and the potential value of the property if it were
to be used in a different way (Smith 1987). When this gap became wide
enough, when the difference between what something would cost, *even
with the amount that would be needed to redevelop it was factored into the
cost*, and the profit that investors assumed they could squeeze out of it
after redevelopment reached a certain point, capital would once again be
reinvested into urban and inner-city neighborhoods. The rent gap at its
apex then becomes the driving force in the economic process of gentrification. So the rent gap is, for investors, a measure of the potential value

of something versus its actual cost at a given time when they feel that the market for it is depressed enough to be at its nadir. However, the rent gap can only be achieved if the area is both materially disadvantaged and ideologically devalued.

All of this takes place where the residents of inner cities are still living. Indeed, Smith shows that in New York City, the focus of much of his work, while global economic processes are being played out in their apartments, bodegas, and city parks, citizens are struggling to make a living and to reproduce their families and ways of life. Social reproduction continues in the face of gentrification, but social reproduction is slowly transformed as the urban residents become the modern-day version of Marx's "agricultural populations." Investors and gentrifiers come to see these residents as something to be overcome in so-called urban renewal. They are cast as outlaws and thieves and socially made as "outside of the natural order of things." What this means is that in connection to material dispossession—when poor urban residents are priced out of their homes as gentrification begins—there is a kind of representational and rhetorical dispossession that must be in place if investors are to accumulate at the rate they desire after they have begun their reinvestment into urban spaces.

One way that gentrifiers and the investors who pave their way into urban areas cast residents who were living there prior to them as "outside the natural order" is through the language of the "frontier" and discourses of "discovery" (Smith 1996). In New York City, gentrifiers and the investors who wish to benefit from the rent gap rely on and perpetuate a form of frontier mythmaking. Newspapers use phrases like "urban homesteaders" and cast these "pioneers" as having a kind of settler mentality—adventurous, brave, and willing to traverse areas and go where they assume no white people have gone before (Smith 1992). Inner cities in these accounts are both dramatic and dangerous, sites where young white settlers can make an iconoclastic life. Smith argues, "The frontier myth makes the new city explicable in terms of old ideologies. Insofar as *gentrification* obliterates working-class communities, displaces poor households and converts whole neighborhoods into bourgeois enclaves, the frontier ideology rationalizes social differentiation and exclusion as natural and inevitable" (Smith 1992). He argues that in New York City in the 1980s, the myth, and the ideology embedded within it, were discursively underpinned by the real estate industry, the culture industry, and the state, in the form of the city's housing policy and agencies.

"The frontier" in this ideology is a place where "savagery" meets "civilization" (Reid and Smith 1993). In New York City these roles were cast with working-class people of color, mostly African American and Latino/Latina households, as the savages and middle-class whites with their desires for loft apartments and coffee bars as the force of civilization (see Reid and Smith 1993:195). At the same time, developers and realtors are "portrayed as 'urban cowboys'—rugged individuals, driven in pursuit of civic betterment—[who] tame and reclaim the dilapidated communities of the downtown urban frontier" (Reid and Smith 1993:193). In writing about gentrification in Harlem, Monique M. Taylor shows us that this mythmaking is also connected to discussions of existing neighborhoods and persons as dirty, pathological, and deviant and portrayals of new residents as stable, healthy, and pushing toward renaissance (Taylor 2002). The myth works to both rationalize assumed social differences, which are seen as natural or immutable, and cast some people as living in a kind of prior state and needing to be brought into a civilized future. This ideology also rests on the kind of temporal fantasy that I discussed above: some people are seen as living with cosmopolitan modernity while others exist in some sort of premodern state of nature. Yet these two temporalities are seen as existing at the same time, a chronotopic fantasy (Bakhtin 1981). As such, this ideology posits certain ideas about human agency (Lipset 2011:21). Povinelli (2011) argues that the communities with which she works are ideologically located in a precolonial past, stuck, in the eyes of the state and others, between that assumed past and an assumed modern future.

The rhetoric and ideology here is the nonmaterial form of dispossession. Through it we can see that the material and economic are always underpinned and presupposed by the ideological, discursive, and semiotic (see Povinelli 2011). While both Marx and Luxembourg understand that how people are cast during the process of dispossession is a part of the process, I argue that the process of accumulation and dispossession in Papua New Guinea today rests on the discursive, semiotic, and visual production of both Papua New Guinea and Papua New Guineans as outside of the natural order of things—with the assumption that the natural order of things is a kind of linear progression fantasy in which everyone, globally, has come to live, or should have come to live, in urban, cosmopolitan ways. The reason that this discussion of gentrification is useful for us is because it clearly connects discursive dispossession as articulated through the rhetorics of the frontier with material dispossession.

This ongoing nature of accumulation and dispossession can clearly be seen in new work on settler colonialism in North America. In both *Mohawk Interruptus* by Audra Simpson (2014) and *Red Skin, White Masks* by Glen Sean Coulthard (2014), we clearly see that the structures emplaced by colonial invasion and settler colonialism work to continually dispossess indigenous peoples. Both authors read the violent transformation of social and economic forms that existed prior to colonization, in what is now Canada, into capitalist forms as an ongoing act of accumulation and dispossession and insist on seeing colonial invasion as continuous and ever present. Invasion continues through current-day policies, development projects, and juridical process, as well as practices around "recognition" and so-called accommodation of cultural difference, which always fail to address the structural inequality that underpins everything in a settler society. Simpson's work pushes farther and theorizes practices of "refusal," focusing ethnographically on Kahnawà:ke Mohawk refusal of American and Canadian citizenship as a form of sovereignty claim. In this analysis of refusal she also argues that anthropologists, and others, in their assumption that colonialism is over, fail to see it as an unrelenting form of dispossession.

This dispossession is, of course, connected to race and the deeply ingrained European, American, and Australian racist ideologies about Pacific Islanders in general and Melanesians in particular (Douglas and Ballard 2008; Clancy-Smith and Gouda 1998; Dixon 1995; Jahoda 1999). In finely grained rhetorics and practices these racist ideologies are embodied on a daily basis for people from Papua New Guinea. These racist legacies are lived and, in various ways, feed into the structural inequality that both creates and limits indigenous modes of being and social reproduction.

Dispossessions Where There Are No Possessions?

Dispossession, broadly conceived, is a taking, a theft of sovereignty over lands and bodies. When the thieves use the stolen land and bodies (usually as labor) to make money for themselves, you have accumulation by dispossession. Because people in Papua New Guinea are granted ownership of their traditional lands by their national constitution, they trouble many materialist analyses of accumulation by dispossession as it relates to land. Additionally, since Melanesians create

FIGURE O.2   Port Moresby. Photograph courtesy of J. C. Salyer.

themselves and others through transactional practices that do not rely fully on Enlightenment notions of the individual as the seat of rights and responsibilities and on philosophical propositions about humans possessing a individual self, Papua New Guinea troubles contemporary philosophical approaches to dispossession and subjectivity.

Much of the literature about possessions in Melanesian societies starts from the position that personhood in the region cannot be theorized in the same way that it is theorized elsewhere. This discussion of person-hood is almost always read into and grafted onto discussions about both material possessions and social change. The European concept of the individual as an ontologically privileged category differs from how it has been construed historically in many Melanesian societies, as most schol-arly work on the region observes (Strathern 1988). This has resulted in the view "that Western and Melanesian images of personhood are fully incommensurable because the West constructs individuals while the societies of Melanesia construct dividuals or relational persons" (LiPuma 2000:131). Here, "relational persons" means people that see and are seen as selves only in and of relations with a plurality others; persons are like mosaics, made up of elements that are performed and elicited in transac-tions with others and not essential or inherent to their "self" or others (M. Strathern 1988). And these "composite beings" are constituted through previous and current "elicitations and exchanges" (Mosko 2008:215). They are produced by both social exchanges and material exchanges— exchanges that are easily recognized by outsiders, such as gifts of land, and exchanges less easily recognized by outsiders, the gift of your wife's mother's labor in the food she grows and feeds you with, for example. Across Melanesia, it is also assumed that most exchanges are meant to be reciprocated. Indeed, the failure to reciprocate is one of the many topics that comes up when Melanesians discuss the difference between their societies and those of their interlocutors.[14]

One critique of this strand of scholarship has been that it essentializes both Melanesian and Western ontology; another holds that it fails to adequately address questions about social change (Biersack 1991; Macintyre 1995; Mosko 2008; LiPuma 2000). There are two crucial correctives to the critiques. The first corrective derives from an attempt to understand how dividual and individual processes of personhood are related. Its aim is to "enable exploitation of the dynamic potentialities of partibility and elicitive exchange as change, and [take] due account of processes analogous to dividuality in introduced dimensions of presumably individualist Western sociality" (Mosko 2010:16) This approach takes seriously that people are "composites of prior interpersonal transactions" and that someone's "composition at any one time indicates his/her potential for future action" (Mosko 2010:17). The second corrective derives from arguments about the historical adoption of particular elements and objects from European culture into Melanesian social lives and practices (Sahlins 1985:23–42, 2005:23–42). It postulates that people in Melanesia acquire objects of all sorts (both "traditional" "introduced" objects) for social reasons and that these objects are put to use in ways that are socially meaningful in relation to already existing ontologies and epistemologies. The incorporation of externally made objects—and it is often commodities that are discussed—does not make systems of world-making less Melanesian; rather, the systems of worlding make objects less Western (M. Strathern 1988:81; Sahlins 2005:29). Indeed, the value of objects comes to be seen through their movement in exchange rather than through quantitative commodity values. Additionally, in many Melanesian societies, for most members, accumulation historically was seen as so antithetical to entrenched demands of reciprocity that to accumulate, or desire to do so, marked you as aberrant (LiPuma 2000:146). This strand of thought takes seriously that historically most material possessions in Melanesia moved from person to person and rarely accumulated with a single person unless that person was a traditional political leader. In that case, the leader would redistribute those objects at an appropriate time or during a ceremony or event.

All of these social and material processes are part of social reproduction. In the chapters that follow we will see how social reproduction, following Katz but drawing on the embedded and ethnographic nature of people's processes of making self and society outlined above, has been reconfigured and altered through ongoing processes of accumulation and dispossession.[15]

What emerges with processes of dispossession, both original and continuing ones, is not simply a new set of economic formations or structures. Nor is it just a new set of images that go along with the commodity economy. What emerges is a "new Symbolic order" and, connected to it, new modes of being, living, making, and knowing the world (see Morris 2016). This process is constant and relentless. What the gentrification literature show us is that there are nonmaterial aspects that always go along with dispossession—the taking of the ability to have community and define community, the marking of people as criminal just for living, and the shaving off of opportunities for social reproduction and representations of and becomings of selves or persons. The ideology and language of "the frontier" and the material aspects of the rent-gap process of creating value and creating a "new" sink for capital that is meant to create accumulation opportunities for some while dispossession for others is what connects Papua New Guinea and gentrifying New York City in this countertopography.

Anthropology and Papua New Guinea

Historically the discipline of anthropology has flourished in Melanesia. Papua New Guinea has been particularly important in the development of anthropological theory since 1922 and the publication of Bronislaw Malinowski's *Argonauts of the Western Pacific*, a book that ushered the discipline into an era of long-term field research as a way to understand both the structures of human societies and the structures of human thought, or consciousness, as they relate to particular phenomena, as well as the relationship between a society's workings and the day-to-day lives of individuals.[16] Indeed, in terms of anthropological "hierarchies of knowledge" Papua New Guinea was, until relatively recently, paramount. In fact, many of the contemporary subfields within anthropology owe their theoretical and methodological origins to work done in Papua New Guinea. These subfields include economic anthropology, psychological anthropology, the anthropology of religion, political anthropology, the anthropology of the body, the anthropology of gender, the anthropology of violence and war, and environmental anthropology (Soukup 2010; see also Foster 1999 and Knauft 1999). Additionally, some of the "hot topics" in the discipline also find some of their origin-building theory in research done in Papua New Guinea—for example, the au courant ontological turn; the examination of the relationship between gifts, commodities, and their circulation; and questions about subjectivity and personhood, reflexivity and cultural analysis, or translation.

Yet today much of the discipline sees the anthropology of Melanesia in general and of Papua New Guinea in particular as a slightly embarrassing link to an anachronistic kind of anthropology. Seventeen years ago, while writing about the future of "cultural areas" and building on Michel-Rolph Trouillot's worry that anthropology's reproduction of ideas about its "others" as somehow "primitive" forced anthropology into a "savage slot"—an imaginary invention central to Europe's thinking about the rest of the world as "other," non-Western, and perhaps more importantly, a locus for a fixation that allowed the West to claim itself as normal and civilized as opposed to this "other" (Trouillot 1991). Rena Lederman warned of the danger of forcing the anthropology of Melanesia and those who do it into a "savage slot" within the hierarchies in the discipline (Lederman 1998:436). This slotting of the anthropology of Melanesia and Papua New Guinea has come to pass.

This disciplinary sense of Papua New Guinea and the anthropology done there derives from four strands of causality. First, anthropologists are part of larger popular-cultural fields, even when they should know better than to be seduced by discursive regimes that have been fully discounted in their discipline. Papua New Guinea has become the ultimate pop-culture metonymic device for a larger set of propositions about time and space that we see throughout Western thought. These propositions are that some people live in a kind of state-of-nature, pristine cultural past and some in a modern, cosmopolitan present (Clifford 1997). This sense that there is a prior state of humanity still "out there" somewhere makes people who assume that they are part of cosmopolitan humanity and who feel guilty for all manner of modern sins—things like overconsuming even when they know the global ecological effects of this sort of behavior—feel better about their structural positions of power and privilege (West 2012: chaps. 1 and 7). Anthropologists fall prey to this belief, just like tourists, aid workers, natural scientists, and oil company employees; all groups of people that I write about in the essays to follow.

Second, since the early 1970s anthropology has been forced to grapple with the colonial legacy of the profession (Asad 1973; Said 1978). One manifestation of this was a rejection of work that was perceived as derived from village-based research questions and research that was assumed to focus on a "culture" rather than on a group of people's connections to larger processes like imperialism, transnationalism, globalization, or neoliberalization. Scholars like Talal Asad argued that village-based work somehow fully embodied colonial power structures that "made the object of anthropological study accessible and safe—because of its sustained physical proximity between the observing European and the living non-European became a practical possibility. It made possible the kinds of human intimacy on which anthropology fieldwork is based, but ensured that the intimacy should be one-sided and provisional" (Asad 1973:17). Ethnography from Papua New Guinea was "slotted," or assumed to be located, within the former domain—myopically focused work that was about culture rather than connection and that was derived, more than other anthropological encounters, from unequal power structures. Additionally, so many of the classic texts within anthropology are about Papua New Guinea—including historically important works by Marcel Mauss, Bronislaw Malinowski, Margaret Mead, and Gregory Bateson, as well as efforts of scholars such as Marilyn Strathern and Roy Wagner—work that derived theory from long-term complex understandings of small-scale cultural articulations. Because such works were hugely influential in the late 1980s and early 1990s, anthropologists trained in those decades assumed that such "foundations" or "history of anthropology" represented the be-all, end-all of Melanesian ethnography, and that there was no new, theoretically engaged work being done in contemporary Melanesia.

Third, much of the ethnography from Papua New Guinea, and Melanesia more generally, even when it is connecting human subjectivities to local sociohistoric propositions and processes, as well as to externally generated processes and circumstances, forces readers to attend to theories derived from local ontological postulates. By this I mean that the ethnography from this region was and is challenging for readers who are unwilling to suspend, even for a second, their own knowledge-making structures. This is because propositions about what "is" in the world and what entities do and do not have power in the world are often quite different for people from

Papua New Guinea than for people from, say, the United States or Europe. And while we are currently within a fruitful and much discussed "ontological turn" within some quarters of the discipline, ethnographies of Papua New Guinea that forced readers from the 1980s to early 2000s to think theoretically from the ethnographic material were slotted as continuing a primitivizing tradition that people wished to move away from.

Finally, there is a subset of current scholarship about Melanesia that works to calcify the place and its people within a much older and much less engaged and dynamic literature about the area. This work is usually based on limited field research, for example, monographs that are based on dissertation research without the scholar having returned over a number of years to the place of work. Or it is grounded in a limited, very old, area literature. When anthropologists see a paper about Papua New Guinea in a flagship journal that grounds the argument in literature from the 1970s and 1980s, with one or two references to more contemporary research in the country, it works to solidify the thinking that there has been a calcification of theoretical contribution from the area.

My evidence for this savage slotting having taken place is hundreds of conversations over the past twenty years with anthropologists who are strangers, colleagues, and friends. For example, when I met a brilliant and lovely colleague many years ago, he said, "Wow. New Guinea, you are a *real* anthropologist."[17] Just this past year, upon my return from three months of field research in Papua New Guinea, another colleague asked, "Did you eat anybody this summer?" The question, although asked in a joking manner, referred to the endless associations between Papua New Guinea and cannibalism. I have had to make the argument for why Papua New Guinea matters over and over in a wide range of professional settings. It is never enough to say that the country matters because the lives of the millions of people who live there matter. In today's anthropology people's lives seem only to matter if they are assumed to teach us something about global processes and assemblages or allow us to theorize something larger than human life, and for various reasons the discipline has come to see Papua New Guinea as not fitting this form.

In the essays in this book, which do not require readers to have prior knowledge of either anthropology or Papua New Guinea to engage, I insist that Papua New Guinea matters because the lives of the people there matter in and of themselves. Yet these essays are also meant to show that the processes and assemblages we see in Papua New Guinea today do have something to teach us about larger theoretical or conceptual questions within contemporary anthropology. Those questions revolve around the creation of inequality through contemporary processes of accumulation and dispossession, questions that have arisen, over and over again, during my anthropological research in Papua New Guinea.

Dispossession and the Ancestors

The first European scholar to undertake what we would think of today as "anthropological research" in what is now Papua New Guinea was the Russian ethnographer Nicholas Miklouho-Maclay, who arrived on the northeastern coast of New Guinea in 1871 (Tumarkin 1993). The second European researcher who focused on anthropological elements of social life in the area was Otto Finsch, a German ornithologist who arrived in 1879. Both of these scholars added to the ethnographic accounts that were being collected by European missionaries around the same time period (Langmore 1989; Moore 2003). While they were not as important in the formation of contemporary anthropology as Malinowski was, they were crucial in the formation of the ideologies that I examine in this book.

Nicholas Miklouho-Maclay was a famous progressive public figure in Russia. He opposed the colonization of the Pacific Islands and argued against it in public forums, like newspapers and lectures, and through political action in eastern New Guinea. He also pushed back against already emerging stereotypes about New Guinea (Tumarkin 1993:35). He opposed sweeping generalizations about "native brutality," slavery, and the slave trade, all the while maintaining a focus on that stepladder theory of human societal development that would come to be known as "unilineal cultural evolution" or "classical social evolution."

Otto Finsch made several trips to New Guinea during which he became convinced that there was great wealth waiting for Germans if they were willing to create colonies there. Indeed, he provided several wealthy and influential bankers with the information they needed to convince Chancellor Otto von Bismarck to establish colonies across the Pacific, and on New Guinea in particular. Finsch used his previous knowledge of the place and its people to locate friendly harbors and acquire land, and the information he provided from his trips in the 1880s created the conditions that Germany needed to begin its period of economic and social dispossession on the main island and in what is now known as the "Bismarck Archipelago." He also provided the Germans, and the New

Guinea Germany Company, with social data that was meant to make dealing with the inhabitants of the island easier. The capital of the German colony was named "Finschhafen" in his honor. In addition to serving as a handmaiden of colonization through gathering ethnographic information, Finsch also collected ethnographic objects, thousands and thousands of them (Buschmann 2009; Penny 2002; Weiss 2012).

These two scholars exemplify two of the forms of accumulation and dispossession that anthropology and anthropologists must account for if we do not wish to replicate the sins of our forbears. The first seems to represent a benign process of accumulation that results in ongoing dispossession. The second, at first glance, appears more pernicious, with a clear link between the scholar's work and material processes of imperialism, which were always about dispossession and accumulation. Finsch advocated directly for accumulation by dispossession, and that is horrible, yet the "benign" version is equally unsettling.

In the case of Miklouho-Maclay, the theory of societal evolution to which he was became the lens through which indigenous people were ordered, understood, theorized, and written about by scholars for the bulk of the nineteenth century and for part of the twentieth century. Even after it fell out of favor with anthropologists, this idea there was a progressive evolution of culture from the simple to the complex, from the savage to the civilized, became the backbone for the "commonsense" understanding of difference in Europe, the United Sates, and Australia (see T. Anderson 2006a, 2006b; Kuklick 2008). Indeed they are the underlying episteme for the European-American-Australian ideology of autochthonous peoples, places, and times. They allow for and reinforce all of the ideologies of the frontier that further both gentrification and dispossession.

These anthropologically elaborated theories can be traced to the Enlightenment and philosophers like G. W. F. Hegel and political economists like Adam Smith. The language of these theorists flowed into early anthropology, and the discipline took categories used by Europeans to explain how people made a living (hunting and gathering, pastoralism and nomadism, horticulture, agriculture, commerce) and ordered them into hierarchies of progress, each generation of early anthropology making the theory more and more elaborate. Even as these theories became seen as obsolete in anthropology and related fields, they held strong in popular ideology. They had so captured the conditions of possibility for seeing others and had so perfectly allowed for capitalist dispossessions that they could not be thought out of (Mirzoeff 2011; Poole 2005).

We still see these representational rhetorics at work today. We see them in the way that the *New York Times* reports about life in the so-called developing world. We see them in the kinds of "development" projects foisted on people all over the world by European and American organizations. They form, today, the ideological locating mechanism that many regular people, nonanthropologists, turn to when they encounter difference. The representational practices I examine in the following pages—among surfers, oil company employees and executives, economists, journalists, and biologists—are all grounded in the history of this set of anthropologically elaborated theories.

How do we ensure that anthropology does not set the stage for dispossession? I recently read a truly brilliant ethnography. It was beautifully written, and I came away from it understanding the ontological and epistemological links between the social and ecological worlds of the people portrayed in it both historically and contemporarily. In it, an indigenous vision of the world and the interrelation of space, time, and experience emerged, yet the ethnography was framed entirely by the works of European theorists of space and place and time, such as Edward Casey, Johannes Fabian, Anthony Giddens, and Martin Heidegger.

What drives both our anthropological arguments today and our production of useful analytic abstractions? Do we, as a discipline, draw theory out of our evidence, or do we only read our evidence through theory produced in other disciplines and at other times? Posing these questions is not a call for a return to an atheoretical anthropology of the past. Rather, it is a serious call to ask ourselves what the politics are of always reading our empirical materials, which are often gathered in places far from the natal homes of European social theory and philosophy, through an increasingly standardized set of analytic lenses. We need to ask about how this standardized set gets produced and validated within the discipline and who doesn't get cited. And do we want to live in a social world and reproduce that social world if it is only conceptually grounded in European, or Western, or Northern Hemisphere social theory?

This brings us to the question of what kinds of worlds we are documenting and reproducing. Some anthropologists would argue that the European phenomenologist philosophers are key to understanding contemporary questions about space and place because of the extraordinary penetration of Western capitalist forms and Western forms of governmentality into the non-Western worlds. This is precisely the question taken up by many anthropologists when they ask about the endurance of local forms in the face of global flows. In *Decolonizing Methodology*, Linda Tuhiwai Smith argues that indigenous peoples have been oppressed by Western social theory (Tuhiwai Smith 1999:28). However, she does not advocate atheoretical research or writing. Rather, she sees the reading of and understanding of Euro-American social theory as a crucial part of decolonizing research methods and writing, but not the end point. For her, the development of theory both by indigenous scholars and by all scholars based on indigenous epistemologies and ontologies is the only path for a truly decolonized profession. She advocates the interweaving of multiple theoretical traditions in ways that do justice to the complexity of people's global lives. Similarly, Diaz and Kauanui (2001) have also advocated for an ethnography of the Pacific that takes seriously indigenous philosophical traditions and ideologies and also excavates the natures of ongoing dispossession. More recently, a scholarly collective has begun to articulate what an anthropology done by indigenous scholars of the Pacific brings to the field today (Tengan et al. 2010).

I've tried to follow what Tuhiwai Smith advocates in this book and elswhere.[8] The global economic system that dominates all our lives of comes to us from Europe and has been theorized by European scholars for a long time, so Western critiques of this system cannot be entirely disregarded. At the same time, indigenous people I conduct research with and the Papua New Guineans that I work with in other capacities hold and develop equally valid theories about this same system and how it intersects with their lives as well as with my life. Additionally, following Michael Jackson, I've tried not to "escape into . . . sympathetic identifications, or [even] political actions that reduce the other to a means for . . . demonstrating what a compassionate person one is, or [for] changing the world" (Jackson 2005:152–153). I do not tell the stories in the book to show you that they bother me but rather to demonstrate the experiences and events that I have taken part in, watched, and discussed. Hayder Al-Mohammad uses the notion of ethnographic being-with to encapsulate this kind of practice: that particular forms of narration might change power relations (Al-Mohammad 2010).

Plan of the Book

This book looks at a few areas where we can see how global forces effect dispossession in Papua New Guinea. Chapter 1 focuses on tourism, chapter 2 on international development and resource extraction-related development, chapter 3 on environmental conservation. Chapter 4 turns things around, so to speak, to focus on indigenous theories of possession, accumulation, dispossession, and sovereignty. The afterword concerns where some of my thinking on uneven development originated.

Throughout the book I return to several themes again and again. First, I look at who employs representational rhetorics to produce images of others in a way that results in dispossession. In chapter 1, surf-related tourists, publications, and businesses all work to make others using specific descriptions of nature, culture, savagery, discovery, and gender. All of this is wrapped up in a set of ideas about temporality. In the chapters 2 and 3 I build on this to show how bankers, the employees of big international conservation organizations, the employees of resource extraction companies, economists, and ecologists all use descriptions exactly like the ones outlined in the previous chapter. Throughout, I tag moments where we can see how these representational strategies draw on ideas first put out there by anthropologists. Concomitant with the images that produce others, I show how all of these actors also work to make selves through their representational rhetorics of others. I show how they accumulate status and senses of their own subjectivity through representations of the subjectivities of others.

Second, I show how these descriptions of nature, culture, savagery, discovery, and gender are used to dispossess. And I think through dispossession both in terms of material dispossession that is happening now and the potential dispossessions of material objects and access as well as dispossessions of sovereignty. I take sovereignty to be multifaceted with aspects connected to power or authority, the ability to self-govern (in the state-related political sense as well as in the sense of rights to make decisions about self, land, family and future), as freedom from domination and control, and as the ability to assert autonomy through daily practice and action (see Simpson 2014).

Finally, I return to the theme of "discovery" repeatedly, for each instance of it I describe is an act of dispossession. Each chapter has a host of actors who in their "discovery" of something or someone in Papua New Guinea creates the conditions of possibility for the kinds of processes described in the rent gap theory. Rhetorics of discovery are never innocent and never apolitical. Make no mistake, the theme of discovery grows tiresome. (Think, as you read this book, about how tiresome it is for Papua New Guineans to be repeatedly "discovered.")

Although each chapter is written to stand alone, they do build on each other. Chapter 1 lays the ground for the representational rhetorics discussed throughout. Chapter 2 connects those rhetorics to the dispossession of both representational sovereignty and material sovereignty today and in the future. Chapter 3 connects rhetorics and dispossessions to a deeper history of the ideology of discovery in Papua New Guinea and introduces some of the indigenous ways of speaking about and thinking about others. In chapter 4, I demonstrate how some people in Papua New Guinea theorize inequality, possession, dispossession, accumulation, and sovereignty. I conclude that chapter with a thought experiment intended to push back against some of the newish theoretical thinking in contemporary cultural anthropology.

1 "Such a Site for Play, This Edge"

Tourism and Modernist Fantasy

At three a.m. on December 21, 2007, I found myself standing in a freezing shower at the Nusa Island Retreat in New Ireland, Papua New Guinea, fully clothed, holding the head of a teenaged Australian surfer as he vomited on my bare feet.[1] He was inconsolable and very intoxicated. He, along with his father, his father's "mates," and their sons had been drinking for the entire day. A friend of mine who works at the Nusa Island Retreat tasked me with looking after the young man. As a woman, I was thought to be able to provide a calming, somewhat motherly, influence. In fact, my presence, as an anthropologist who works in Papua New Guinea, incited him to say, between gasps for air and the expelling of copious amounts of vomit, "It's just so, you know, man, so real. It's so real here. . . . I mean they are just so, like, they just live. . . . It's just, like, a man and his hut and the sea and the waves like forever. . . . I'm never going back home."

The young man had accompanied eight other men on a surf holiday to Papua New Guinea. They were all Australians, from Brisbane or other smaller Gold Coast towns, and they were all accomplished surfers. While on Nusa Island, they surfed, drank astounding quantities of South Pacific Lager and Bundaberg Rum, fished, ate, and then surfed and drank more. And they enjoyed every second of it. Earlier in the day, prior to my unexpected shower, I had spent several hours with the young man, whom I will call Brendan, poring over *Surfing, Surfer, Surfer's Journal*, and *Carve*, four of the top-selling international surf-related magazines, talking about Papua New Guinea, anthropology, and his future. Brendan, his father, and their friends exemplify the people who come to Papua New Guinea as surf tourists. They are male, they have visited multiple surf-tourism destinations, they are from Australia, they are between the ages of twenty and sixty, they are voracious consumers of surf-related media, and they all identify themselves as "surfers."

At four p.m. on June 18, 2013, I was sitting on a curb in the downtown area of Kavieng, sharing a South Pacific Lager (white can) with a longtime friend of mine who is from Mussau Island. I had met him the first time I visited New Ireland, in 2005. At the time he was the star bartender at a local resort. By 2013, he was without a home of his own (although he will always be welcome in his natal village), divorced and denied access to his two young children by their mother's mother's brothers, jobless, and recently released from the provincial hospital. When I asked him what he was going to do for work, he said, "I'd like to go back to bartending. It was such good money. But they won't hire me back. I don't know what I'm going to do, but I've been thinking about opening my own bar. But I can't get a bank loan, and I can't get in touch with any of my mates in Australia for help."

When I first met this young man, whom I will call Thomas, he lived in the staff housing complex of the resort, worked six nights a week at the bar, and swam or kayaked around the island every morning. We became friendly during these early morning outings, as I am a swimmer also, and even after I established a base elsewhere in the province, we stayed in touch, and I spent time with him whenever I was in Kavieng. Thomas is a person who exemplifies the men from Papua New Guinea who work in the nation's surf tourism industry. He is between twenty and thirty years old, comes from one of the islands in New Ireland, is well educated, is a great surfer, and sees his labor in the industry as a starting point for a life in business.

In 2009 an Australian surfer who was a repeat customer at the resort where he worked invited Thomas to accompany him to Australia. Thomas was enticed by the idea of exciting travel to exotic places. He was also lured by the promise of a job that would pay what he termed "expatriate-level wages." He quit his job and went to the Gold Coast where he went to parties and bars and spent his days surfing and meeting his friend's mates. From what Thomas says, everyone he met thought it was amazing to meet a man from Papua New Guinea who was an excellent surfer with perfect English-language skills, lovely manners, and a serious desire to work and make money. He told me stories of how Australian surfers repeatedly asked him about cannibalism, "the island lifestyle," and "undiscovered waves" and how they all seemed disappointed in him because of his answers. Sadly, there were no jobs offered. Thomas's Australian friend quickly grew tired of his presence once "the novelty wore off" (Thomas's words, not mine). He found himself without work (indeed, Papua New Guineans are not entitled to obtain work permits in Australia, and he would have been deported if he had tried to work illegally), without a place to stay (his mate's girlfriend got tired of him living with them), and without the money to return home. Thomas finally got home, almost a year later, but he had no job and few appealing prospects for the future.

In what follows, I examine the relationship between the production and circulation of mediated images of Papua New Guinea, the production of ideas about nature and culture (place and people in Papua New Guinea), and processes of self-fashioning by people who visit Papua New Guinea as these processes are enacted with regard to surf-related tourism. The surf tourism industry in Papua New Guinea depends on, and then reproduces, fantasies about the relation between primitive and civilized peoples, places, and times, projecting this fantasy through notions of "discovery" and "frontiers." Such fantasies are a form of dispossession that ultimately result in material dispossession and the creation of or enhancement of inequality. These fantasies then drive the production of place and space in Papua New Guinea and set the conditions of possibility for what tourists actually experience when they are in the country. Subsequently, the tourists reproduce these fantasy formations in their own self-fashioning, replicating the narrative forms that scholars have seen in primitivist travel writing for hundreds of years. With this, surfing as sport-tourism becomes another avenue for the reproduction of modernist forms and ideas about Western selves and "others."

This chapter draws on ethnographic fieldwork and participant observation in New Ireland Province, Papua New Guinea, survey data collected from 239 surf-tourists who have visited Papua New Guinea, e-mail interviews with 45 surf-tourists who have visited Papua New Guinea, and textual analysis of surf-related magazines. The focus here is on fantasy and tourism lives of men because the vast majority of surfers who come to

FIGURE 1.1
New Ireland Province.
Photograph courtesy
of J. C. Salyer.

Papua New Guinea are male. Women surf tourists tend not to visit Papua
New Guinea. Of the 239 people surveyed, eight were women. Of the
forty-five surf-tourists interviewed by e-mail, five were women. During
my ethnographic fieldwork in New Ireland only nine surfers I encountered were women.[2]

Surf Tourism in Papua New Guinea

The traditional stories of coastal peoples in Papua New Guinea,
like most places in the Pacific, include tales of riding waves in canoes, on
housing timbers, and on other flat bits of wood. There was not, however,
the kind of stand-up surfing most people practice today until the 1960s
and 1970s, when Australians working for the colonial government brought
manufactured surfboards with them to what is now Papua New Guinea,

which was then an Australian colony. In the early 1980s, both expatriates and Australian-educated nationals began surfing in earnest the breaks near Port Moresby, Vanimo, and Kavieng. By the late 1980s, these surfers had established the Surfing Association of Papua New Guinea (SAPNG), a national body to regulate the industry and develop strategies for how surfing might contribute to the Papua New Guinea economy, and the Vanimo Surf Club, modeled on Australian surf clubs and meant to promote the sport in and around Vanimo. After its legal incorporation under Section 7 of the Associations Incorporations Act in December 1996, the SAPNG sponsored national surfers in the South Pacific Games and the Oceania Indigenous Surfing Competition.

Because of the growing interest in Papua New Guinea as a surf-tourism destination (2005 saw 1,200 people come to the country specifically to surf), in April 2006 the SAPNG presented the Pacific Enterprise Development Facility of the International Finance Corporation with a proposal for the development of a formal, national "surf management plan." In both Vanimo and Kavieng, the local surf clubs had already established local "management plans." The plans do three things. First, they limit the number of surfers permitted in the water at any one time. Second, they charge a levy or tax on each surfer for each day surfed and distribute this money back to the communities who hold the area surf breaks in traditional marine tenure. Third, they provide a small income for the local surf clubs that is intended to help them grow and promote the development of local surfers.

The SAPNG has ten goals, and the development of these "management plans" is meant to help them meet several of them (Abel and O'Brien 2015). According to one SAPNG board member, the plans are meant to "promote sustainable development of the industry and make sure that locals get some benefit from it" (SAPNG n.d.; see also O'Brien and Ponting 2013). Additionally, although stated outside of the official SAPNG rhetoric, the plans are meant to, according to one of the plan's architects, "make sure we don't become another Indo, with overcrowded breaks and too many international operators taking advantage." This is the first and only functioning management plan for surfing in the world (Abel and O'Brien 2015).

Prior to the adoption of the surf management plan, between 1987 and 2003, Papua New Guinea, as a surf tourism destination, was profiled in the following print magazines: *Pacific Longboarder*, *Surfing Life* (three times), *Surfers' Trip* (three times), *Niugini Blue* (three times), *Paradise Magazine* (six times), *Surf Trip*, *Surf Europe*, *Blue Edge Magazine*,

Island Business, Surf 1, and *Sports Scope.* Since 2004 it has been profiled in *Surfing Magazine, Gold Coast Surf, Surfing Life, Surfer Magazine,*
the *Surfers' Journal, Surf Magazine, Island Business, Tracks* ("the Surfers'
Bible"), and *Surfline's Water.* Additionally, since 1980, it has been covered
in 73 newspaper stories (including in all the major Australian and New
Zealand newspapers). The vast majority of these magazines mention
the surf management plan. They also cast Papua New Guinea as exotic,
unknown, undiscovered, secret, primitive, wild, lost, and beautiful, and
the men who surf there as intrepid explorers, echoing Regis Tove Stella's
excavation of the terms used during the colonial period in Papua New
Guinea (Stella 2007).

The Ocean as Modernist Fantasy
and Circulated Medium

The sea has long been a medium over which people travel
physically and a medium through which they travel aesthetically, with
literature, poetry, and art. The sea inspires, expands, and reflects certain
fantasies and fears. In the past century or so the sea has metamorphosed
from a world of the deep, dark unknown to a world of science, technology,
and recreation (Ford and Brown 2006; Helmreich 2007). Its shores have
been violently transformed from the home-places of indigenous peoples,
to colonial and postcolonial ports, to working-class slums, to opulent sites
for the conspicuous display of wealth. (For details of this process across
the Pacific, see Finney 1996; Baugh 1990; Wills 2007; Douglas 1998;
J. Kelly 1992; and, especially, Sahlins 1989.) For many people, the sea
has gone from "something to be inhabited" to "something to be contem-
plated as an expensive backdrop" (Taussig 2000:258). Its inhabitants, the
creatures who find their home-places in it, have been transformed from
fantastic, unknown monsters into commodities. Today, sea creatures gal-
vanize harrowing direct action in environmental campaigns and are used
to depict the impending planetary doom that is global climate change.

Although most people use objects and products that come to them
across oceans on a daily basis, they rarely think about the sea as a medium
for movement. The ships that deliver toothbrushes, dental floss, glass
cups, and coffee, and the people that work to make those objects or move
goods from production to distribution sites, fail to cross people's minds
as they brush their teeth, rinse their mouths out and then ruin the whole

process with a second cup of coffee (West 2012). Euro-Americans are more likely today to experience the sea as recreation and restoration than they are as networks across which commodities move around the planet. In addition to the things of daily life that circulate over the ocean, the sea also serves as a medium for the movement of people. In the Pacific, especially, this has been the case for a very long time.[3] Today, there is less ship travel than in the past, but the sea lures many of the millions of tourists who travel from the global North to the global South each year. The World Tourism Organization estimates that there were 935 million international arrivals at tourism destinations in 2010 (UNWTO 2011).

Surf tourism is one of the most robust sectors of the tourism industry (Warshaw 2004). It is also an economic lynchpin for the global surf industry (Kampion 2003). The industry, which caters to 10 million surfers globally, is a multibillion-dollar business that includes the production of material commodities, like surfboards and clothing; the distribution of those commodities, through retail sales; and the organization of professional sporting events and contests, like the Rip Curl Pro, the Roxy Pro, and the Quicksilver Pro (see Buckley 2003:407 and Reed 1999). It also features multiple forms of tourism, including high-end resort-tourism and eco-tourist ventures. All tourism depends on mediated images to drive consumer desire (Urry 2002; see also Croy et al. 2009; Foale and Macintyre 2005; and Kahn 2011). The surf tourism industry depends on internal, industry-generated and -owned media (surf magazines, "documentaries," and websites), as well as externally produced media, like surfing movies (Bettie 2001; Buckley 2003; Henderson 1999; Ormond 2005; Ponting 2009; Rutsky 1999). The media associated with surfing produces images of kinds of people and types of places. The people are, overwhelmingly, white male surfers cast as brave and intrepid explorers who are carefree, alternative minded, and nonconformist. The places typically are exotic, uninhabited (or lightly inhabited), undiscovered (or recently discovered) sites with perfect waves, delicious food, a chance of danger or intrigue, beautiful bikini-clad women, and uncrowded breaks.

Surfing magazines have always been the major form of media though which images circulate to and from surfers.[4] These magazines range from general-interest publications, like *Surfer,* to special-interest ones, like *Pacific Longboarder,* and they are circulated through subscriptions and through distribution at newsagents and surf shops (Buckley 2006:453; see also Ponting 2009). All surfing magazines have information on contests and on the celebrity surfers who participate in these events, advertisements for all manner of surf-related items—everything from surfboards to clothing, wetsuits, tours, and stories about surfing localities and destinations. They are heavily illustrated with photographs taken by professional surf photographers (Buckley 2006:453). These magazines are directly connected to the tourism industry, both in terms of the vertical integration of various surf-related companies that own magazines, resorts, and tour companies, and in that these magazines drive touristic desires.

Tourism, Image, Media, and Space

Tourism takes standard forms that rely, in part, on mediated images.[5] Contemporary scholars of tourism and media often use John Urry's notion of the "hermeneutic circle" of tourism to analyze the relationship between images, forms, and actions (Urry 2002; see Canton and Santos 2008g and Jenkins 2003). For Urry, tourism is a social form that is based on the visual consumption and reproduction of images (Urry 2002:135). Images circulate, they are imbued with certain meanings, and then these meanings are shared through further circulation (Urry 2002; see also Hall 1997). These images then drive touristic desires and practices. In his analysis of images and surf tourism, Jess Ponting argues, drawing on Urry, that images are transmitted to tourists through surf-related media, that these images inspire travel, that the tourists work to find "the icons of symbolic elements seen in the projected images" and record them themselves, and that finally, the tourists then display their own images in ways that work to inspire others to travel (Ponting 2009:176; see also Preston-Whyte 2002:313). Ponting calls the surf images "nirvanic" and shows, with ethnographic material from the Mentawai Islands of Indonesia, that mediated images of perfect waves, uncrowded conditions, soft adventure, and exotic, tropical environments drive surf tourism there. Tourism operators know exactly what images they need to produce, on the ground, to enhance the tourism experiences of their guests. They are conscious of the media images and work diligently to make sure that the surfers' experiences mirror the ideals of the media-induced fantasy (Ponting 2009:178–182).

These touristic images are tied to older images of people and places, or the environment and society. Miriam Kahn examines the ways that colonial and postcolonial images of nature and culture have worked to produce space and place in the Pacific Islands in general and in Tahiti specifically (Kahn 2011). Tahiti is not just imagined as exotic and tropical, as much of the Pacific is; it is the site of origin for the exotic and the tropical, for European ideas about utopian worlds populated by noble savages living in harmony with nature, and for the dusky maidens that have fueled the sexualized fantasies of Europeans since the 1700s (Kahn 2011:32–60). Kahn shows that for the contemporary tourists who visit because of these fantasies, only certain kinds of activities and images are allowed into their already existing fantasy formations of space, place, nature, and culture. They literally do not see places, peoples, and events that sit outside of the fantasy. This is, in part, because of the ways that tourism operators structure experience and, in part, because of tourists' limited field of vision. To this analysis of image and tourism Kahn adds an analysis of the worlds of Tahitians and how they experience and produce space, place, nature, and culture. She shows, very clearly, that tourists and Tahitians live in "parallel, but disconnected, worlds" (Kahn 2011:15). Additionally, Kahn highlights the material manifestations of image and fantasy with a sophisticated analysis of the production of space in Tahiti. It is not simply that fantasy endures or that images motivate travel. Rather, fantasy and image, when intertwined with economic and political power, help to bring spaces and places into being (Kahn 2011:97).

Touristic fantasy and image as they relate to space are intertwined with modernist ideas about temporality. David Lipset and Rupert Stasch have both used Mikhail Bakhtin's notion of the chronotope to examine spatiotemporal understandings and representations of peoples living in New Guinea.[6] Bakhtin argued that a chronotope is "the intrinsic connectedness of temporal and spatial relationships that are artistically expressed in literature" (Bakhtin 1981:84). Writers create worlds that reflect the spatiotemporal reality of their own worlds, or at least of how they experience their worlds. In his analysis of the circulation of the figure of the primitive in print media, Stasch uses the chronotope to describe three different scales of spatiotemporal understanding that are displayed in travel writing (Stasch 2011). The first scale is the "narrated chronotope," or the narrated sequence of the writer's interactions with seemingly primitive peoples; the second is the "chronotope of textual performance," or the set of material, ideological, and linguistic relations between the writer and the reader; and the third is the "mythic chronotope," or the "mythic relation between contrasting primitive and civilized humans" (Stasch 2011:3). This final chronotope maps a spatiotemporal scale that mirrors notions of unilinear evolution and forms a set of engrained ideas and images concerned with the relationship between modern media consumers, like tourists, and people, like the indigenous inhabitants of New Guinea, considered by the consumers to be "primitive" (Stasch 2011:6–9). Elsewhere I have argued that he shows that "so-called 'primitive people,' who are the people, according to these travel writers, found on the island of New Guinea, are lost Stone-Age, childlike cannibal savages who are losing their culture, on their way to modernity, living in an ever-shrinking world, on the last frontier which is a hell-on-earth, Jurassic Park–like jungle that exists on the edge of humanity. The narrators, on the other hand, are intrepid, thoughtful, current-day Michael Rockefeller–like adventurers who are primed for the discovery of untouched nature and culture and who, like the tourists they inspire, can cross chronotopes" (West 2012:63). Stasch follows these chronotopes, and the images they rely on, produce, and reinforce, as they circulate, arguing that their repetitiveness makes them persuasive and that their persuasiveness helps to drive primitivist tourism desire (Stasch 2011).

Lipset's work shows clearly that chronotopes are more than just a "category" or helpful "unit of analysis" for ordering events in time and space; rather, they engender action and agency. He argues in places like Papua New Guinea, sites where modernist institutions may or may not have the grounding and solidity that they have in sites in the global North, chronotopes may give rise to "rival chronotopic claims about human agency in time and space" (Lipset 2011:21). Through his analysis of climate-related events and ideas in Papua New Guinea, he shows that rival claims about agency then drive particular kinds of actions and the unfolding of events in a particular sequence in particular places.

Other kinds of fantasies about subjectivity and place also stimulate tourism. In discussing the psychological work that our imagination of "the frontier" does for us, Vincent Crapanzano develops the idea of "the beyond" (Crapanzano 2004). He sees frontiers as imaginative formations that offer up a set of images of self and trigger a strong set of desires. People strive to reach these desired places and things and the desired selves that we associate with them, but they are always out of reach (Crapanzano 2004:14). They exist in a place of full fantasy, and once we access a real place, object, or set of interactions that we imagined previously, the beyond has moved a tiny bit forward, causing us to always have a melancholy longing for something more.

Australian Surfing, Media Circulations, and Fantasy Formations

Surfing is an indigenous practice in Moana, or Pacific Island, societies.[7] The locality best known for a documented history of surfing is Hawai'i. Most scholars trace the first European description of surfing to Captain James Cook at Kealakeku Bay in 1788, but this description is short and tells only what Cooks sees, not anything about what the surfers are surfing for. The indigenous newspapers of Hawai'i, published in the Hawaiian language, had numerous descriptions of surfing and many accounts of how the practice was part of a larger social system of ontology and epistemology (see Kamakau 1991; Nendel 2009; and Walker 2008). In Hawai'i, surfing brought together art and artistic production, spirituality, aesthetics (in the sense of bodily experiences), and a set of propositions about the relationships between nature and culture.

Board surfing came to Australia in 1914 when Duke Kahanamoku, the famous Olympic swimmer from Hawai'i, visited the country (Booth 2002:36; Walker 2008). On December 23 he gave the first Australian public demonstration of surfing at Freshwater Beach, just beyond the Sydney Harbor (Booth 2002:38). His trip was part of the beginning of a colonial refashioning of Hawai'i and "Hawaiian culture" by nonindigenous promoters who sought to grow the tourism industry there.[8] In Australia, after Kahanamoku's demonstration, surfboards were initially, albeit hesitantly, associated with lifesaving as rescue craft, but many shied away from surfing because it was thought to be "a hedonistic practice" that derived from exotic and *other* Hawai'i and as "menacing" for beach bathers (Booth 2002:39). However, by the 1930s, the Surf Life Saving Association (SLSA) had incorporated boards into their rescue-related paraphernalia, and by 1946 surfboard paddling was included in the national surf lifesaving titles contest (Booth 2002:87). This sanctioned use of boards was part of a seemingly wholesome and healthy set of practices undertaken by a set of seemingly wholesome and healthy young men, men who were concerned with personal fitness and the safety of Australia's beaches.[9]

In the 1950s in Australia, the post–World War II boom "produced a generation of overstimulated over-consumers that looked for continuous thrills and fun" (Booth 2002:91). These young people consumed the images of surfing from California and Hawai'i rapaciously (Booth 2002). The 1959 film *Gidget*—based on a 1957 book by Frederick Kohner recounting the real-life exploits of his daughter, Kathy Kohner, a Malibu teenager who learned to surf from and spent time with well-known Malibu surfers Miki Dora, Terry "Tubesteak" Tracey, Billy "Moondoggie" Bengston, and Bill Jenson—solidified the image of surfers as off-the-grid, anti-mainstream, laid-back pranksters (Rutsky 1999). The film portrayed surfing as an alternative lifestyle while at the same time making it appeal to postwar, middle-class desires for consumer culture (Booth 2002). It and other surf-related films sent the message that surfing was a form of "freedom" (Ford and Brown 2006:59). For example, *Endless Summer* (1964) conflated travel, youth, freedom, and the search for "the perfect wave" with a narrative of discovery (Ormrod 2005:42). Rutsky argues, "In these films, the appeal of surfing and surf subculture is often based on the attractiveness of nonconformist, irreverent, and anti-bourgeois attitudes cobbled together from elements of teenage culture, rock-and-roll, bohemian philosophy, and beat culture and mixed with a heavy does of parody. This appeal is, moreover, linked to the allure of non-Western cultures, derived in large part from surfing's own Pacific Islands origin" (Rutsky 1999:13).

These films made their way around the globe to Australia, as did less mainstream or even anti-mainstream films made by California and Hawai'i surfers. The films portrayed young men "who rode waves and traveled endlessly, and who never worked or worried," and with this they "carried the potentially subversive message that surfers were less predictable, less trustworthy, and not so ready to fall in line" (Booth 2002:95). In the late 1950s, Greg Noll and other well-known surfers brought Malibu boards to Australia and brought more films and images of surfers to Australia with them.[10] By 1962, Sydney surfer Bob Evans was making his own surf movies, screening them around Sydney, and he had founded *Surfing World*, a publication meant to publicize his films.[11] *Surfing World* evolved into the magazine *Surfer*, which by 1970 had a monthly circulation of 100,000 (Booth 2002:96).

In the late 1960s, attitudes towards surfer in Australia began to change drastically. In the 1950s and early 1960s, surfers, for the most part, belonged to surf clubs. These clubs were organized around lifesaving, but they were more like homosocial civic clubs. In the mid-1960s, numerous men who were not members of the clubs began to take up surfing. The baby boomers were college-aged, and as many of them went off to college, as in the United States, they became disillusioned with what they saw as "the establishment." Part of the 1960s counterculture worldwide was a disillusionment with the state, with corporations, and with other kinds of institutions thought to have power. According to David Harvey, as "various counter-cultural and anti-modernist movements" arose in the 1960s "antagonistic to the oppressive qualities of scientifically grounded technical-bureaucratic rationality as purveyed through monolithic corporate, state, and other forms of institutionalized power (including that of bureaucratized political parties and trade unions), the counter-cultures explored the realms of individualized self-realization through a distinctive 'new left' politics, through the embrace of anti-authoritarian gestures, iconoclastic habits (in music, dress, language, and lifestyle), and the critique of everyday life."[12]

In Australia, one of these "iconoclastic habits" was surfing, and "soul-surfing" or "riding waves for the good of one's soul" became the mantra for the counterculture surfers (Booth 2002:112). By the 1970s, Australian surfers were representing themselves as "hedonistic" and "unconventional," a "sub-culture," juxtaposing themselves with lifesaving club members who were "conformist" and "establishment types" (Stedman 1997:77; see also Pearson 1979). The sport was becoming a key site for the self-fashioning of alternative identity, and magazines played a pivotal role in this (Stedman 1997).

The pioneers of the Australian surfing industry, the magazines *Surfing World* and *Tracks*, used the counterculture to sell magazines and used the magazine to sell the counterculture (Booth 2002:113; Stedman 1997). The seemingly alternative practice was being used to "advance capitalism by pioneering new commodity forms, particularly in music and leisure" (Booth 2002:117). The images and fantasies that young people attached to the counterculture in Australia were mapped onto the constellation of objects that came to be associated with surfing. And these objects soon became the commodities that were marketed to people as crucial to their alternative lifestyles (Booth 2002:117). The surfing "community" that read magazines noticed this, and the 1970s and early 1980s saw numerous letters to the magazine editors that complained about people buying the image without understanding the lifestyle (Stedman 1997:80).

By the mid-1970s, most of the world's best-known surfing counterculture figures were taking part in international surfing contests sponsored by big corporations. By the 1980s, these contests were an indispensible part of surfing-as-sport, and they were directly tied to the marketing of surf-related commodities, like mass-produced boards, clothing, wetsuits, and other items. As the industry grew, so did surf tourism, which the magazines promoted as well. At the same time, the companies that were commodifying every aspect of surfing were selling rejections of commodification back to the community in the form of alternative "lifestyle choices" (Stedman 1997:81; Lanagan 2002). Counterculture surfers grew uneasy with the fact that by buying a t-shirt, factory-produced board, or reading a magazine, one could identify as a "surfer," not to mention that almost all of the professional surfers with corporate sponsorship were highly skilled athletes and not "alternative" figures. So surfing companies began to market separate lines of products, magazines, and experiences for the "authentic" and "alternative" surfers.[13]

The surf magazines also provided a basis and a constant referent for self-fashioning (Stedman 1997:77). They fostered a sense of community, created and policed the boundaries of the subculture, encouraged the notion that they provided a forum for communication among members of the subculture, and became "the most important site for the maintenance of collective identity" (Stedman 1997:78; see also Ford and Brown 2006:59). Magazines are so important that definitions of who is and is not part of the surfing subculture now depends not on who surfs but on who is portrayed and represented in the specialist surf media. Leanne Stedman says, "It can now be argued that the subculture as it is simulated through magazines and films *is* the surfing subculture" (Stedman 1997:78).

Today, while there are young people learning to surf in record numbers, the population of surfers who travel is growing older and becoming wealthier.[14] Because of crowding at mainland surf breaks in Australia and the United States (the two nations with the largest number of surfers), these older, wealthy surfers are creating an increasing demand for overseas surf holidays.[15] In the South Pacific, the major destination for Australian surfers, this has resulted in the growth of the surf tourism industry. Sumatra (the Mentawai Islands), Bali, Samoa, Tonga, Fiji, and the Maldives have all had established surf tourism destinations and operators for some time now. Generally the "discovery" of new destinations follows this trajectory: professional teams or groups sponsored by surf-related companies travel to new areas and surf large and difficult waves there. These trips are documented by professional photographers and videographers and are presented in magazines and documentary-style promotional films. Next, charter boats begin to bring guests on live-aboard charters to the areas. These guests surf smaller, less spectacular breaks. Subsequently, international operators come in and open resorts and lodges (Buckley 2006). While there are some small-scale surf travelers who travel to surf but stay in local accommodations and use mainstream transportation, the vast majority of the industry today is organized by specialist surf tour companies who sell packages to prime locations via live-aboard charters or through specialist surf resorts (see Buckley 2006:193–195). Two of these major companies are the Indies Trader and World Surfaries. They cater to "cash-rich, time-poor surfers" and carry them to seemingly "inaccessible" and uncrowded breaks (Buckley 2006:195). They also cater directly to those who want to experience "undiscovered" "frontiers" in this watery world.

Discovery and Masculinity

Martin Daly is a fifty-one-year-old Australian who, in collaboration with the surf industry giant Quicksilver, undertook a five-year long "exploration of the world's oceans" called "The Crossing." The project made him, among some surfers, "to the reef passes of the Indian and Pacific oceans, what Ernest Shackleton was to Antarctica." One of the pioneers of surf tourism, and the man credited with turning Indonesia's Mentawai Islands into a global surf destination, Daly now laments the current state of surfing in Indonesia because of "surf taxes, licensing proposals, international airports, and private ownership of the most popular waves" (Patterson 2008:59).

Joel Patterson, a native Californian who is now editor of the magazine *Surfer*, interviewed Daly for Surfline's *Water* magazine in the summer of 2008.[16] The sixteen-page spread is an interview accompanied by thirty-two color photographs taken by professional surf photographers Ted Grambeau and Dave Sparks. The interview centers around Daly's musings about Indonesia as a contemporary "destination" and a trip he took with "the Rip Curl team to explore and document . . . a group of islands in the Western pacific" (Patterson 2008:59).

In the interview, Daly seems appalled that Indonesians have begun to regulate surfing and build small and not-so-small locally owned businesses around surfing. He says, about the industry in the Mentawais,

It's getting really heavy. Basically, it's come down to the business end of surfing versus the surfers. There are people out there—and I like to think of myself as one of them—who own and operate boats and live the surfing lifestyle. And then you have this non-surfing, capitalist-pig element that is just there to take money out of our thing, and they're making things really hard right now. They're trying to impose taxes on every surfer who goes there, they're colluding with the Indonesian and Mentawais governments, trying to put up fences and get exclusive rights for all the waves. Surf camps are trying to get rid of charter boats. I see it as freedom versus the establishment. (Patterson 2008:70–71)

Daly also laments the way that younger surfers approach surf travel, drawing a line between people of his generation who surf for pure reasons and want authentic experiences and younger people who surf for fashion and want packaged tourism: "I get a lot of people out there who totally get it, and the there are a lot of people, who, unless it's served to them on a plate, they just aren't prepared to put up with the waits, the bad weather, and the floggings that it takes to make it all come together. I guess it's just human nature. Our society these days is all about 'now, now, now' and 'gimme, gimme, gimme' and instant gratification" (Patterson 2008:66).

Daly acknowledges his role in the commodification of surfing. "For me, it's sometimes a case of 'oh my god, what have I done?'" (Patterson 2008:66). However, this reflection is more about the development of the younger consumer surfer who wants perfect waves, amazing live-aboard service, and easy access with no difficulties and less about his role in creating the very industry in Indonesia of which he is now a critic. Patterson asks, "What's your view on how the Mentawais surf experience has changed in recent years?" Daly replies,

It hasn't changed at all when there's no one around. The magic's still absolutely there, and it's not as crowded as everyone says. We surf by ourselves all the time out there. A lot of people take it all for granted, and when they fly in they don't realize that they're going to one of the most remote places in the world. They see it in the magazines, they see it fully marketed and prostituted—as we do—and they think it's this well-trodden, safe area. I remember when I first went out to the Mentawais how far away from everywhere I felt, and that's the same feeling I get in these islands we took the Rip Curl guys to. I feel responsible somewhat for exposing the Mentawais to the world, but if I hadn't done it, someone else probably would have ten minutes later. (Patterson 2008:67)

He goes on to say, "Surfers don't like regulations and rules. I mean, that's the whole reason we like surfing, right? Freedom. That's the whole idea of a boat . . . it's a freedom machine" (Patterson 2008:71).

The notion of "freedom" is merged in the language of surfers with discussions of moments of "transcendence in which the subject—the surfer—and the object—the breaking wave—merge as one."[17] One former world champion surfer says, "You go into oblivion. Suddenly all your life is there in this long, long stretched-out wave; you're removed from the past, everything that has been on your mind has become immaterial, everything gone to jelly, and you feel completely removed from the world around you. Nothing matters any longer but you and the board and the wave and this instant of time."[18]

Martin Daly says, about Indonesia and the sites there that he turned into surf tourism mecca, "It's the bad things about Indonesia against all the things that we hold dear. It's kind of like watching a bunch of seagulls fighting over a chip. I see it as freedom versus the establishment" (Patterson 2008:59). Because of this lament over the loss of "freedom" in Indonesia, Daly set out in the mid-2000s to find "new destinations." During this voyage he "discovered" several new breaks and a "group of islands in the Western Pacific." When asked if he would reveal the name of the islands, Daly said, "I'd rather not. I mean, it's a bit out of reach for the average bloke, unless he's got a really good boat. It's not like the Mentawais where anything that floats will work. It's the Northwest Pacific Ocean, and the winds and weather are what's saved it all these years, but I'd still rather leave the exact location out of this" (Patterson 2008:59).

Daly continues by saying that the unidentified islands are hard to access because the airlines and shipping lines are often not working. The islands are "remote," and they are "a lot more challenging than Indonesia because of the sheer distance, the lack of shelter, the size of the waves, and the amount of swell" (Patterson 2008:63). But he likens the islands to Tuamotu Island and the Maldives because of similar reef structure and surf. He goes on to describe the area as having an "untouched" marine environment: "You put your head under the water and look around and it's like it was supposed to be. I spent a lot of time in North Queensland [Australia] when I was a kid, and I used to go out to the [Great] Barrier Reef to go diving in all these places that no one had ever dived or fished before, so I kinda know what a tropical marine environment should look like . . . around these islands the environment is pristine—there are huge fish everywhere, the coral's alive, endless underwater visibility, seabirds are nesting all around. It's refreshing to see a place in such great shape environmentally" (Patterson 2008:63).

Daly mentions that there are inhabitants on the islands, but he only talks about them in terms of whether they surf or not. The only photograph of an island inhabitant is of a man standing in front of a small hut surrounded by hundreds of open coconut halves. Daly says that only a couple of the local people surf. He also mentions that during his boat trip, he went to places in the western Pacific "where people had never seen surfers before" (Patterson 2008:63). When asked if he is going to run trips to this "new area," he says that it is expensive and difficult to get there, but he would "like to establish a low-key deal where we just go out there and do it without whoring it out to the rest of the planet" (Patterson 2008:71). It turns out that one of the places that Daly "discovered" on that trip was Nusa Island, New Ireland Province, Papua New Guinea, a place where the Australia–Papua New Guinea Keene family has owned a surf-related business for decades.

Untouched Nature, Culture, and Surfers

Back to the vomiting teenager with whom I began this chapter. Brendan and his fellow surf tourists came to Papua New Guinea to surf waves that they, as a group, described as "empty" and "pristine" and to interact with people whom Brendan's father described as living "a simple life without the headaches of modernity" and whom one of his friends described as "primitive" and "simple." They also want to interact with other surfers who understand that there is an authentic or real "surfing vibe" that can still be found in places like Papua New Guinea.

Brendan's father and his lifelong friends have been taking surfing related holiday trips together for twenty years and have been on surf holidays to Australia, New Zealand, California, Hawai'i, Bali, the Mentawais, the Maldives, Sri Lanka, and Costa Rica. They are between the ages of forty-five and sixty, and their occupations range from owner of several franchise restaurants in Brisbane to CEO of a major Australian company, electrician, and carpenter. They all met through Brendan's father, and unless there is some family or business emergency they all go surfing together for two weeks, twice a year, each year. They leave their wives and girlfriends at home. The older men have converged on Nusa Island previously; however, 2007 was the first time that they brought their sons.

Brendan and one of the other young men had just graduated from secondary school, and they were taking a year off before attending university. Everyone considered the trip a sort of coming-of-age celebration for the young men. All of these men, both young and old, express fantasies about people, place, and time when they describe what draws them to Papua New Guinea, what they find when they get there, and why what they find is valuable. They are exemplary of almost all of the surf tourists I have interviewed during the research for this project.

The first way that surf tourists express their understandings of place is through their discussion of the "village" they live in while in New Ireland. In 2007, the "village" of the Nusa Island Retreat was a series of ten tourist-ready bungalows, two shower blocks that included self-composting toilets, a main office that doubles as the owners' house, and a restaurant and bar building. The retreat is located on Nusa Lik, an island about a five-minute boat ride from the main port in Kavieng, the capital of New Ireland province. In addition to the retreat, there is also a local settlement on the island. It is separated from the retreat by a chain-link fence.

The "village" experience of the tourists is free from children, pigs, chickens, and the constant stream of visitors and activities that make up social life in Papua New Guinea. It is quiet, with manicured tropical plants, and with various rescued tropical birds populating the trees and bushes. Its inhabitants are all workers. They are English-speaking Papua New Guineans who are getting paid to be friendly, happy, and interested in the tourists. The vast majority of tourist interactions with the staff are with the expatriate surf guide, the owners, the boat drivers, and the bartenders. All of these people maintain what the surf guide calls the "it's all good attitude" with guests at all times. Tourists experience all of this in predictable ways. In interviews many tourists discuss village life as "laid back," "chilled out," "easy," "fun," "beautiful," "natural," and "quiet." However, many of them draw temporal conclusions from their experience. One of Brendan's father's friend expresses this when he tells me that people living in New Ireland are living "like people lived a thousand years ago."

Place is also discursively produced in terms of the surf breaks, the environment, and Papua New Guinea as a nation-state. The surf breaks are described by one visitor as, "undiscovered breaks where nobody but the locals have ever surfed before." A limited number of surfers allowed on them at any one time. The number of surfers on the break is the key factor in discussions about them. Being, as one fifty-year-old man described, "practically alone" on a break fulfills the fantasies of these lifelong surfers. They all express to me, in groups and one-on-one, the frustration they feel surfing now in Australia. This is connected back to the locals and local-surfers one finds in Papua New Guinea. Elsewhere, breaks are too crowded and there is often a "locals only" mentality that privileges people who surf the breaks daily and marginalizes visitors. But this is nothing, they argue, to the "locals only" mentality that exists in Hawai'i and is emerging in Indonesia. Hawaiian and Indonesian surfers are accused by many of having a "tribal mentality." Papua New Guinean surfers, by contrast, are admired for their growing ability. (Jim, a forty-two-year-old man from Sydney who works in the surf industry says, "Some of these kids will be hot one day. . . . There is some real raw, primal talent here.") Interviewees also admire how they have maintained their "traditional" way of life. This discursive production of Papua New Guinea and its inhabitants is often expressed just prior to some sort of caveat about the place as "the last frontier," "feral," or having, according to a businessman from Perth, "a feel like the wild wild west . . . where anything can happen." What this means to the surfers is that you have to be a particular kind of person to embark on the journey to Papua New Guinea.

This assumed maintenance of "tradition" also connects to the environment that surfers find in Papua New Guinea. Tourists describe it as an "untouched paradise," "an aquatic Eden," a place where people have not "squandered their resources" or "overused their resources." Again, for many interviewees this is given a temporality. In an interview at Nusa a twenty-six-year-old from the Sunshine Coast said, "Papua New Guinea is like the last place in the world. It is the last place without development." One of his friends quickly added, "Yeah, but it is totally threatened." When I asked what he meant by that, they both agreed that there is a worry that Papua New Guinea will develop too fast and that locals won't be ready for "modernity."[19] With this, images of the environment connect with images of natives. Both are cast as in danger, threatened by modernization or development.

New Islanders are thought to be living in authentic and traditional ways that reflect the ways that their ancestors lived. Tourists repeatedly told me that people there live practically like they did in the Stone Age and by falling to the corrupting influence of money they would lose their idyllic ways of life.[20] By taking up the desire for commodities and what one man from Melbourne called "Western bullshit," natives are seen as in danger of destroying their communities and their environments. They are also perceived as not ready for development and in need of what an Australian aid worker living in the Highlands of the country calls "a helping hand to navigate the complex modern world." Thirty-seven of the surfers interviewed used the phrase "they are not ready yet" in their discussions of development in New Ireland. In fact, according to the vast majority of interviewees, the rest of the country already evidences this. New Ireland is compared, repeatedly in interviews, with both Port Moresby, the capital of the country in which none of the surfers spent more than one day, and the Highlands, a region where almost none of the surfers have ever been. These two places are cast as "dangerous," "rough," "awful," and, for Port Moresby at least, "the asshole of the planet." The people there are seen as violent criminals that have been corrupted by modernity. They steal, they drink, they are sick with HIV and AIDS, and they drain on the Australian government and the taxes of the Australian people.

The people in New Ireland that surf tourists discursively produce in interviews and conversations are of two types: locals and surfers. There are, however, local-surfers and surfer-locals. The locals are natives who are thought to live in idyllic villages, pass their days, according to a sixty-year-old man from Darwin, "fishing, fucking, and napping," and who have not been, according to a forty-nine-year-old man from the Sydney suburbs, "polluted by all that capitalism bullshit." The man from Darwin put it clearly: "Their life is so simple here, like it used to be everywhere. It is what we should all aspire to. They don't have to worry about anything." The man from the Sydney suburbs asked me, in my capacity as an anthropologist, "What do they think about? There is nothing to worry about here—no mortgages, car payments, tax—and they don't talk about anything complex. Its not like they are debating politics or anything!" In almost all of my interviews, Papua New Guineans are cast as compliant, laid back, and apolitical, being contrasted with people in Hawai'i, Fiji, and "Indo," where locals have been "polluted" and are "heavy." The local-surfers are authentic in their surfing ability and in their lifestyle, which has not been corrupted by the surf industry, as it has been in Australia: "You watch them out there, and there is this natural ability. I saw a kid the other day on a broken board, and he was hot. He didn't need some fancy board to thrash. He was there with the waves, and he was in the zone. I hope that they don't buy into the whole product thing, you know? I mean he was just as good on that old broken board as he would be on a new one. All that gear has really changed the mentality of surfing in Australia and Indonesia. All the kids want the gear and don't get the lifestyle. It is about you and the swell and the ocean, not about the gear."

The men that I spent time with in New Ireland and interviewed online discuss themselves, as surf tourists, and others who brave Papua New Guinea in order to surf in a standardized set of ways. They talk about themselves and others in New Guinea as set apart from the men and women who go to easy surf destinations in Australia and the United States and as similar to, yet more enlightened about surf tourism than, surfers who go to international destinations like Indonesia, Fiji, and Costa Rica. Twenty interviewees use the phrase "doing it for the right reasons" and more than fifty discuss travel to Papua New Guinea as, to quote a twenty-four-year-old man from Melbourne, "getting back to what it is really all about." When I asked them to explain what "all about" is, they replied: "being free," "saying fuck you to the man," and not buying into that "Rip Curl, Billabong, industry image." A man from Coolangatta, who refused to give his age, says it is tied to "what it was like when my old man was young. Before it became all about aggression and contests and product. When it was pure and about you and the waves and your mates."

The surfers who come to Papua New Guinea also discuss the surfer-locals, Australian surfers who live full time in Papua New Guinea. They are viewed as having made profound decisions about "how to live" because they have, according the Coolangatta man, "tuned out" and "made the call to live an alternative lifestyle." They are, he continues, "free." These men are to be envied because they have a freedom that is not possible in Australia, and they are men that are imitated when the surfers get back home. During an interview in Brisbane, a forty-four-year-old tourist I had spent time with in New Ireland told me,

> I try to take [one of the expatriate owners of the Nusa Island Retreat] and [the expatriate surf guide at Nusa Island Retreat] with me wher-ever I go. They have the life there, and they do it for the right rea-sons. They do it for the waves and nothing else. I'm a businessman and have a hectic life here and sometimes I forget the whole reason I started surfing. I started young and I did it for the right reasons. Now, when I do get a chance to go here, I'm almost aggressive, and then I close my eyes and think, okay, what would [the surf guide] do? How would he be right now, and then I center myself. I'm more like who I was when I was a kid. That's why we keep going back to Nusa. It brings me back to what matters.

Consumptive Selves

Globally circulated mass-mediated images of places and practices shape surfers' expectations, experiences, and understandings of Papua New Guinea. Media-borne fantasy structures the consciousness of tourists; it limits what they see in part because tour operators draw on it in crafting the experiences they offer and in part because the spaces they experience come to be because of the fantasy. All of this fantasy turns on a set of propositions about time. However, it is not simply the mythic chronotope at play in Papua New Guinea's surf tourism industry, this fantasy is crucial to surf tourism. The surfers who come to Papua New Guinea are not just searching for mythic, premodern, primitive culture and nature. They are also seeking a prior and pure self. That self is an ideal of the intrepid adventurer and a fantasy formation based on the image of the "soul surfer." The search for the soul surfer, a character who may or may not have ever existed, ties together the mythic chronotope; media; the production of space, place, nature, and culture in Papua New Guinea; surfer self-fashioning; and capital. All of these elements come to them, in part, through media.

Surf tourism in Papua New Guinea draws on the mythic chronotope in obvious ways and on the idea of "the beyond" in two, less obvious ways that are intimately tied to this mythic chronotope. First, surfers are always looking for the next big thing, the newest place, the unknown or undiscovered site, the unsurfed spot. This is the *future beyond*. They try to find this future beyond through surf tourism, and there is a whole industry, built by people like Martin Daly and by surfing magazines, around perpetuating this notion. The industry works to create and sustain this beyond but also to make it unattainable. Part of its unattainably is that it replicates the mythic chronotope, a time and space that people can't really find. They discursively produce it in their descriptions of Papua New Guinea, what they thought was "the final frontier," but they know that the true untouched primitive and unsurfed break is out there waiting for them on another frontier.

Second, surfers also focus on the beyond that is in the past. A sort of authentic surfing of yesterday that was more about the waves and less about the gear, that was more closely tied to "soul surfing," populated by fewer people, and unpolluted by aggressive young surfers. They desire the imagined past—a past that none of them actually experienced because it never really existed. It was, from the beginning of the surf industry, a product sold to consumers. It is this desire for the *previous beyond* that drives the attempts to access the *future beyond*.

Counterculture identity draws on an imagined past that is supposedly more authentic and pure. The music, the clothing, the things people had and what they did have supposedly been polluted today by capitalism and commodification. But when people reference this supposedly authentic past they do so through talking about alternative versions of the same commodities that made surfing what it is today—alternative brands (like Fox), alternative contests, or alternative destinations (like Papua New Guinea). The authenticity that is lamented as lost is just as tied to consumer capitalism as the modernity that is distained.

The chronotopic fantasies of *the beyond* drive contemporary exploration, and exploration has always and continues to lead to dispossession. Neil Smith (2002) argues that with the closing of absolute space there is a realigning of space and who controls it. When the frontier is closed, new frontiers are opened and new sets of local actors are disposed by the accumulative desires and actions of people with capital and power. The discovery and pushing of the surf site frontier is a form of accumulation by dispossession or uneven development. Tourism, with its constant production of new illusions of the further "beyond" (i.e., sites and frontiers that are not ruined by tourism), is a never-ending form of accumulation by dispossession. It is relentless in its search for new images and new destinations; however, these newly discovered places are not really ever new at all.

Claims of discovery are really at their base political claims. There is no real discovery going on. By claiming to have discovered a place you are editing out the people who live there from your representations of that place and thus attempting to disempower them. This disempowerment, this erasure of people from sea and landscapes, leads to the fantasy of these sites as empty and therefore open to transformation by outsiders. In arriving by sea on his boat, the *Indies Trader*, Martin Daly bypasses the modern and cosmopolitan aspects of many of the countries in which he surfs. Surfers see themselves as part of an imagined, diasporic community, a "global tribe," an "ecological nation." They tell a particular history of that nation, which makes sense insofar as their diaspora nation, like other nations and other circulators of capital, has worked to dispossess people in many places of land and sea-based rights. Their diasporic nation has also worked, in ways similar to those described by Miriam

Kahn (2011) with respect to Tahiti, to produce space and place in Papua New Guinea.

There has been a great deal of discussion in the tourism literature about "authenticity" and the ways in which tourists seek sites where they can experience some sense of it (see West and Carrier 2004). In his early, seminal analysis of how the search for authenticity drives tourism, Dean MacCannell argues, "Modern man has been condemned to look elsewhere, everywhere, for his authenticity, to see if he can catch a glimpse of it reflected in the simplicity, poverty, chastity, or purity of others" (MacCannell 1976:41). His argument is that the "authentic" people seek is not the authentic other (although that does drive some tourism) but rather the authentic self. Surfers, like most modern Western tourists, assume that the present replaces the past. By discovering places like Kavieng they can step back into the past and access not only what they assume to be the prior-other but also what they assume to be a prior-self. The seeming authenticity of the future beyond allows them imaginative access to the previous beyond. This tourism is not about Papua New Guinea at all; it is about a search for a pure, unpolluted, Australian self. That self, however, is the social production of surf magazines, the surf industry, and the very forms of capital that these men attempt to escape and to deny the citizens of Papua New Guinea.

Surfer fantasies create and structure the conditions of possibility for Papua New Guineans to directly access the vast storehouse of international capital that would allow them to direct their futures or even to direct the future of the surf tourism industry in Papua New Guinea. The enduring, endless search for the previous beyond and the future beyond inextricably couples the fantasized subjectivity of Australians and Papua New Guineans within this mythic chronotope. The found "primitive" justifies the assumed modernity and superiority of the Australian. These fantasies are an enduring, pervasive form of representational dispossession that has extreme material consequences.

These fantasies also endure in part because they sell; their value accrues in the stories that people tell about Papua New Guinea when they get home. These stories give the trip and the place a particular sort of value. People enjoy their trips, but they enjoy telling stories about them even more. Brendan had already heard fantasy-fueled stories about Papua New Guinea before he visited—from his father and from magazines. And I'm sure he has told many of his own over the past few years. Today he is a happy, successful twenty-something living in Brisbane, working hard, and spending his holidays going surfing with his mates in places like Papua New Guinea.

Thomas is back to work, but he can't get a bank loan to open his own bar because he is too "high risk" for any of the Australian banks that dominate the banking world in Papua New Guinea. He is considered, by the assumed nature of his being, the assumed nature of his subjectivity, to be *lacking*. Thomas, like others in New Ireland, is assumed to be— and here I quote various bank officer whom I interviewed during several "financial capacity building workshops" and "small business development workshops"—"lazy," "easygoing," too focused on "traditional culture," and apt to spend resources on maintaining that "traditional culture" at the expense of paying off a bank loan. Like others in New Ireland, Thomas is thought to be "not ready" to manage money and in need of "financial literacy lessons" and "capacity building." Luckily, there are right-thinking international development consultants and experts who can provide, for the rate of AU$1,000 a day, workshops to bring Thomas and his fellow New Irelanders into the light of modernity via capacity building workshops.

2 "We Are Here to Build Your Capacity"

Development as a Vehicle for Accumulation and Dispossession

I nudge Seku in the ribs with my elbow to persuade her to ask her question. Or rather to ask the question she and I and five of the other women attending the "financial capacity building workshop" had come up with during our tea-time discussion. We are collectively confused about some of the implications of qualifying for credit. Commercial banks in Papua New Guinea rely on a person having "fixed assets" to be eligible for small business loans. We are all taking a multiday government-sponsored course to help us build small businesses. Seku and the other women from New Ireland Province are trying either to start new businesses or to grow their existing businesses. I am sitting in on the workshop to learn more about how Papua New Guineans are imagined, portrayed, and cast by institutional actors—like banks, aid organizations, and nongovernmental organizations—involved in development programs and projects linked to "capacity building."

We are in Kavieng, the capital of New Ireland Province, being "trained" by Papua New Guinean representatives from three of the country's commercial banks. Between 2011 and 2015 I attended similar workshops in Port Moresby, the capital of Papua New Guinea, and Goroka, the capital of the Eastern Highlands Province, and the trainers included Papua New Guineans, Australians, and New Zealanders. During the course with

Seku, all the participants are from small communities like Meteran, a village of about a hundred people on far coast of New Hanover / Lovangai Island and a five-hour boat ride from Kavieng; Panachias, a village with about 300 on the west coast of New Ireland Island and a two-hour drive from Kavieng; or Lovangai, a settlement with about 700 people on the close coast of New Hanover / Lovangai, about a three-hour boat ride from Kavieng. There are also a few participants from town, women who are from a range of natal homes but who, for various reasons, now live in the suburban center of the provincial capital. The trainers are from Port Moresby, a city with a population of over 400,000 residents that is an hour-and-a-half flight from New Ireland.[1]

My little group of small business owners and I are confused because the banks require that people have fixed assets if they wish to apply for loans. A fixed asset, as opposed to a current or liquid asset like cash, is one whose future economic benefit is probable to flow into the business, that is not easily liquidated, and that can be easily and reliably marked with a value or price. In the training fixed assets were defined for people as land deeded to the individual, homes or buildings built on deeded land, motor vehicles, and machinery. We are confused because almost nobody in Papua New Guinea has assets of this kind. We are especially confused about the remarks that have been made about "deeded land." Over 90 percent of the land in Papua New Guinea is "customary land." This means that extended family groups hold land title collectively over multiple generations and that land is often thought to be inalienable. Indeed, specific family relations to land and sea are often thought to be genealogical, meaning that people have an actual kinship relation with aspects of their surroundings (Narokobi 1999). Additionally, many peoples in Papua New Guinea have deep ontological relations with their lands and the assemblages of creatures, plants, and features on it (see J. Bell 2009a, 2009b; Halvaksz 2008; Jacka 2015; Lipset 1997; and West 2005b). Across New Ireland Province, land and sea title have been historically passed between women, as the ethnic groups living there are mostly matrilineal (Billings 1969; Powdermaker 1933).

Finally, Seku asks the question: do banks allow cash in the bank to serve as a stand-in for fixed assets if the women don't own land as individuals, have deeds to their homes, or own equipment or vehicles. One of the trainers, a man, answers, "No, because people here will just loan their money out to wontoks [family] or spend it on grog [liquor], so the banks don't trust people." Quickly his colleague chimes in with a comment about how women, in particular, can't hold on to money in Papua New Guinea because of pressures from their male relatives. Another trainer, a women, interrupts them and explains that the banks understand that fixed assets are hard to come by but that their reluctance to allow people to use cash as a stand-in stems from their observations that Papua New Guineans "lack the capacity" to manage money in a way that assures secure savings accounts and long-term financial solvency, and that we are there for that reason, to have our "capacity" built.

In this chapter, drawing on this ethnographic example and three others, I examine capacity building as one nodal connection between the colonially anchored, yet fully contemporary, fantasies about nature, culture, savagery, discovery, temporality, and gender. Through the ethnography I show that the notion of people "lacking capacity" is always conjoined with the notion of people who are living in a prior, primitive state. This has created, and continues to foster, a set of conditions whereby contemporary Papua New Guineans are dispossessed of material objects and money, their rights of representation—or what I call their "representational sovereignty"—and sovereignty over land and its futures in Papua New Guinea. Ordinary Papua New Guineans are constantly met with the exhausting task of being asked to prove that they are not living in the realm of the primitive. This notion of lacking capacity also allows for

FIGURE 2.1   New Ireland fishers, Kaselok Village. Photograph courtesy of J. C. Salyer.

Papua New Guinean experts to be given lower material compensation for labor and education equal to their international counterparts. Finally, I demonstrate how discussions of *capacity* often pull anthropologists into the role of "savage slotting" Papua New Guinea in the ways I critiqued in the introduction.[2]

We have seen how tourism, as an economic and social form, relies on mediated images, how these images drive touristic desire and practice, and how these desires and practices then drive the material configurations of the tourism industry and the enforced behaviors of tourism workers, thereby giving tourists the exact sense of experience that they initially desired. The previous chapter focused almost entirely on the experiences of men and the notions of expatriate and national masculinity that are intertwined with deeply held Euro-Australian-American fantasies of discovery, danger, and virility and demonstrated the connection between touristic fantasy and dispossession. All semiotic-material cycles of dispossession depend on racist, colonial, ideologies to set the conditions of possibility for seeing Papua New Guineans, international circuits of capital to move images and people, and the frontier myth to hollow out the real lives and bodies of Papua New Guineans thereby opening up space for external investments of various kinds. International development interventions transform this semiotic-material cycle into a diagnosis of Papua New Guineans having a profound "lack," which calls for technical solutions and interventions from elsewhere and encourages ignoring the structural constraints and conditions that entrench inequality in Papua New Guinea.

Natural Resource Extraction, Environmental Conservation, and National Expertise

Papua New Guinea is in the midst of a profound social, economic, and environmental transition. The Papua New Guinea Liquefied Natural Gas (PNG LNG) project, which ExxonMobil initially conceptualized in 2004 and began in earnest in 2008, entailed the construction of 450 miles of pipelines, multiple gas-processing facilities, and a major gas storage facility. The project moves 6.9 million tons of gas out of Papua New Guinea to China and Japan each year and will do so for the next thirty years. The initial phase of the PNG LNG project brought an estimated US$15 billion into the country's economy, and the first gas shipment happened in May 2014.

In July 2011, a few years before the gas and its revenues began to flow, an American big international nongovernmental organization (a "BINGO") that focuses on environmental conservation visited the Eastern Highlands Province with representatives from ExxonMobil. The BINGO brought these Exxon representatives to Goroka to hold a series of meetings to discuss the administration of a proposed Biodiversity Offset Fund to be associated with the PNG LNG project. The Biodiversity Offset Fund is a mandated condition for the financing of the project. The international financial institutions and commercial banks that are lending ExxonMobil the funding for the project are bound by the principles of the International Finance Corporation's "Performance Standard 6: Biodiversity Conservation and Sustainable Natural Resource Management" (IFC 2012). Performance Standard 6 states that all new major resource extraction projects must create and maintain a fund to offset the project-caused loss of biodiversity over the life of the project. If companies do not follow these standards, neither international financial institutions nor commercial banks will lend them money. It is estimated that the Exxon PNG LNG fund could be as much as US$100 million over the next thirty years.

Exxon Mobil approached the BINGO for advice about how to create, maintain, and administer this fund for Papua New Guinea. To mitigate the negative effects of biodiversity loss, the money was meant to support large- and small-scale conservation projects and large- and small-scale conservation research, both at sites along the pipeline and at other national sites. As of the July 2011 meeting, the BINGO had already received US$600,000 to help ExxonMobil plan for setting up the fund. The BINGO brought Exxon to Goroka to meet some of the national scientists that the BINGO contracts with to do their work in Papua New Guinea in order to show that they understood the landscape of biodiversity conservation in the country.

Since 2004 I have worked with a group of colleagues in and from Papua New Guinea on a long-term project centered on providing opportunities for young people from Papua New Guinea who want to become scientists and anthropologists. In 2007 we cofounded the Papua New Guinea Institute of Biological Research (PNG IBR) an NGO dedicated to this objective. We find the best and brightest undergraduates in the country, invite a small set of them to come and live in Goroka after they graduate from university, and prepare them to compete for international scholarships to masters and PhD programs. While with us, they earn an honors degree through one of our partner national universities. Our staff advises their honors projects and their applications to scholarship programs and graduate school. We are the only NGO in Papua New Guinea or outside of Papua New Guinea that focuses on national education in the sciences and anthropology with the goal of enrolling students in international programs and then facilitating their return home to work in national conservation. We also provide employment for many of the people who come back to Papua New Guinea with advanced degrees in the fields we specialize in. These national scientists then work with small-scale conservation initiatives in communities where they have longstanding ties. They consult with communities regarding conservation projects that they have identified as urgent, help the communities find funding for the projects, and help them understand the ecological and social conditions at play in the local use of various elements of biological diversity. One of our founding principles is the proposition that the conservation of biological diversity in Papua New Guinea can only be achieved if Papua New Guineans have full sovereignty over that diversity.

During the visit to Goroka, representatives of Exxon and the BINGO requested to meet with the directors of PNG IBR. I happened to be in town and am on the board of directors, so I was invited to join the meeting. On a sunny morning we all sat together on the patio of the PNG IBR offices, we were seven board members and senior staff of PNG IBR (two white women and the rest national ecologists), four BINGO employees (one a longtime Papua New Guinea researcher and three of whom had never been to the country before), and two representatives from Exxon. PNG IBR staff were asked, with no prior warning that they would be asked this, how they would spend $100 million on conservation in Papua New Guinea. After the question was asked, I watched my colleagues from Papua New Guinea sit in complete silence for a while. Finally, they began to throw out ideas based on what PNG IBR already does: train students, work with communities to create small but effective conservation areas in places where our students and staff have long-term field sites, partner with communities to help them understand the population ecology of prey species that they are concerned about in terms of loss of biomass associated with hunting and habitat loss, and repatriate biodiversity sovereignty to national scientists and landholders living in rural, highly biologically diverse, areas.

About an hour into the meeting, one of the BINGO representatives spoke up and said that he really thought the PNG IBR staff ideas were interesting but they showed, clearly, that PNG scientists and NGOs didn't have the "vision" to manage a biodiversity offset fund. Then, right there in front of my national colleagues, the four BINGO employees shifted the discussion to a conversation about how Papua New Guinea "lacks capacity." The following things were said—and these are all direct quotes—in the following order:

"Papua New Guinea does not have the internal capacity to manage and administer a fund of this size."

"Most people in Papua New Guinea live in precapitalist societies where people do not understand money and have a cargo cult mentality."

"Handling this much money would just disrupt society."

"Most well-educated people in Papua New Guinea who work for the government or for most of the organizations that do deal with large amounts of money are corrupt."

"The government of this country is totally corrupt; it's just a worse version of big men and the wontok system."

"National management of this fund would be a disaster."

A second example of how capacity building rhetoric is deployed in Papua New Guinea revolves around a close friend of mine who is from Papua New Guinea and has a bachelor's degree from a prestigious university in Australia and two international master's degrees, one from Australia and one from Germany. Esso Highlands Limited, the arm of Exxon that runs the day to day of the pipeline in Papua New Guinea recently interviewed her for an environmental consulting contract. Her expertise is the sustainable development of natural resources and in particular she focuses on helping participants of informal markets so they can learn to capture some of the benefits of oil and gas development without turning to unsustainable harvesting of their natural resources. In a recent project she worked with rural women fishers to help them set up businesses to sell mud crabs to mining companies working near their natal villages, helping them both access these markets and understand issues around sustainable harvesting and crab reproductive biology.

The standard consultant rate in Port Moresby for expatriates is a minimum of US$1,000 per day (not including housing, food, and transportation, which are also part of the standard pay package for expatriate workers in Papua New Guinea). Esso Highlands offered my friend the position at a salary of $200 per day (all inclusive). When she pressed them on the rate, they said that they were not authorized to pay a national consultant more than that because, as a rule, "nationals" do not have the "capacity" that expatriate workers have.

A third example links capacity rhetoric and rhetorics of prior, autochthonous peoples. When I am in Port Moresby my old friend Malcolm "Mal" Smith, the former governor of the Eastern Highlands Province, asks me on occasion to accompany him to some kind of event. Smith was born in Scotland, immigrated to Australia as a child, and flew helicopters for the Australian army in Vietnam between 1963 and 1967. After leaving Vietnam, he moved to what is now Papua New Guinea and has lived there ever since. He is now the owner of Pacific Helicopters, a company he started with one helicopter in 1975, and a citizen of Papua New Guinea. During the second week of August 2011, he asked me to accompany him to dinner with some people he called "gas execs" at the Bacchus Restaurant at the Airways Hotel. The Airways Hotel in Port Moresby is the go-to hotel for the oil and gas industry elite in the country. Our hosts for dinner that night were several employees of a small petroleum exploration and development company focused on developing oil and gas reserves in Papua New Guinea, Poland, Canada, and the United States. We had dinner with the company's country manager, its president for exploration, and its vice president for exploration.

The dinner was delicious, the conversation was lively, and the bill was well over US$1,000 for five people eating and drinking.[3] During dinner, as the waiters brought us delicious dish after delicious dish, and bottles upon bottles of wine, we talked about many different things, but most of the conversation focused what my dinner companions called "culture" in Papua New Guinea. The vice president for exploration had never been to Papua New Guinea before, so his colleagues asked me, as an anthropologist, to give him an introduction to "culture" that specifically included explaining the "wontok system," the "big man system," "brideprice," and "compensation"—all anthropologically generated terms that have become part of the day-to-day discussion of "culture" in Papua New Guinea. During our discussion after my forced lesson, both of the company's employees who had spent time in Papua New Guinea invoked the image of the "primitive" as conjoined with these assumed "cultural" complexes in Papua New Guinea repeatedly. One of them told a story about meeting a "tribe" in Jiwaka Province who had never before "seen a white man"; the other talked about places where "people don't even wear clothes."

Finally, their conversation turned, as it always does with this sort of crowd, to why working in Papua New Guinea is "so hard," why landowners are so "difficult to deal with," why "compensation ruins progress and keeps people in poverty," and why projects "fail" in Papua New Guinea. I was, again, looked to as the go-to expert on all culture in Papua New Guinea and asked to explain "all the tribal problems," why "locals can't manage money," why there is a "shortage of skilled labor" in Papua New Guinea, and why, in general, both locals and the state "lack capacity." Once the these floodgates had been opened, Mal and I sat back and listened to the rest of the conversation, which shifted in focus to the various ways autochthonous peoples everywhere "lack capacity." The executives moved with alacrity between their critiques of people in Papua New Guinea, the First Peoples of Canada, and Native Americans in the United States.

Capacity Building

The term "capacity building" has a reasonably short history in development discourse. Used sporadically in the 1970s and 1980s, it came to prominence in the 1990s when it was directly connected to internal and external United Nations assessments of why technical solutions to development problems did not seem to work (see UNDP 2009). The general assumption on the part of development practitioners was that all problems of development had a potential technical or technological fix. Once that technology was found and implemented, the problems identified would cease to be problems and *development* would occur. Technocrats were put in charge of defining, visualizing, describing, and assessing development problems, and their techno-visions set the conditions of possibility for solutions. They saw technological lacks and came up with technological solutions. These solutions seldom included people. When assessments began to show that development—as measured by agreed-upon indicators—was not happening (even though of course the ethnographic data had shown this for decades), the idea of capacity building came to the fore in development planning. Technology was still seen as the ultimate answer (with lack of technology being the ultimate cause).[4] But the proximate cause was that the "underlying human and organizational capabilities" of people in underdeveloped places and in the organizations that managed development needed to be "strengthened" (UNDP 2009). Capacity development schemes were thought to be appropriate for all scales: individuals, organizations, and whole societies. A 2008 European Center for Development Policy Management study defines capacity as "the ability of individuals, institutions and societies to perform functions, solve problems and set and achieve objectives in a sustainable manner," as "the ability of people, organisations and society as a whole to manage their affairs successfully," and as "the ability of an organisation to function as a resilient, strategic and autonomous entity" (Baser and Morgan 2008:22).

Scholars of development have written about capacity building as a buzzword (Eade 2007) and as a new development fetish (Clarke 2010), locating it, to some extent, as another twist in the endless reimagining of development speak and policy. Cook and Kothari (2001) show how it has become seen as a kind of moral obligation in the wider development practice of "participation." LaHatte identifies the larger political economy of capacity building and argues that "positioned as a technical, apolitical solution to development's intractable failures, capacity building is part of the broader neoliberal development agenda that has come to dominate development practice. Within this agenda, capacity building occurs through education, training, human resource development (HRD), and new managerialist activities all aimed to instill 'good governance' and ultimately increase development effectiveness" (LaHatte 2015:2; see also Kenny and Clarke 2010). Like other forms of neoliberal ideology, practice, and policy (see Castree 2010), the focus is on individuals and individual agency, and there is a sleight-of-hand dismissal of structural constraints and structural histories of all kinds. There is also a secondary sleight of hand in which the long-articulated colonial notion of indigenous peoples and colonized peoples having an inherent lack is brought back into official development language and practice. This notion has, of course, been ideologically present in all development interventions, but the term "capacity building" smuggles it back in as a modern rhetoric. The ideology inherent in capacity building—that there is an inherent lack in non-European persons, institutions, and social systems—is almost always operationalized as a set of technical solutions (trainings, structures, audit cultures) that do not address the structural causes of inequality. This historic, persistent, and insidious notion of lack drives all intervention done under the guise of capacity building. Three scholars working on capacity building bring ethnographic specificity to this development ideology, policy, and practice.

The Community Health Planning and Services initiative in Ghana, which Harriet Boulding discusses in her recent work, stems from the results of a research project that found that "providing resident nurses increased the interactions of community members with health services by eight times that of district health centers" (Boulding 2015:1). So the health services created an initiative to place nurses in direct, daily, contact with women in rural households. Additionally, the project took as part of its premise that these nurses would be more effective if they had additional training (on top of their clinical nursing training) to help them build "relationships with community members" and gave them "counseling skills" (Boulding 2015:2). This was a "capacity building" initiative focused on individuals as well as on "enabling environments," and it was built on a reasonable idea: creating social ties between health workers and women would make women more likely to utilize health services if they had health problems (Boulding 2015:4). If you have ever worked in a rural community, this may seem a bit of a no-brainer. But Boulding's work shows that the standardized and structured guidelines given to the nurses during the capacity building trainings actually foreclosed any ability they might have to create real social ties with women and some households. The standardized data collection they were taught to do and the structured temporalities they were taught to maintain did not reflect the sociality or the temporality of the communities in which they worked. Boulding demonstrates that they also didn't reflect a deep knowledge of the local ways of maintaining and creating social networks. Indeed, she shows that *building the capacity* of these nurses was meant to result in their working outside of historic, local, structure, practice, and convention.

Kristin LaHatte's work investigates acts of capacity building in Haiti as well as the ideological underpinnings of capacity building as a nodal practice in neoliberal development interventions (LaHatte 2015). She shows us that by focusing on the individual as the locus of change and advancement, capacity building replicates the notion that inequality is not a structural systemic failing but rather a failing at the level of individuals that can be fixed by altering individuals. She also points to a subtle aspect of capacity building that is not talked about in USAID manuals: that the ultimate goal is to produce new kinds of persons and that, in doing so, it is assumed that new kinds of institutions and societies will follow. In the push to produce new kinds of persons there is an inherit critique of prior kinds of persons and of the social worlds that those persons inhabit and "consider socially and morally appropriate" (LaHatte 2015:20). In Haiti capacity building, while ostensibly a technical apolitical solution to the failures of development, is actually an attempt to radically alter social reproduction (see Katz 2002).

Christopher Hewlett demonstrates that the notion of lack inherent in the idea of capacity building is historical, based on an Enlightenment notion of how people and society are meant to be ordered and organized. Using historic and ethnographic work from Peru he argues that part of capacity building's origin is in the colonial push "to bring indigenous people . . . into the modern world and allow them to participate in (Peruvian) modern society while maintaining their cultural identity" (Hewlett 2015:22). This is also the origin of a form of recognition politics we see in settler societies today (see Povinelli 2002 and Simpson 2014). Hewlett highlights a historical set of assumptions about individual and societal lacks among indigenous peoples. He shows how well-meaning individuals created interventions ostensibly meant to incorporate indigenous peoples into productive modern society. Yet underlying all this well-meaning do-gooder-ism, there is an inherent focus on creating particular types of state-citizens and particular types of relations to land and natural resources that set the stage for ongoing dispossession.

LaHatte, Boulding, and Hewlett also show us that the peoples being targeted by capacity building have their own senses of where capacities and responsibilities sit in and with and between entities. For Amerindian groups, capacities sit in corporality and bodies and the forms of transferences and exchanges between bodies (and here we mean human and nonhuman bodies). When these transferences and exchanges are translated into "knowledge" or "practice" and targeted for alteration by missionaries, development practitioners, or the state they are diminished (Hewlett 2015). For Haitians, capacities are located in the very set of social relations of obligation and person making that development interventions seek to change: the all-encompassing set of social relations that are people's "security blanket" in life (a phrase LaHatte heard when her interlocutors discussed local ideas about capacity building). Social relations that are seen as, and described as, "corrupt" by development interventions are targeted for intervention and change (LaHatte 2015). In rural Ghana, capacities sit in the rhythms and temporalities of village life. To foster better health care for women, rural health workers would have to move with and in these often irregular, seemingly disorganized, rhythms and temporalities of village lives. Yet the very structure of the capacity building interventions works against this movement (Boulding 2015). So capacity building work done in these places is also meant to be a process of transformation. *It is about creating new persons, new forms of social reproduction, and new social networks.*

Recently, this rhetoric of capacity building has thrived in Papua New Guinea. Between 1950 and 1970 there were only two scholarly citations (including published papers, government reports, and United Nations reports) that mentioned "capacity building" and New Guinea.[5] Between 1970 and 1980 there were three, between 1981 and 1990 there were twenty-nine. But between 1991 and 2000 there were 941, between 2001 and 2012 there were 7,200, and between 2012 and 2015 there are already 4,020 references. Less than half of the AU$483 million of Australian Aid money that goes to Papua New Guinea yearly goes to Papua New Guinean individuals or institutions.[6] In fact, 46 percent of aid goes to "technical assistance programs" to bring in Australian and other experts to help "build capacity" (ACFID 2010:14). In 2010 Australia had 1,204 technical advisers in the aid program and, "according to AusAID, the average cost for long-term expatriate advisers was $20,015 per month and for short-term advisers, $1,618 per day."[7] A 2010 review commissioned by the governments of Australia and Papua New Guinea found that "the heavy reliance on technical assistance for capacity building in the Australian aid program to Papua New Guinea is its most controversial aspect" and that these programs do not seem to be working.[8] Yet capacity building is still an entrenched representational rhetoric that has gotten loose from "bank speak" (Moretti and Pestre 2015) and become one of the rhetorics through which ideologies of autochthonous peoples are made in this material-semiotic-hermeneutic circle of frontier-discovery-dispossession.

Capacity Building, Environmental Conservation, Resource Extraction, and Sovereignty

There is a particular international structure to funding for the conservation of biological diversity. Since the neoliberalization of most national economies in the 1980s and 1990s, national funding structures for in situ conservation have been truncated to the point of near nonexistence (see West 2012: chap. 2). Today, the global North sets the agenda for environmental conservation everywhere and funds most conservation globally. The major funders for international conservation are multilateral organizations like the World Bank, the World Trade Organization, and the United Nations. Ostensibly made up by various countries, these funders are dominated by the global North and by bilateral organizations like USAID and AusAID, organizations that receive their funds from governments in their home countries and use those funds for international work that is meant to benefit those home countries. The secondary funders for conservation are large private foundations, most of which are located in the United States and Europe. Some of these are the Gordon and Betty Moore Foundation, the MacArthur Foundation, and the Ford Foundation. These foundations usually have boards of directors for their conservation programs that are made up of American and European scientists. Increasingly, corporations, like mining companies, fund the funders or serve as "partners" in particular funding agendas (Robinson 2012). Indeed, the Convention on Biological Diversity, the multilateral treaty meant to conserve global biodiversity, included corporations in its list of partners as early as 2002 after its COP 6 meeting (CBD 2005).

Periodically all of these institutions—primary and secondary funders as well as "corporate partners"—send out calls for proposals. The calls are based on strategic plans, programmatic initiatives, and the results of international meetings like the meeting of the International Union for the Conservation of Nature (an international conservation organization that spun off from UNESCO in the 1950s) and the biennial meetings of the directorate for the Convention on Biological Diversity. The calls for proposals circulate internationally, and many organizations apply. The vast majority of these major conservation grants go to the BINGOs: the World Wide Fund for Nature (WWF), Conservation International (CI), the Nature Conservancy (TNC), and the Wildlife Conservation Society (WCS). These four huge organizations apply for every grant that is offered for conservation in Papua New Guinea.

These organizations have professional grant writers, full-time accounting offices, and famous board members (for example, the actor Harrison Ford is the vice chair of the CI board of directors and Rob Walton, of Wal-Mart fame, is the chair of its executive committee). They have huge professional staffs in their head offices. They also have huge endowments. Their in-country programs, however, are often responsible for paying for their entire office operations with external grants that they apply for from large funding organizations. In Papua New Guinea the in-country programs were developed in the late 1980s and early 1990s as an open attempt to capture the revenue flows that were coming into the country from international funding for Integrated Conservation and Development Projects (see West 2006). To be clear here—the global North sets the agenda for conservation, then funds that conservation, employing, for the most part, outsiders, even when organizations like

CI, WWF, and WCS have "national offices." This process dispossesses Papua New Guineans of sovereignty over biodiversity in their country, currently and in the future.

Once grant money is in hand, the projects actually have to be carried out. The vast majority of work done in Papua New Guinea by the BINGOs (including their national offices) is contracted to national NGOs. The national NGOs are contracted to do the labor of the grant but not to administer or manage it. All small NGOs in Papua New Guinea take part in these agreements to do the work promised to funders by the BINGOs. It is rare that the national NGOs or their national staff have been consulted in the grant-winning process, and the proposals funded often go against the grain of what national scientists think are the paramount issues in their countries as well as the experiences of what works in conservation in these countries. These contracts rarely pay overhead costs (things like rent, insurance, utilities, audit fees, car and truck costs, and insurance); nor do they tend to pay for office staff (receptionists, office managers, accountants, directors); nor do they pay for staff superannuation, salary taxes (which the employer must pay in Papua New Guinea), housing allowances (which all decent national employers pay in Papua New Guinea), or insurance; nor do they pay fair wages to national scientists. BINGO contracts tend to pay a per diem rate with the assumption that your salary base will be paid by the NGO that you work for. These per diem rates tend to be slightly above the minimum wage for the country. The result is that national scientists serve as waged labor in conservation, again having little sovereignty over conservation futures.

As a board member of PNG IBR I have had the opportunity to speak with funders about why we didn't get a grant we applied for when one of the BINGOs did. On more occasions than I can count I have been told that that we just don't seem to have the capacity to carry out the work we have detailed. And on many of those same occasions I've been told that our scientific staff will benefit from, learn from, and begin to move toward that capacity, by working with BINGO staff. Our staff are "just not ready yet" to manage projects, grants, and the like, or to define conservation agendas for their country. Ultimately, for many of these projects that we have applied for and not gotten the grants for, the BINGOs ask us to contract our staff to do the labor on the grant project.

My colleagues at PNG IBR, and other truly national conservation-related NGOs, are constrained from moving freely within this structure—they lack access to the social, economic, and political resources that would allow them to compete on a level field with the BINGOs. Additionally, the representational rhetorics place a kind of semiotic structural constraint on my colleagues, which feeds back into why they don't have the social, economic, and political resources that would allow them to compete.

Let us return to the comments the BINGO employees made to the Exxon employees while they were sitting with five internationally gradu-ate-trained national ecologists and two American board members of PNG IBR. First, the comments centered on *capacity*, focusing on the idea that people in Papua New Guinea do not have the ability to manage large amounts of money, had an almost "bank-speak" tone to them, as if we were all, jointly, discussing the *lack* of certain forms of "development" in Papua New Guinea. Almost immediately, the one BINGO employee who had previously worked in Papua New Guinea switched to a voice of having-been-there authority. He described "most people in Papua New Guinea" as living in "precapitalist societies,", not understanding money, and having a "cargo cult mentality." He sets his authority by using the term "cargo cult"—a term generated and popularized by anthropologists that has become one of the most frequently used bits of rhetoric for people

FIGURE 2.2   Papua New Guinea Institute of Biological Research scientists, Sera Research Station. Photograph courtesy of J. C. Salyer.

attempting to show the lack of modernity among people in Papua New Guinea (see West 2005b). He then moved to a paternal tone, worrying that Papua New Guinean "society" would be "disrupted" by the burden of managing money, echoing the colonial writers Regis Tove Stella (2007) directs us to (as well as the statements made by many of the surfers I discussed in the previous chapter).

This specialist's comments about what forms society takes in contemporary Papua New Guinea—as he sat at a table with elite national scientists—are a rhetorical strategy of hollowing out. Indeed, they are an identical form of hollowing out to what I proposed in the introduction to explain Neil Smith's rent gap theory (Smith 1992). A quick reminder: the rent gap describes the disparity between the current rental income of a property (its real current value) and the potentially achievable rental income (what could be its value if certain semiotic and political work is done to lower that current value to a point where nobody will want to invest in the property). The real estate agent, or in this case, the BINGO employees, then swoop in and buy up the property when its price is at its nadir. They depress the market for a site so that they then can profit from investing in it themselves.

The BINGO employee used the notion of a "precapitalist society" to cast Papua New Guineas in a way that erases the expertise of my colleagues— national scientists who know their country's biological diversity and who are well placed in terms of guaranteeing its conservation—and produces an image of autochthonous peoples, places, and times. "Precapitalist societies" is a proposition, through rhetoric, that the real citizens of Papua New Guinea are prior and exist in a "mythic chronotope" that mirrors ideas about unilinear evolution and assumes that some people, like Exxon and BINGO employees, live in the present while others, like "most people in Papua New Guinea," live in the past. As I illustrated in the previous chapter, using the work of Rupert Stasch (2011) and David Lipset (2011), that chronotope is not just a discursive form for ordering events in time and space; it is a rhetorical strategy meant to engender action.

Having located "most people in Papua New Guinea" in another, parallel temporality, the BINGO employee then, again invoking anthropological vocabulary to enhance his authority, refers to "big men" and "the wontok system." He uses these terms to highlight the failings of the government and "corruption," in case he has not yet effectively erased the expertise of my colleagues and set the conditions whereby his colleagues will be viewed as the appropriate stewards of biodiversity in Papua New Guinea.

This rhetorical turn scales up from the level of the individual to the level of the institution and calls to mind scholarly work done on "failed states" and "corruption" in Papua New Guinea that the Exxon employees would certainly know. He transfers the lack from the individual to the state and then ends by invoking "disaster."

His goal with all of this rhetorical representation is dispossession. First he wishes to take money that might go to a national NGO, so he is focused on financial dispossession. This is actual financial dispossession. Second, he wishes to dispossess my colleagues of sovereignty over the future of biodiversity in their country. The projected value of the fund at the time (US$100 million) is more than has ever been spent on environmental conservation in Papua New Guinea. The fund has the potential to radically transform biodiversity conservation in the country. By attempting to grab the fund, the BINGO was effectively saying that Papua New Guineans should not have sovereignty over their own lands, plants, animals, and systems. The BINGO employee also usurps representational sovereignty from my national colleagues during our meeting. Because they know better, they would never characterize *all* Papua New Guineans as anything. They would, as they often do, carefully discuss the nuances of science education in the country and where and how that connects with indigenous ontological worldings as they concern plants, animals, and systems. They would, as they often do, discuss how one must navigate the structures of the Papua New Guinean public service—and the reality that dishonest individuals work in some of the offices—when dealing with government offices connected to forests, oceans, and resource extraction. They would, as they often do, discuss how small-scale funding for small-scale projects with small groups of people tend to produce better conservation outcomes than the mega-projects favored by the BINGOs. My colleagues would also have lively debates about the anthropologically generated terms that the BINGO employee mobilized during his attempt to show his authority in and over their home.

The third level of dispossession embedded in the BINGO employee's comments bring us back to the question of land titling and ownership and how these things are connected to "development" in Papua New Guinea. By scaling up his rhetoric from individuals to organizations to the state, he follows the path by which this "bank-speak" term gets loose from policy and practice and moves into ideology and then back into policy and practice. International institutions, like commercial banks, work to create structures in which only certain forms of title and ownership (fixed assets, for instance) matter in ways that will allow people to access institutional help, like loans, that might help them move out of structural positions of inequality. These structural barriers are tied to a larger system of dispossession that threatens to encompass Papua New Guinea.

Customary land in Papua New Guinea cannot be sold. Its title however, once registered with the state, can be leased—through either a grant or a sale—to an outside party for a fixed number of years. Historically under the British, German, and Australian colonial governments, while there was land alienation in some places for the construction and expansion of cities and towns and for the creation of plantations for coconuts and coffee, there was little disruption of historic land tenure or longstanding familial ontological relations between rural peoples and their lands. For decades now, AusAID has been focusing on land titling and administration projects in Papua New Guinea as a way to alleviate poverty (see T. Anderson 2010). Its leaders, along with many neoliberal economists, argue that land alienation will alleviate poverty by resulting in outside economic investment, which will lead to "development" (see AusAID 2000; Hughes 2004; and Lea 2004). In much of the international literature about development in Papua New Guinea, land alienation is configured as one way to combat the assumed failures of the state and the assumed corruption of the state (Gosarevski et al. 2004; Hughes 2004). These assumed failures of the state are also often connected to economists' "readings" of "culture" in Papua New Guinea (see Fukuyama 2007 and Gosarevski et al. 2004). These economists argue that in a place like Papua New Guinea, which is rich in natural resources but has a system whereby "the country's resources are inefficiently exploited and badly distributed, as a result of a highly dysfunctional political system," there is a "lack of fit" between European institutions and the underlying "society" (Fukuyama 2007:2). Culture and society become cast as a barrier to economic development with the markers for culture articulated as "ethnolinguistic fragmentation" (Fukuyama 2007:9), the "big man system," and "communal land ownership" (Gosarevski et al. 2004:136). All of these elements are then seen as barriers to "savings, investment, and productivity" (Gosarevski et al. 2004:136).

Through AusAID the Australian government has invested a great deal of money into projects connected to the alienation of land, natural resource, and biodiversity in Papua New Guinea (T. Anderson 2010:2). Some of these projects have been focused on "land mobilization," which is a bank-speak term for organizing customary land to be leased or shifting lease systems into systems where land can be sold to outsiders. When "mobilized," "the customary character of land breaks down completely" (T. Anderson [2010]:2; see also T. Anderson 2006a and 2006b). Elsewhere land registration by colonial and seemingly postcolonial governments results in the ongoing dispossessions we see globally (see Coulthard 2014; Simpson 2014; and Trask 1999). The system is not perfect, but because of the enshrinement of customary land tenure in the Papua New Guinean constitution, the majority of the country's citizens, even while facing the structural barriers that foster economic inequality, can produce, hunt, or gather enough food and natural materials to live (T. Anderson 2006a, 2006b; Bourke and Vlassak 2004). This means that people like Seku, my friend from the capacity building workshop, even without individual title to the terrestrial and sea areas she utilizes for both her business and her family's subsistence, can make a living off of her customary property. The rents that Seku, or any other rural landholder, might receive for leased land are nothing value-wise—for example, between 20 and 100 kina per hectare per year in the case of oil palm company leases—compared to subsistence and small scale economy value of customary land which Anderson estimates at 13,400 kina per year.[9]

With Australian-backed land registration pushes in Papua New Guinea, land is registered by people claiming to represent a customary group of landholders; then, through "lease-leaseback" schemes, it is leased to the national government and leased back to a national custodian who can then lease land to a logging company, an oil palm company, a tourism development company, or any other corporation that custodial party wishes to do business with. Once leased in this manner, even if—and this often the case—the person originally claiming to represent the customary group did not, in fact, represent that group or only represented a portion that group, it is impossible for customary landowners to revoke the lease (see Oakland Institute 2013). The commercial returns for the land-leasing company are extraordinary. For example, the same hectare in Papua New Guinea for which Seku might receive 100 kina per year if she were part of a local landowner lease group would garner a commercial return for an oil palm company of as much as 24,671 kina per year (ITS Global 2009).

What this slight diversion into property issues in Papua New Guinea shows us is that the rhetorical strategy used by the BINGO employee—associating Papua New Guineans with a prior savage state and then linking the nation-state to the same rhetoric—connects with this larger system of international development schemes for and of the dispossession of

FIGURE 2.3   Papua New Guinea Institute of Biological Research Decolonizing Methodology seminar, 2015, Goroka, Eastern Highlands Province. Photograph courtesy of J. C. Salyer.

people's sovereignty over land. Recall that capacity building can be targeted to three scales: the individual, the institution, and the state. In Papua New Guinea, all three scales are, after being conjoined with the notion of a lack, rhetorically tied to the primitive, and that formation is used to foster dispossession. The intended results of capacity building are the creation of new persons, new forms of social reproduction, and new social networks. In the end, in terms of policy, practice, and ideology, capacity building is about transforming Papua New Guinea into something else: a vessel for external investment, which will provide high rents to investors, whether AusAID, commercial banks, companies, or conservation organizations.

The rhetorics around "culture" that are deployed in these examples mask structural constraints and structural histories, and they bring us back to the role of the discipline of anthropology in fragmenting social worlds in Papua New Guinea. Linda Tuhiwai Smith writes of the "systematic fragmentation" of indigenous societies and their "systems of order" through imperialism, colonialism, and the forms of research that grow out of these processes (Tuhiwai Smith 1999:28). Her focus is on the carving up of "indigenous worlds" by academic disciplines, but her analysis can be extended to analyze the carving up of worlds into analytic-descriptive bits by anthropologists. Cargo cults, big men societies, the wontok system, brideprice, compensation—all of these analytic-descriptive fragments of indigenous ontological and epistemological worlds are the creations of anthropology. As a field of knowledge production, Melanesianist anthropology made itself relevant to the rest of the discipline through these disarticulated forms. I am not suggesting that the social relations that were described, in part, by these terms are not real but rather that these terms, in all of their partial-truth-ness, like the term "capacity building," "got loose" from anthropology and have now become weapons of dispossession. They help some of the people who use them to smuggle in the notion of the primitive in that sleight of hand that moves our attention away from structural inequality.

Closing the Workshop

After the workshop with Seku and my other women friends from New Ireland, I went for drinks with the bank employees who had run the training, and when I asked them about the refusal of banks to grant loans to people with robust bank accounts but without fixed assets, the bank employees, all Papua New Guinean, gave me reasoning that could have easily come from any international consultant working in development or conservation, as well as from any tourist visiting the country. One man, from Port Moresby, confided in me, "You have worked here a long time, you know these people. They live out in the village, and they don't understand money. They would just as soon give it to someone for a brideprice as they would keep it in the bank to guarantee their loan." A woman who lives in Port Moresby but who is from Lae said, "These people are not developed; they are islanders. They have that cargo cult mentality." When I asked her what that meant, she replied, "They just can't be trusted. What you need down here—because there is so much opportunity—are more people from Australia or from Port Moresby who know how to build a business and won't mix that up with all that village business." Her colleague chimed in, "People out here are simple. They don't know how to manage money; they don't understand that they need to go through the land registration process. And here it's all through the women, so it's even harder." The evening proceeded with these same sentiments expressed over and over again. As people got drunker and drunker, the shorthand term they began to use was *kanaka*, a word originally used to refer to workers and slaves from the Pacific Islands employed in and held in British colonies in the late nineteenth and early twentieth centuries. It is derived from the Hawaiian *kānaka 'ōiwi* or *kānaka maoli*, meaning "from Hawai'i" and was exported along with colonial business interests across the Pacific. It is extraordinarily derogative when used in Papua New Guinea as it connotes backwardness, savagery, and stupidity.

Every morning Seku awakens before dawn. Her house, on New Hanover / Lovangai Island, faces the sea and is close to the Catholic church. Seku tells me that her first thoughts every day are about God and how blessed she is to be his child; then those thoughts turn to her fishing business. She runs a business that consolidates the fishing efforts of numerous men and women around New Hanover / Lovangai and then moves the catch to Kavieng daily so that it can be sold in the town market. The fish must be caught early in the morning, packed in coolers, and then transported on small open skiffs called "banana boats" to town. The boat she uses has a 90 horsepower outboard on it, so on a day with calm seas the travel time between her house and Kavieng takes about an hour and a half to two hours. She will get the best price for her fish, and the fish of the people who she consolidates for, from the two or three hotels that buy local products in the Kavieng market, and those buyers will be at the market before six a.m.

Seku manages the fishers in her village, the transport of the fish to town daily, the fish sellers who move her product in the market, and the money that must be collected daily and paid out to her fishers. She also tends to do shopping for people back on the island when she is in town, deposit money into people's bank accounts, and run other errands that need to be taken care of. She also manages buying fuel for the boat she uses and protecting that fuel once it gets back to New Hanover, a place that depends on boats for all travel yet has no fuel station of any kind, the closest one being in Kavieng.

Seku attended the financial capacity building workshop to learn how to apply for a bank loan to finance the purchase of a freezer. When seas are rough, the trip into Kavieng takes significantly longer than two hours. Her fish don't garner as good a price on these days, so she decided that having ready access to ice would help keep the catch fresh during transport. She also needs a solar power set-up to power the freezer and had hoped that the bank loan could cover this cost also. She told me that she was sure that the workshop would help her to understand what she needed to do to "earn" the bank loan.

During the workshop after Seku asked about "fixed assets"—something she does not have—she was told that the workshop would help "build her capacity" so that she could build her business. Yet Seku will never get a bank loan. This extraordinary businesswoman who is providing what appears to me to be economic development to her neighbors on New Hanover is met with structural constraints, and as with my colleagues from PNG IBR, when those constraints begin to come into view, they are veiled over with rhetorics of lack and primitivism, casting the blame for inequality on them and not on larger systems of structural oppression and dispossession.

3 Discovering the Already Known

*Tree Kangaroos, Explorer Imaginings,
and Indigenous Articulations*

In 1880 the British naturalist A. R. Wallace characterized the entire island of New Guinea as "the country of the cassowary and the tree kangaroo . . . where the foot of civilized man had never trod" (Wallace 1880:494). Tree kangaroos (Macropodidae *Dendrolagus*) are large (15 to 32 pounds) arboreal marsupials that are found only on the island of New Guinea and in far northern Queensland, Australia. Today, there are three species of endemic New Guinea tree kangaroos on the International Union for Conservation of Nature's endangered species list (*Dendrolagus scottae*, *Dendrolagus goodfellowi*, and *Dendrolagus matschiei*), and the animals have, along with birds of paradise, become emblematic of the island's biological diversity and the perceived and real threats to it.

For research ecologists, tree kangaroos are a fascinating little-known-to-science family (Macropodidae) with only fourteen species members.[1] Although "discovered" in 1826 and named between the 1850s and 1890s, these animals have remarkably little written about them—indeed, a new species, *tenkile* (*Dendrolagus scottae*), was "discovered" in 1990. This makes them alluring research subjects for students who wish to embark on PhD studies that are exciting (because they take place in forested rural areas on the island of New Guinea) and that allow them to contribute to science with just about everything they find (since there is little known by Euro-American-Australian scientists about the animal's behaviors in the wild).

For conservation-related actors, tree kangaroos are emblematic of the kinds of little-known-to-science animals that are being lost because of anthropogenic forces. Conservation scientists working in New Guinea see them as critically endangered because of human population growth, hunting, and habitat loss from logging, mining, and palm oil plantations. Because of the scale at which conservation scientists work in Papua New Guinea, and most other places, they tend to target human hunting and human use of forests materials, which they term "habitat destruction," as the behaviors and actions that must be altered in order to "save" these animals.[2] Conservation marketers working at big international conservation organizations like Conservation International see tree kangaroos as possible "points of funding." These animals are cute. They are small and plush furry, with extremely long tails, pink noses, eyelashes, paws that resemble human hands, and pouches. Inside these pouches are tiny replicas of the larger animals. Donors, both large foundations and individual citizens, are swayed in conservation funding by the charismatic nature of the nature and tree kangaroos are charismatic in photographs and on Web pages.

For economists interested in conservation and development, these animals have value because they are part of "biodiversity," and biodiversity has economic value that contributes to human livelihoods and economies. Increasingly economists have a say in conservation planning and the development of conservation ideology. They tend to see value in biodiversity because it contributes something to humans in economic terms. It "provides or enhances" four areas: ecosystem productivity, insurance, knowledge, and ecosystem services (Heal 2000). Tree kangaroos provide economic value in several ways, according to the logics of economics. First, as "ecosystem productivity" they add to system diversity, and diverse systems are more productive (they produce more biomass, e.g. more species per experimental plot, which means more biomass grown and more nutrients available). Second, as "knowledge" they may have genetic material that could help with veterinary medicine. Third, as "ecosystem service," they are keystone species and their removal or extinction may cause other unforeseen changes in the systems in which they live. Economists also see biodiversity as bits of nature that can contribute directly to markets. For tree kangaroos these markets are tourism (for people who wish to see the animals in the wild and are willing to pay to do so) and research (for scientists who wish to see the animals in the wild and are willing to pay to do so).

For zookeepers, tree kangaroos, like other marsupials, are a draw for children because of their "cuteness." For the animal-interested public, tree kangaroos are a curiosity. Yet they pose a problem in that they don't do much in captivity. When in the wild the animals, spend their time foraging, mating, and caring for young. When in zoos and nature parks they just sit. They are neither "playful" nor particularly active at all. This means that although visitors are attracted to photographs of them, when they see them in (lack of) action, they are left with a feeling of disappointment. To counter this disappointment, zookeepers and zoo education specialists have begun (in zoos in Sydney, Brisbane, and Seattle) to link the animals more and more with the indigenous people who are their "number one predators," as is stated in material from the zoo in Sydney. This linking creates an exciting and seemingly exotic story about the animals that draws zoo visitors into a narrative in a way that tree kangaroos sitting quietly in trees does not.

For many of the indigenous peoples of New Guinea, tree kangaroos are fleeting materializations of the sacred. They play roles in people's philosophical understandings of the world, in their epistemological strategies, in the social relations between the living and the dead, and in poetic expressions that encode bits of history and landscape knowledge, and that at times also bring the world into being. They also, in some places, play an important role in subsistence, as they are often the largest mammals hunted.

In this chapter I offer several examples of the structure and form of the dispossessions that come with the external engagements with the plants and animals that live in coproduced landscapes with Papua New Guineans. Each of these examples focuses on tree kangaroos. The first example is based on ethnographic material that I have collected with Gimi-speaking peoples in the Eastern Highlands Province of Papua New Guinea since 1997. The second example is focused on the history of the European "discovery" of tree kangaroos. I then move to two contemporary narratives of "discovery" connected to tree kangaroos. I use all these examples to flesh out my argument in the introduction of this book: that Papua New Guinea is a site of constant discovery and that that constant discovery has a certain narrative form, a certain set of representational rhetorics associated with it, and that it is always a site of accumulation and dispossession.

FIGURE 3.1   Kile, Goodfellow's tree kangaroo (Dendrolagus goodfellowi). Photograph courtesy of J. C. Salyer.

Gimi World Making

The part of the Gimi world where I have spent the most time is a place called Maimafu.³ While called a "village" by outsiders, the place name encompasses fifteen ridge-top settlements and has about 800 residents. The Maimafu Gimi speak a dialect of Gimi known as Unavisa Gimi.⁴ Gimi hold the forests surrounding their settlements in traditional tenure, and their land spans a topographic range from lowland rainforest to montane cloud forest. Maimafu is in the shadow of what its residents call Bopoyana, or what others call "Crater Mountain," the highest peak of an extinct volcano that last erupted in the Holocene. Maimafu's residents are sedentary shifting horticulturists who rely on hunting for their protein needs. In their gardens they grow sweet potatoes, taro, and other tubers; a variety of leafy greens; and various introduced vegetables like corn, cabbage, beans, onions, squash, pumpkins, and tomatoes. They also cultivate sugarcane, bananas, wild mushrooms, and other food items. Today their major source of cash income is coffee cultivation. There is no road to Maimafu, which makes it difficult for the government-run community school to retain teachers and for much-needed medical supplies to get to the village aid post. There is a grass airstrip, which people use to get their coffee to market, but flights are extremely expensive. There is a small-scale gold mine half a day's walk from Maimafu. The site (EL 1115) is in the Unavi district on land held by the 2,487 Mihive Gimi-speaking people from the Guasa settlement.

The Maimafu Gimi live in the shadow of a failed externally generated and funded environmental conservation project that was known as the Crater Mountain Wildlife Management Area (CMWMA). The project began informally in the late 1970s–early 1980s and was solidified by national and international conservation policies and practices in the 1990s. In October 1994 the Papua New Guinea Department of Environment and Conservation (DEC) declared the area a national wildlife management area under the Faunal (Protection and Control) Act of 1976. The act establishes the mechanisms by which "Wildlife Management Areas, Sanctuaries, and Protected Areas" are set up and maintained. It provides for a set of formal institutionalized mechanisms to regulate wildlife harvesting, possession, and trade in these areas. The CMWMA effectively ceased to exist in March 2005 (West and Kale 2015), but its material and social effects are still felt today.

The ideology behind the wildlife management area was that indigenous peoples of New Guinea do not naturally "value" the biodiversity on their lands but that they could be taught to value it by outsiders who worked to show them that under the right circumstances they could derive economic benefit from that biodiversity. Those circumstances relied on the creation of "conservation enterprises," which linked conservation to development. The WMA program was funded by the Biodiversity Conservation Network (BCN), a part of the larger Biodiversity Support Program (BSP) a USAID-funded program focused on the Asia-Pacific region that funded community-based businesses that depended on biodiversity. "BCN is testing the hypothesis that if local communities receive sufficient benefits from a biodiversity-linked enterprise, then they will act to conserve it" (BSP 1997:iii; see also BSP 1996). Therefore, BCN took as its premise that commodity production and economic incentives that tie people to commodity-based systems are the strategies that would promote the conservation of biological diversity. The hypothesis testing began in earnest with a $20 million commitment from USAID in 1992 and was planned to last for six and a half years ending in March 1999. Part of that money was used to create the CMWMA and to implement programs that would link conservation to development in the minds of Gimi peoples. These programs included creating local businesses revolving around biological research, tourism, and handicraft production; training local men to work with biologists; teaching local men biological diversity and conservation; and implementing a monitoring system to measure the results of bio-diversity conservation. Almost all of these projects, save the handicraft production, were undertaken with Gimi men, as it was understood by the outsiders that forests and the biodiversity in them are part of men's lives and not women's.

Before its demise, the 2,700-square-kilometer CMWMA encom-passed lands that are home to both Gimi and Pawaia peoples, peoples who believe that their day-to-day lives and social relations with the living and dead bring their forests and the plants and animals in them into being. The spaces encompassed by the CMWMA matter to the Gimi and Pawaia because they sustain them and are sustained by them, because they hold and tell their history, and because they are the source and the sink for their cosmological relations with the past and the future. Although neither of these sociolinguistic groups thinks of the world in terms of Western notions of "value," conservation scientists, activists, and practitioners deemed their ancestral lands "valuable" for three main reasons. First, the area is covered with forest that is highly biologically diverse with high rates of endemism. Second, the area is large enough to cover the landscape between lowland rainforest on the Purari River and montane cloud forest on Bopoyana, thus creating a protected area that encompasses multiple natural systems under one project. And third, because there are low human population densities around Bopoyana, it was assumed that human-generated changes to the landscape were slight.

They were not wrong about these biological facts. Gimi territory is extremely biologically diverse, even by New Guinea standards. Although species lists are incomplete for the area, biological surveys have revealed 286 species of birds (100 of these endemic), 84 mammals (20 of these endemic), 71 frogs (5 of these occurring nowhere on the planet besides the slopes of Bopoyana), 28 lizards, and 17 snakes. In forest test plots, botanists found 228 species of trees per hectare. In addition, five major vegetation types and seven major terrain types have been identified at Bopoyana. What conservation-related actors never took fully into account, however, was that Gimi have a set of social relations with their surroundings that far surpass what outsiders think of as "value." One of the kinds of creatures that share the world with Gimi peoples are tree kangaroos.

Gimi relations with tree kangaroos are connected to Gimi philosophies of transaction, coproduction, and the relations between the living and the dead. The Gimi view their own subjectivity as attained through transactive relationships between living people, mutual recognition between people and other species, and exchanges between living people, ancestors, and others (both other creatures and other nonhuman agents). For them, everything that "is" and that ever will be is the physical incarnation of their ancestors' life force. They believe that people are made up of flesh, which is made by their social relations and transactions with the living, and *auna*, which is made by their social relations and transactions with the dead. Auna can be thought of as the force that animates a living person. When a person dies, her auna leaves her body and migrates to the forest. Once there, the auna slowly turns into *kore* ("ghost," "spirit," "ancestor," and "wild") and lodges in plants, animals, streams, mountains, birds, and other bits of what we call forests. The life force of a person becomes the forest, with the "wild" parts of the forest becoming filled with and "animated by" the kore of deceased Gimi. Once the auna goes to the forests and begins to infuse itself into wildlife, it becomes part of not only the forest but also the never-ending cycle of Gimi existence. The auna was merely the form that kore took while the person was living, but it always was, and always will be, the kore that animates the forests. Kore might animate a tree kangaroo, a mushroom, a Pandanus tree, a stream, or any other forest element. This makes all elements of structure and process in a Gimi forest the momentary manifestation of this never-ending cycle. And there is profound indeterminacy in this cycle. That auna that animated a creature could have, in the kore form, become anything, anyone, and anyplace. It could have been reinfused into the never-ending cycle of exchange in endless configurations.

The Gimi world then is produced through social relationships between beings. These beings are people, ancestors, spirits, plants, and animals. These social relations are not neutral and economic; they are familial and poetic. In societies based on gift exchange, like Gimi society, identity and personhood are made through social relationships with others. People's capacities are seen as they relate to others and their identities are understood as a composite of the sources that went into making them. Personhood is located at the confluence of relationships that encompass certain knowledges, social capacities, and practices that can only be expressed and utilized with reference to others. Because people are constantly entering into new social relationships, they are always making and remaking identity. The idea of who they are at any given time is only realized through their relations and transactions with others. And that identity is only momentary—it is crystallized in a transaction and then changes and shifts and moves. It is always in process, always becoming. And it is not actually the identity that is important; it is the affinity or multiple affinities that are possible as people, plants, and animals network in and out of each other, the past, and the future.

Men come into the world and bring the world into being through their relations with wild (kore) things in their clan's forests.[5] They bring tree kangaroos, cuscuses, cassowaries, echidnas, megapodes, and other creatures into being through hunting and singing. Unavisa Gimi men hunt marsupials both purposefully and opportunistically, yet highly prized marsupials live at high altitudes and are difficult to find without well-trained hunting dogs. In the past, much marsupial meat was taboo. However, during the drier parts of the year, men went in clan-based hunting parties to the high forests to kill large numbers of marsupials for rituals, and marsupial meat was the only meat consumed during these important social events (Gillison 1993:38). Today, people spend much of their labor time and energy during the dry season harvesting coffee. This has shifted the practice of hunting parties to the wetter season. Since they no longer associate marsupial consumption with rites and rituals exclusively, when animals are encountered during trips to gardens or trips to the forests for other purposes, people are likely to kill them. Marsupials often killed in this manner are ground cuscus or *hama* (*Phalanger gymnotis*), northern common cuscus or *jabe* (*Phalanger orientalis*), common spotted cuscus or *ota* (*Spilocuscus maculates*), and several species of echymipera and bandicoot or *hau*. Even with the local availability of these species and the modern lack of association of marsupials with sacred ritual, men still make special trips to high forests to hunt tree kangaroos because they are highly prized as meat and because the animals are rarely found close to human settlements.

Gimi narratives about marsupials are found in theatrical performances, creation myths, divination and initiation rituals, and songs. Theater was frequently performed in some Gimi areas (Gillison 1993:72–75) until the 1980s when there was a push by missions to do away with "pagan" rituals. Now it is very rare. Since the mid-1970s, when Adventist missionaries began activities in and around Maimafu, the Maimafu Gimi have not performed the ritual enactment associated with male initiation. However, Gimi also describe the behaviors of marsupials when discussing divination rituals associated with sorcery, which is on the rise in the area. Additionally, people describe marsupials and their behaviors in songs. Many of the marsupial songs are composed by individuals and then perhaps become known by others (Gillison 1993:262). Many songs recount a certain historic event on the composer's land and are concerned with property rights, animal behavior, and the social relations between humans and animals.

The following song about *kile* (Macropodidae *Dendrolagus goodfellowi*), shared with me in July 2003, celebrates the animal's resolve, when shot by an arrow, to go as high as possible in a tree:

> *Gomo kile kola kola amene abo*
> *lepetepe me hulu o.*
> *Gamogo asitai hulu siba kereamune*
> *lepetepe me hulu o.*
> *Gomo kile kola kola amene abo*
> *lepetepe me hulu o.*

> The kile (that I see with my own eyes) is bleeding, is bleeding,
> his blood runs down, it runs down, but he goes up the tree.
> He wants to go up to the *gamogo* leaf (that I see with my own eyes),
> his blood runs down, it runs down, but he goes up the tree.
> The kile (that I see with my own eyes) is bleeding, is bleeding,
> his blood runs down, it runs down, but he goes up the tree.

The translation makes clear that it is a song sung about a specific kile, the phrase *amene abo* indicates that the singer has seen this kile with his "own eyes." It is not a kile that lives in collective memory but rather a kile that is in a specific tree, at a specific place, at a specific time. This is important because it indicates that this song is not simply "indigenous knowledge" that can be recorded and passed on. The kile in the song sees the composer, and the composer sees the kile. It is in that moment of recognition that hunter and hunted form a social relationship of exchange. The kile as food makes the hunter's body while the kile as embodied ancestor or kore makes the auna of the hunter. This moment constitutes Gimi, other, past, present, and future and reveals Gimi as being-in-the-world in ways that are absolutely not about economic valuation of "natural resources."

Regarding animal behavior, bringing Gimi forests into being, and relations to clan ancestors and the past, the composer of the song says,

> When you shoot kile or *kama* [Macropodidae *Dendrolagus dorianus*] with an arrow, the first thing that happens is that blood comes down from its nose. That is when you know that you have gotten it. When it begins to bleed, and it knows that you've gotten it, it always goes higher and higher and higher in the trees. It knows and it goes. It knows and it goes. Kile and kama always go to the same tree when they are shot, they try to find the *gamogo* [a kind of tree]. So you know when you shoot one and you lose it, it has gone to the *gamogo*.
>
> Usually, when you see them, or when the dogs find them, they are *ya-ahmipi* [sitting at the base of a tree] or *milivi* [down in a low place where they can find food]. They sleep *ya-ahmipi* and they find most of their food *milivi*. At night they get cold sleeping *ya-ahmipi*, so when they wake up in the morning, they go *yahalagapi* [to the top of the trees]. They stay there and warm themselves in the warm sun all morning. At *folaelae* [midday] they come down to eat and they find their food. If the female has a baby it is easy to catch her, she is thinking about her baby and not about other things. The baby is in her *ahme ko* [pouch; lit., breast + net string bag] and she is slower than usual. They are always together, *bana* and *badaha* [male and female]; they are like people and they get married. . . . When my ancestor, Lioni, came to this place [in the song] first, he was the first one, he killed kile, and the blood from his nose dripped on this ground. Since then, this has been Lionisuwana [my family's ground].

The first part of this explanation is about the mutual recognition between hunter and animal. The animal and the hunter know each other's behaviors because they have both done this before. The hunter has done it during his life and during his ancestor's lives, and the animal knows the behaviors because it is the physical embodiment of the kore of the hunter's ancestors. The second part of the explanation is about producing forests as spaces of animal and human action. The composer discusses the animal's behavior in detail to show that the creature has a way of life, that it is not simply an animal that acts randomly but a being that has customs. As such, the animal is much more than a "resource";

it is a being that has social relations with other beings and a set of tem-
porally guided behaviors. The final part of the narrative shows how clan
grounds are claimed and how these claims are reasserted through the
actions of hunters and animals. People claim ground through use—
current, historic, and in traditional stories. The hunting and killing of
kama and kile is often recounted when one asks a man why his clan holds
a particular piece of ground. The composer explained to me, "We know
that the ground is Lionisuwana because my ancestor killed kile here. He
could have only killed kile with the help of his ancestors. They showed
him the way to this place for the first time. They led him to this part of
the forests because they were already here."

Songs can also be more specifically concerned with moving the dead
into the forests:

> I want to see the Yauw-one waterfall
> kama and *waya* [Papuan lorikeet, *Charmosyna papou*] we see you go
> up the waterfall
> I want to see the Tiruwa-one waterfall
> kile and *hane* [little red lorikeet, *Charmosyna pulchella*] we see you go
> up the waterfall.

The composer of this song explained that when he sings it he thinks
of his daughter who died while she was walking in the forest when a
tree toppled over and crushed her. The composer knows that sorcery was
responsible for her death because she was walking on his clan's ancestral
land and because the tree was one that he was going to use to build her
brother a new house—the very tree he had picked because it was close
to where his own father had once killed kile. The land is close to their
hamlet, so he was certain that his father's luck in finding kile there had
to do with the kore of his ancestors. Logically, a place like this could not
cause his daughter's death through ordinary means. Her death by sorcery
is a constant source of pain for him, and the song helps to lessen his
pain, it is about healing the living and helping the dead. After I recorded
the song, in October 2005, he explained to me: "When I sing this song it
brings back the pain of her death. It takes me there to the place where she
died. I sing about the Yauw-one and Tiruwa-one [the waterfalls] because
if I could drink from the water on my ground, I could begin to lose my
sorrow. I composed the song right after she died. I went to the place and
I sang to lose my sorrow."

Gillian Gillison, writing about the actions taken after a death to ensure that the auna leaves the person's hamlet, says, "Waterfalls are called *kore abe* or 'ghost urine,' a euphemism for semen, because, like mountains, giant trees and other forest monuments, they represent ultimate transformations of personal auna into kore" (Gillison 1993:122). Ine's song is a mourning song that worked to draw his daughter's auna into the forest.

When the auna of the dead "penetrates" marsupials, animals that it seeks out in particular, it reenacts events from traditional women's mythology and comes to be part of this cycle (Gillison 1993:92–95, 122). Marsupials can also be used in divination rituals: After a person's wandering kore has been "housed" (Gillison 1993:122) in an animal, it can help living relatives find their killer through divination rituals involving the live animal being questioned by elder men. So marsupials are not simply animals to Gimi, they are the literal embodiment of ancestors, and what has been translated as "environment" is not simply a place filled with floral and faunal resources waiting to be used or made into commodities, it is a place of social relations between the living and the dead.

Song about marsupials are salient in terms of birth, life, death, and afterlife. For older Gimi, "hunting marsupials" is a metaphor for conceiving a child (Gillison 1993:211). In the past, if a man's wife had a baby, he would venture to the forests and kill many marsupials, guided in his hunting by his own dead parents (Gillison 1993:236). Marsupial meat was also intimately tied to Gimi systems of head payments, rites, and relationships between family members that contribute to the growth of a child through exchange relations. These relationships tie a man's clan and his wife's father's clan tightly together, thus reproducing the social relations between them. Ine's song encodes the relationship between children, life, and parents onto the forests and the tree kangaroos. These songs show that Gimi see themselves as having social relations with animals in similar ways to their social relationships with people, relations of exchange and transaction. They also show that Gimi produce their forests as meaningful spaces through exchanges and transactions with animals, plants, people, and spirits.

When Gimi think about and interact with the forests, there is a constant dialectical relation between organism and environment that is directly connected to how they make themselves and others through transactive relationships and through the sort of mutual recognition that creates subjectivity. With no Gimi there is no tree kangaroo, and with no tree kangaroo there is no Gimi; with no Gimi there is no sweet potato,

FIGURE 3.2   Anna, Maimafu Village. Photograph courtesy of J. C. Salyer.

and with no sweet potato there is no Gimi. Ancestral spirits enliven Gimi forests, but it is, in part, the mutual recognition between Gimi hunters and hunted animals or the merging of the auna of a woman and the auna of her cultigens that creates subjects, produces space, and lies at the heart of Gimi politics of the production. This transactional being-in-the-world, in which subjectivity is constantly being produced, is the way that Gimi see "self" and "other"—be that other another person, an ancestor's spirit, a sweet potato, or a tree kangaroo.

Tree Kangaroos and Their "Discovery" by Europeans

In 1825, on the long journey by sea from New Guinea to France, a tiny tree kangaroo threw itself overboard.[6] I imagine the little animal confused by its surroundings of smooth wood, salt smells, and strange sounds and wondering where its mother and father are (the animals pair bond and raise their young as a social and subsistence unit). I can see the French surgeon, René Primivere Lesson, who had collected it on his voyage around the world between 1822 and 1825 letting the little animal out of its cage for a bit of fresh air. I see it as it hops up from the deck to a crate, then to another, then to the rail, trying to find the highest point available, the tops of these strange trees, and when it could go no further, flinging itself into the deep black below.

"*Merde!*" shouts Lesson, as his prized curio's pouch fills with water and he watches it descend into the ocean.

Lesson's anguish, in my imaginary vision, is tied to his knowledge that when he arrives home and tries to describe this wondrous creature to his naturalist colleagues, they won't believe him. My imaginary Lesson is right to worry.

In 1826 Lesson published his description of the animal, which he called *Kangurus veterum*:

> The animal we provisionally name kangaroo of Aru (*Kangurus veterum N.*) is called Podin by the Papuans of the Port of Dorey, New Guinea. It differs from the Australian kangaroos by the dimension of its limbs. Size is that of a common hare: its ears are proportionately shorter than other species. Head rounded, muzzle more conical, less shortened than the "oulabat" (the swamp Wallaby, *Wallabia bicolor*). Neck less slender. Forelimbs more elongated, stronger, more robust; hindlimbs less long, bigger. Tail is one third shorter. Pelage is uniformly brown on the upper parts, passing to grey on underside. (Flannery et al. 1996:2)

Lesson, even with this description that shows us that he had examined the animal, become intimate with its limbs and ears, its nose and mouth, would not be able to truly identify the new species because he did not have a specimen. Two Dutchmen would bring the first specimens to Europe after a collecting trip to the Dutch East Indies from 1826 to 1828 instigated by the director of the natural history museum in Leiden, Holland, and meant to expand the Dutch scientific knowledge of the natural history of the Netherlands Indies. The director had convened the "Natural History Commission for the Netherlands Indies" himself, and it was a pet project that took the lives of thirteen of his employees between 1820 and 1836 (Flannery et al. 1996:3).

In June 1826, Dr. Salomon Muller, a Dutch knight, and Heinrich Christian Macklot set out in a final attempt to bring the unruly natural history of the territory under control—and to survive the trip. Muller lived to bring back four tree kangaroo specimens that the pair collected in 1828 from the southwestern coast of New Guinea. Macklot met an untimely demise in Java in 1832, but Muller arrived safely home in 1836.

The animals (*Dendrolagus ursinus*, Vogelkop tree kangaroo) obtained by Muller and Macklot would have certainly been pets in the villages from which they were collected (Husson and Rappard 1958). They were purchased by the pair and loaded onboard the ship, a prize for science and a tasty treat for the crew. Three of the tree kangaroos were eaten, their bones carefully preserved, and one was allowed to live so that she could be observed. Indeed, Muller and Macklot, before his death, kept her as a pet. She traveled with them when they left the ship and lived with them when they resided in the Moluccas and on Timor (Husson and Rappard 1958). In addition to discussing her behaviors, their detailed accounts of life with her describe her personality as "extremely tame and trustful, jumped into our lap, and let itself be patted and scratched, in a word, allowed us to treat it as a lap-dog. It seemed not to dislike such caresses either. It followed those who lured it, ate from the hand and with its slightly rough tongue licked our hands and face" (Flannery et al. 1996:3).

Muller and Macklot were by no means the only early naturalists to keep tree kangaroos as pets. Flannery et al. (1996) mention six scientists who kept them, and Flannery himself describes several he has kept over the years. This is rationalized, by early and contemporary scientists alike, as one way to observe the animals. By all accounts they make rather joyous household companions for Europeans.

The first European claim to the island of New Guinea was in 1828 when the Dutch claimed the western half of the island while Muller and Macklot were in the middle of their collecting trip. Muller's return to Europe set off a bit of a frenzy over the island, and the 1850s saw a flurry of activity around it, including A. R. Wallace's famous voyage around the Malay archipelago (1854–1862).

In 1858, Salmon Muller addressed the March meeting of the Royal Geographic Society of London (Müller 1858). In his address, he describes the history of Dutch exploration, the physical conditions of the coasts, his impressions of the high mountains visible from the coasts, the climate, the geography, the river-mouths that meet the coasts, the soil types present (here he cites the work of his now-deceased friend Macklot), the fossils found, and the flora. "Very remarkable is the want of mammalia in New Guinea," he notes, going on to describe the six species of mammals they found, all marsupials. Three of the species were "unknown": one "a little carnivorous pouched animal of the race Phascogale" and the other two, kangaroos, "which differ very characteristically from all others of the class hitherto described, in that they live upon trees." And that for that reason and because of the physical differences, "we have formed them into a new group, under the name Dendrolagus" (Müller 1858:269).

After Muller's talk, which was translated by John Yeats, Sir Roderick I. Murchison, the society president, led a discussion of the merits of scientific exploration of the island. Mr. Crawfurd, a member who "has studied, not only the natural features of the adjoining regions, but also the character and language of the people" (RGS 1858:183) was wholly against the continued study of the island: "Although Providence no doubt had wise objects in view in creating such an island, I believe it to be, as far as we know, the most useless large portion of the globe" (RGS 1858:184). Its jungle was too dense: "It does not contain a single animal useful to man, except a few that have been imported, the hog and the dog," and while it may be interesting to geologists, it was less interesting than nearby Bali. More importantly, its inhabitants were "in an exceedingly rude state," and the only valuable product there was nutmeg. The "rude" natives were, in Crawfurd's opinion, "equivalent to what the Spaniards call the *Indios bravos*—that is the untamed, uncivilized Indians" (RGS 1858:185). The birds of paradise were, of course, important, but not enough to recuperate the island itself to being worthy of further investigation. Here, early on, we see the twinning of the kinds of representations of nature and culture that Regis Tove Stella (2007) points us toward. These rhetorics establish, *scientifically*—in terms of the science of the day—that there is no or little value in the natural world or the cultural world on the island of New Guinea, that it is empty of what should compel a natural scientist.

What is also interesting in the discovery of the tree kangaroo is the emphasis placed on having and watching. Seeing a new kind of animal "in the wild" or even having on one's ship for a while did not give one the authority to describe it. One must possess it, compare its bones and skin to that of other possessions, and locate it within a larger collection before it can be given a particular scientific meaning and value. Newly discovered animals come into being for science first through bones and behaviors. But once they have been gotten and watched, they had to be described. The describers were not the same as the collectors. In anthropology we call the early social anthropologists "armchair" anthropologists. In natural history their counterparts, mostly men living in the Victorian era in the United Kingdom, worked to fit new animal bodies into existing systems of classification. In order for people to visualize these strange creatures, they had to be illustrated and brought visually into being for Europeans. All of the images in the 1800s and most of the ones from 1900 to 1960 were based on dead specimens or animals in captivity.

A Land of Constant "Discovery"

Scientists return to Papua New Guinea over and over again on voyages of exploration and discovery that are connected to tree kangaroos. The rhetoric they use to describe their investigations mirrors the frontier language of gentrification (see the introduction) and their stories and actions intersect with various portrayals of Papua New Guinea's nature and people. These representational rhetorics of discovery empty out the previous meanings attributed to places by people who actually live there. In this way, scientists' rhetorics of discovery are no different from those of the surf-related tourists, development-related actors, and other "discoverers" of Papua New Guinea. Moreover, these scientists practice forms of representational erasure. All of the expatriate research teams I have ever known working in the country rely on the expertise of national scientists, yet these local researchers' names rarely occur in the narratives of discovery. Nor do the indigenous peoples, who are more often than not the ones who alerted the scientists to the presence of an unusual or important creature.

In December 2005 a team of scientists from Conservation International undertook a rapid assessment of biological diversity in New Guinea's Foja Mountains. The trip was part of Conservation International's Rapid Assessment Program (RAP), whose purpose is to "deploy" scientists and "experts" to places in the world that are "poorly understood" in order to assess the biological diversity of the area quickly categorize it as a hot spot or not.[7] The trip to the Foja Mountains was successful beyond the dreams of the organization and the scientists on the trip. The team, made up of people from Indonesia, Australia, and the United States (with no Papuan or Melanesian scientists included) found animals that are "new species" or "undiscovered species," including frogs, butterflies, plants, the first new bird to be "discovered" on New Guinea in past sixty years, and a "new species of tree kangaroo."

Dr. Bruce Beehler, then vice president of Conservation International and head of the Melanesia program, led the trip. "It's as close to the Garden of Eden as you're going to find on Earth," he said of the area.

"We could reach down and just pick up Long-Beaked Echidnas, right in camp" (BBC 2006).

The trip was particularly significant because of the new bird species, since New Guinea is known throughout the conservation world for its birds, and because of the tree kangaroo (*Dendrolagus pulcherrimus*, the golden-mantled tree kangaroo). In Conservation International's press releases surrounding the "expedition," in all the print-news stories that reported it, on National Public Radio in the United States, and on the BBC in the United Kingdom, the discovery of this "new" tree kangaroo was reported as a wondrous discovery, a reminder that there are things out there yet to be known to science, that there is still a chance of finding "Eden" on Earth. In each of the radio reports I listened to, the "discovery" was reported to be a "new species" of tree kangaroo. *National Geographic* and the BBC even hailed the trip as having "discovered" a "lost world" (National Geographic 2006; BBC 2006).

In fact, *Dendrolagus pulcherrimus* is not a new species. It is the smallest member of the Goodfellow's tree kangaroo complex, meaning that it is a subspecies of *Dendrolagus Goodfellowi* (*Dendrolagus goodfellowi pulcherrimus*). It was first named by Tim Flannery in 1993 and first spotted by Flannery and Lester Seri in 1990 in the Torricelli Mountains of Papua New Guinea. Seri and Flannery, in their talking with old men living along the eastern mountain range, heard stories of *weimank*, a tree kangaroo that looked like Goodfellow's but was smaller and more gracile. They began a search for it sending local hunters out over to the western Torricelli range. The hunters returned with a specimen and Flannery, the world's foremost expert on tree kangaroos (and some would actually say all marsupials) identified it as a new species. Seri and Flannery also collected oral history information from hunters in the area and concluded from this that the animal once had a range that was about 95 percent larger than the range they had identified in 1990 after finding the first specimen (Flannery et al. 1996:108–109). One of the first living members of the species seen by scientists, one of the two brought to Flannery and Seri in 1990, when dissected was found to have a shotgun cartridge in its stomach, having eaten it and been unable to excrete it (Flannery et al. 1996:109). At the time of the "discovery" *National Geographic*'s website read:

> The golden-mantled tree kangaroo is just one of dozens of species discovered in late 2005 by a team of Indonesian, Australian, and U.S. scientists on the island of New Guinea. The animal is the rarest

arboreal, jungle-dwelling kangaroo in the world, the researchers say. This was the first time the mammal was found in Indonesia, making it only the second site in the world where the species is known to exist. The kangaroo was discovered on an expedition in the Foja Mountains of Indonesia. The National Geographic Society, Conservation International, and the Biology Research Center of the Indonesian Institute of Sciences supported the expedition. (National Geographic 2006)

Indigenous peoples analyze and remember these trips of "discovery" differently from the expatriate scientists or *National Geographic*. The following story is based on interviews with residents of Maimafu after one scientific expedition. Isabelle and Jean-François Lagrot, trained veterinarians and "travelers" visited Maimafu (a village they describe as "lost in the mountains") in 2002 (Lagrot 2003:42, 48). They came to conduct what they termed "scientific research" and look for tree kangaroos (Lagrot 2003:46). They published the "results" of their visit in the March–April 2003 *Asian Geographic* magazine. In their story they discuss their fascination with the "unknown-to-science" tree kangaroos; their research sponsorship by the firm Merial, which they call "a French-American vet lab"; and their success finding three tree kangaroos in a two-week period (Lagrot 2003:48). They also discuss a number of "magic words" that the "Papuan hunters" they worked with have for animals (Lagrot 2003:48). Two of these "magic words" are *kama* and *kapul*, words that are not magic at all—given that Gimi do not have a notion that any language is "magic" or that individual utterances have the power to change relations between humans and the spirit world.[8] The words simply mean Doria's tree kangaroo in Gimi and tree kangaroo in Melanesian Pidgin, respectively.

Before they went out to Maimafu from Goroka, the capital of Eastern Highlands Province, the Lagrots told the conservation scientists working for Wildlife Conservation Society and the Research and Conservation Foundation of Papua New Guinea that they were a "French film crew" making a documentary on tree kangaroos for French television. They stated that they were under strict time pressure and that they would have only a few days in the Crater Mountain Wildlife Management Area, where Maimafu is located, to film the animals. They told the Wildlife Conservation Society that they were trained as veterinarians but that they were not in the country to work with the animals in any medically related way, only to film them.

Both the Research and Conservation Foundation and Wildlife Conservation Society talked to the Lagrots about Maimafu, tree kangaroos, and the Crater Mountain Wildlife Management Area. Wildlife Conservation Society ecologists, having conducted biological surveys throughout the Crater Mountain area, showed the Lagrots where they thought that they might have the best chance of seeing tree kangaroos in such a short period of time. The Lagrots filmed the Wildlife Conservation Society staff pointing to the location on a topographic map in the Wildlife Conservation Society office. The staff also explained to the Lagrots that Gimi have a good success rate hunting tree kangaroos because they use dogs to track them. They also explained that dogs always either kill or injure the animals. Upon hearing this, both the Lagrots promised that they would not use dogs or even allow the men that they hired to trek with them to bring their dogs with them.

According to my Gimi friends who discussed their visit with me the year after they visited, the Lagrots seem to have forgotten this promise the minute they left Goroka. J. F. Lagrot says in his article that they were much more "successful" in finding tree kangaroos than the American biologists who have been working around Maimafu for the past several years. He explains that the Americans had had little success because they had failed to work with "Papuan hunters" who use dogs, but that he and his wife had spent "a lot of time training the hunters and explaining exactly what [the dogs] were there for."[9] This claim about spending "a lot of time" with the hunters training the dogs is not backed up by Gimi men who accompanied the Lagrots. These men say that once a dog is of hunting age it is as trained as it can be—that you can not teach an old dog new practices.

The locals' recollection of the Lagrots' trip to Maimafu and their work with its residents have several other inconsistencies with Lagrot's own portrayal. One of the men who took them to the summit of Crater Mountain—where they say they captured, photographed, filmed, took blood and hair samples from, and then released several tree kangaroos—sat down with me in the summer of 2003 to discuss the Lagrots and their visit to Maimafu. This man, whom I call Marcus, tells a very different story about the hunting trip and the capture of the animals.

Marcus says that from the beginning of the Lagrots' visit, people in Maimafu were concerned about what they were being asked to do, and about the Lagrots' safety. The couple brought their four-year-old daughter with them to Maimafu and although they mention her in their publication, they do not mention that people initially refused to take her to the top of Crater Mountain. Marcus says, "It is not a walk or a place for a child. It is difficult and dangerous, especially for whites who are not good in the bush. We did not want to take her but they told us that we had to do it." Lagrot says that Marcus, "the team leader," would not let anyone else carry the child (Lagrot 2003:49). Marcus told me that no one else would take the responsibility of carrying the child. At the time Marcus was desperate for cash, and he convinced all the other men from Maimafu to accompany him on the trek.

Lagrot states that the trekking party located the Doria's tree kangaroos on the top of Crater Mountain because they did not want to interfere with the American team's research site. Marcus contends that while they did climb Crater Mountain, they found the tree kangaroos directly in the center of the Wildlife Conservation Society 1998 survey site. He also says that while he and other local men repeatedly told the Lagrots that it was illegal and wrong for them to hunt the tree kangaroos with dogs in the research site, the Lagrots told them that Wildlife Conservation Society had told them that it was OK. As mentioned above, however, they were told the exact opposite: that dogs always either kill or maim the animals and that when this happens, the hunters kill the animals and eat them. This is precisely what happened; the animals the Lagrots found were indeed mauled by the dogs. Marcus told me that after the Lagrots went to sleep at night the hunters easily tracked the injured animals and killed and ate them. He argued that their actions were much more humane than letting the animals die in the forest "for no good reason."

Kangaroo Dispossessions

My Gimi friends and teachers and their ancestors have known tree kangaroos as long as they have known their forested surroundings. They have affective, visceral connections to them (Deleuze and Guattari 1987) not only because these creatures co-produce Gimi bodies through hunting and ingestion but also since they are quite literally made of the substance and makers of the substance of Gimi past, future, and present. Gimi and tree kangaroos come to be in-the-world through the bodily and aesthetic relations that they share. This is, of course, not the only way that Gimi know and make and relate to the creatures. Gimi are hunters, perhaps less so today in a world of Christianity and focus on national schooling, but they are hunters nonetheless, and hunters "know" creatures because of what ecologists would call observed behavioral ecology. Take, for example, my teacher Kabe. He knows these animals in the abstract: he can tell you about their behaviors throughout their life-span. He knows these animals in the specific: he can take you to places where you can see and observe the signs of their being. He also knows them in the poetic, in the forms and structures through which they are brought into the aesthetic worlds of Gimi.

When a scientist or a tourist-scientist, as I have called the Lagrots, comes to Kabe's world and invokes this Western practice and narrative of discovery it is not simply an unintentional oversight (see West 2008). It is a dispossession. While these scientists and others may well not understand Gimi relations to their surroundings—never mind that Gillian Gillison and I have been writing about Gimi-worldings collectively, although not together, since the 1970s *and* since all of our work is easily available to people—there is no way that they would ever encounter these creatures without information and guiding provided by Gimi and national scientists. This is the case with all biological expeditions in Papua New Guinea. There are indigenous experts from the sites of "discovery" and from various national institutions who guide and facilitate all the work that is done by outsiders. These "discovery" trips—whether in surfing, development, or science—erase both the knowledge and labor of people from Papua New Guinea so that outsiders can come to be seen as experts and so that narratives about intrepid chronotope-jumping white men can add value to the lives, bank accounts, and structural positions within scientific hierarchies of power for these men.

This historic narrative of "discovery" gives us a distinct perspective on the two more recent narratives. First, although we can glean certain things about the early scientists working in what is now Papua New Guinea, we only see partial aspects of their expeditions. We see them narrated through a particular rhetorical form—the adventure story of the scientist and his voyages of discovery. Yet we catch glimpses of the fuller story in the attention paid to the personality of the animals or the arguments about the value of place, space, creatures, and peoples when stories of them are returned to Europe and ordered as part of the growing hierarchy of discovery—compared with the bits of nature and culture that have been extracted, stolen, and disappeared from across the colonial world. With the story about Conservation International, we see the modern expedition—how it is cast in the press using the same narrative forms and tropes as all other stories of "discovery" and how it is manipulated to garner support for the larger goals of international conservation organizations. With each press clipping, with each "discovery" these BINGOs (see chapter 2) dispossess. They solidify the narrative that they are the proper stewards of biological diversity futures in places like Papua New Guinea, and they set the stage for the structural constraints that lead to the ongoing dispossessions associated with conservation funding.

The story of the "expedition" to Gimi worlds fleshes the picture out even more fully. It shows us how nonwhite expedition members (Gimi hunters) viewed the people who came to their lands, what they were asked to do, and the outcomes of the engagements. It reinforces for us the sense that in any narration of these "expeditions" by outsiders, only part of the story is told. It also reminds us that dispossessions come in so many forms—the actual taking of animals being one of them.

Tree Kangaroos and Multi-Species Worlds

American cultural anthropology recently has witnessed a vigorous return to a disciplinary interest in the relationships between people and their surroundings. While many scholars have been writing about this set of relationships for decades in the subdisciplinary fields of human ecology, political ecology, and environmental anthropology, this resurgence in interest has been flashy. Some of the new work builds on older anthropological engagements with questions of humans, human nature, and political economy, expanding it and brining new conceptual tools to ongoing conversations (see Kirksey and Helmrich 2010 and Helmrich 2009). Some of it claims anew the work that scholars have been carefully crafting for decades (see Latour 2004).

Much of the new, and valuable, work on what Kirksey and Helmrich (2010) term "multi species ethnography" draws heavily on the philosophical work of Deleuze and Guattari, especially their notion of "becoming"—the proposition that nothing is, it is all coming to be, and that new engagements between agents hold within them endless possibilities for political change and nonhierarchical futures (Deleuze and Guattari 1987:241). Donna Haraway (2008) took these ideas and comingled them with her long-term work on social interactions between different species and her interest in hybridism and new forms of the human. One of the conceits of this new work is that prior to this "turn" most anthropology attended to the nonhuman only in terms of things to be eaten or hunted. This conceit has been "theory-ed up" through Giorgio Agamben's notion of what is there to be killed or the killable ("bare life" in his phrasing) (Agamben 1998), and the argument has been made that aside from a few intrepid souls, almost everyone else has written of the creatures and processes and forms that humans share their worlds with in reductionist terms, as if humans mattered only.

Yet this literature articulates what my Gimi teachers, friends, critics, and collaborators and their ancestors have known for a long time, that humans are not the only agentive beings in the tropic cascades of life (see West 2005, 2006 and Gillison 1993). Gimi have always been "multi species ethnographers," as have many other indigenous groups.

This attention to indigenous worldings has also been extra-present in contemporary cultural anthropology. This shift in attention has been ushered into the thinking of younger scholars through the extraordinary work of Eduardo Viveiros de Castro (2004a, 2004b, 2014) and Philippe Descola (1994, 1996, 2013), and it is always deeply connected to the work of Marilyn Strathern (1988). The conceit of this so-called ontological turn is that we should (and some of us have) moved away from a kind of epistemological focus in anthropology—a focus on how knowledge is made, produced, and enacted—and toward an understanding of situational affect that is emergent and deeply emplaced. This is precisely how I see and attempt to write Gimi worlds. However, the failure of this new trend in anthropology, which, again, like the multispecies turn is not a new trend but a group of smart people returning to a careful examination of what particular analytics bring to our understandings of alterity, is that it tends to fail to shed light on the kinds of dispossessions that affect Papua New Guineans and others daily.

4 Indigenous Theories of Accumulation, Dispossession, Possession, and Sovereignty

An old and fundamental anthropological question has been challenged of late. That question has three parts. The first part asks, *How do people live their world?* How do they see, smell, taste, hear, feel, sense, move through, make meaning out of, find meaning in, represent, narrate, know, perceive, think about, remember, imagine, desire, and empathize with all that they experience as surrounding them? The second part asks, *How do different ways of living-in-their-world affect how people understand, engage with, and act toward others?* The third, *What happens to people's modes of living their worlds when people living their worlds in radically different ways interact?*

I tend to think about this tripartite question as a phenomenological one. As an ethnographer, I have tried to answer it by talking to and spending time with people in order to develop understandings of their conscious experiences. I also describe and analyze experience, as well as interpret how others describe and analyze experience. Additionally, I am interested in phenomena and people's experience, narration, and understanding of phenomena. Throughout my career I've tried to think about this enterprise that I'm engaged in as trying to understand people's "being-in-the-world" (Heidegger 1962), how new "modes of being" (Heidegger 1982; Marx 1975) emerge, how different modes of being intersect in particular times (West 2006, 2012), and how these modes of being produce particular spaces (West 2005b, 2006).

The scholars posing the recent challenges to this question argue that they are taking issue with both the "being-in-the-world" and the actual ethnographic enterprise parts of it. They propose that there is not "the-world" but rather many worlds (Viveiros de Castro 2004a:6), and they argue that our anthropological goal should not be to understand humans through our examinations of their contextual relationships with people and things in the word but instead to understand the worlds that people are living, in the terms that they are living them. We should examine the worlds that are, they contend, the worlds that exist. These scholars are part of what is being called by outsiders "the ontological turn in anthropology" and by insiders "recursive anthropology" (Holbraad 2012). Some of these scholars claim that their approach takes phenomena and objects seriously in a way that is above and beyond other approaches within the discipline of anthropology (Henare et al. 2006). Eduardo Viveiros de Castro insists that the central organizing goal of anthropology or "value" of it is "working to create the conceptual, I mean ontological, self-determination of people[s]" (Viveiros de Castro 2003:4).

I said that this fundamental anthropological question has three parts: *How do people live their world? How do different ways of living-in-their-world affect how people understand, engage with, and act toward others? What happens to people's modes of living their worlds when people living their worlds in radically different ways interact?* It seems to me that the scholars who are invested in the recursive approach to anthropology have approached the first part of this question only, so I want to consider the second and third parts from a perspective that takes the question of ontology seriously. I approach these questions through the political ecology of conservation interventions. I also examine the particular question of ontology with a sense that the place of indigenous philosophy is not adequately addressed in much of that literature and that it has not paid attention to dispossession adequately. In its push to move toward recursive understandings, it has, to some extent and in some cases—but not all—failed to see that indigenous worldings almost always engage with ongoing dispossessions on a daily basis and that indigenous peoples are constantly revising and rupturing their epistemes in order to understand these dispossessions (see DiNovelli-Lang 2010).

Political Ecologies of Dispossession

Political ecologists have been developing a robust theory of accumulation, dispossession, and environmental conservation since the late 1990s (see Davidov 2013; Büscher and Dressler 2007; Doane 2014; Grandia 2012; A. Kelly 2011; McDonald 2010; Peluso 1996; Sullivan 2013; Tsing 2004; and West 2006, 2012). The majority of these scholars work in places, like Papua New Guinea, where sites that are seen as important global biological assets overlap with very poor communities. These scholars elucidate the relationship between contemporary global political-economic process and local social, political, and ecological processes and livelihoods. Much of this scholarship takes as its starting point David Harvey's argument that one of the hallmarks of contemporary neoliberal economic life is the privatization of public assets—or the "redistribution of social wealth"—to individuals, corporations, and other entities (non-governmental organizations, for example) (Doane 2014:235; see Harvey 2005, 2006) and that much institutionalized environmental conservation carries the structures and forms of privatization even if lands do not "officially" transfer ownership.

The anthropologist Molly Doane argues that "institutionalized conservation—embedded as it is in a dominant market culture system—operates as a system of accumulation. Accumulation by conservation is a form of symbolic accumulation that adds value to our market-based cultural, political, and economic system, by asserting that it is a source of, or force for, ecological sustainability" (Doane 2014:234). Conservation forces indigenous peoples off their traditional lands (Dowie 2009), radically alters their land use patterns (Grandia 2012), compels them to become part of markets (like tourism) that will never provide the promised benefits (West 2006), and benefits corporations who wish to show their environmental concerns to the wider public (Doane 2007, 2012). While there are examples of indigenous people refiguring dispossession in a way that allows for new political actions and alliances (Cepek 2012), this is usually not the case.

In this chapter, I attempt to bring to this political ecology of conservation as dispossession some of the theories concerned with inequality and its causes. These indigenous theories of accumulation, possession, dispossession, and sovereignty have emerged during my work with Gimi-speaking peoples, and they connect to the large literature on how Papua New Guinean peoples see, know, make, embody, experience, and produce

their surroundings. This literature, which is concerned with the environmental philosophies among indigenous peoples in Papua New Guinea,
shows that while people there are always drawing on older ontological
propositions about the world and how it works, they are also constantly
undertaking epistemological practices that produce new forms of understanding (for examples, see J. Bell 2006; Gegeo and Watson-Gegeo 2001;
Jacka 2009, 2010, 2015; Halvaksz 2003, 2006a, 2006b; Halvaksz and
Young-Leslie 2008; Lipset 2011, 2013; and West 2005b).

In what follows I present four stories that are suffused with Gimi theories of accumulation, possession, dispossession, and sovereignty. The
first is an old Gimi story—one that has been told for as long as anyone
can remember. It is, among other things, a Gimi philosophical analysis of
possession and dispossession. It is not a static telling but rather a rhetorical form and formulation that is deployed in various contexts to various
ends. The second and third stories are my ethnographic recounting of two
events from my time living in the Gimi world. One is about my teacher
Kabe and his sons and how their analyses of their own experiences tell us
something about Gimi ideas about dispossession and what it means to
hold the power to know worlds. The other is about how people theorize
what dispossessions come to the Gimi world with conservation interventions. The fourth story also takes up this theme—how Gimi see and live
in a world shot through with conservation and how they, in turn, make
sense of the present in light of new forms of knowledge and new philosophies of life that they encounter. I do *not* present these stories as indigenous knowledge, traditional ecological knowledge, or any of the other
fragmenting categories often used to conceptualize indigenous peoples
engagements with their surroundings (Cruikshank 2005). I offer them as
examples of theories derived from philosophy, and I take philosophy to
be the study of the nature of reality or existence. I do not submit them as
ontology alone; while they often encompass understandings about meta-
physical relations, they are not limited to that. I do not put them forward
as epistemology alone; although they do contribute to the production of
knowledge, they are not limited to that. I present them as co-produced
articulations of Gimi philosophy (see Turner 2006a, 2006b).

I conclude the chapter with a thought experiment in which I take historic events that I wrote about in the previous chapter and re-narrate them
through my understanding of the Gimi philosophies of life. With this, I
ask us all to try and imagine an anthropological world where the analytic
forms we choose might be derived from Gimi philosophy as easily as they

FIGURE 4.1   Kobe and Ellen, Maimafu Village. Photograph courtesy of J. C. Salyer.

are derived from continental philosophy, critical theory, Marxist theory, or any of the many other analytic frames to which we, as anthropologists, have had allegiances over the years. I also ask us to imagine what writing ethnography or history might look like if we relied less on Euro-American-Australian forms of narration and more on other forms of narration. I do this to help us imagine what anthropology might be with a more diverse set of philosophical frames.[1]

Women, Birds, and Worldings

Many older people have recounted the following story to me over the past eighteen years. The anthropologist Gillian Gillison (1993) also collected multiple versions of this story as have Ben Ruli and the ecologist Enock Kale. I collected the version I recount here from a sixty-five-year-old woman named Kobe in 1998. The story as it is written here is not a direct quotation—it is my translation of the story that she told me. I distinguish between the two because there are nuances lost in translation and because the voice I hear when I read aloud the story that follows is neither Kobe's nor mine. It is a comingling of our voices. Elsewhere I have explored the idea of the coproduction of knowledge that happens in the ethnographic encounter (West 2005a, and I return to this question at the end of this chapter.

One day a widow said to her two young children, a boy and a girl, "You stay here near the banana tree while I go to the forest to collect ferns. We have to have ferns for the *beheda ada* [the Gimi death ritual where the auna or soul of the deceased is coaxed away from the living and back to their lineage's sacred grounds]." She told them to stay near and if they heard ripe bananas falling from the tree that would be a sign that she was dead. She told them to listen hard, and then she went through the forest up to the garden that her husband had been clearing when he died. The garden was not fully cleared and the sticks he had been sharpening for fence posts were not fully sharpened.

The garden was on the banks of a river, and she decided to go up the river to the head. So she went out of the garden and went up, noticing along the way that it seemed that her husband had gone that way before he died. She went up and up into the mountains. Along the way she caught frogs and collected ferns. She put the ferns and the frogs in her net string bag. All the way up she collected ferns and frogs, frogs and ferns. As she climbed higher and higher she thought she heard another person.

She came to a clearing, and there was an old man sitting by a fire as if he was waiting on her. He had just split open a rotten tree and was sitting eating grubs. She asked him who he was, and he answered with a question for her. He said, "Who are you, and why are you here on my ground?" She replied that she was gathering greens for herself and her children. He asked where her children were, and she told him they were at home, but she did not tell him they were under the banana tree. He said that she could collect greens there, or she could follow him and he would show her where there were more ferns and some yams for her to dig. She followed him higher and higher.

As they walked he asked her for the frogs in her net bag. She gave them to him and he ate them. He asked her for the frogs she put under her head covering (a covering she was wearing because she was in mourning). She gave them to him and he ate them. He asked her for the frogs she had hidden under her skirts. She gave them to him and he ate them.

They came to a place where there were yams, and she began to dig. He watched her and then told her to bend over more. That the yams were wild and that she had to stick her rear up more in the air to get the leverage to dig the wild yams. Then he went off to do other things. When she looked up again he was standing over her with a sharp stick. It was covered in blood and guts. The old man impaled her right then and there on his stick. He killed her and afterward he put her skin on and he became her. He put her legs on like pants and put her arms on like a shirt. After he put her on he put her clothes on and took up her net string bag. Then he went back down the mountain.

He went down and down and then came to her house. He called out to her children, "I am home with ferns, and I've brought you a rat to eat." The old woman's daughter ran out and said, "We were worried about you," but she did not say anything about the banana tree. The man, disguised as their mother, said, "I am fine but I am thirsty from the walk up up up the mountain. You must go and get me water to drink. Water to quench my thirst." So the young girl left her still younger brother with the man she thought was her mother. She walked to the river all the time still knowing that she had heard the bananas fall but not knowing that her mother was dead.

While the young girl was gone to the river, the man killed the small boy. He killed him and put his body in the roof of the house. Then he returned to a fire he was building. When the girl came home with the water, the man was cooking the ferns that her mother had gathered. He told her that her brother was asleep in the net bag that he was carrying on his head, the net bag he had stolen from the dead mother.

The young girl sat down at the fire with the man, and soon the man fell asleep. He slept and he slept while the girl worked her net bag. As she worked she thought that she felt rain coming through the roof, but then she remembered it was not raining. She wiped the "water" away that was dripping on her and she saw that it was blood falling from the roof of the house. She looked up and saw her brother. Immediately she knew that the person sleeping was Kore Bana and that he had led her mother high into the mountains and killed her. She took her brother down and wrapped his body and put it in a net string bag. She called to the dog and then she burned down her father's house. As she ran from the house she heard the old man screaming and screaming.

She then went to the forest with the dog and her dead brother. After a while in the forest she wanted to find a husband, so she sent the dog to look for him. She told the dog that he should run to the ridge tops in the distance and look for her husband. She told him that if he found her husband he should come back and wag his tail to show her the way. She sent him off and soon he returned wagging his tail, so she followed him to a garden house that was close by. In the house she found her true husband.

When she entered the house the man inside asked her why she was there. She did not answer with a question. She told him the story of her father and mother and brother. She stayed with him from then on. He gave her shell necklaces, sweet potatoes, cassowary feathers, the pelts of marsupials that had been killed on his lineage land, and some pork, and then he was her husband.

After they were married they took the things from their wedding and threw them in a tree. They also put the dead brother in the tree. Then the husband went hunting. He told the new wife that no matter what she heard she should not try and get into the tree. Then he went on his way.

The woman stayed in the house until she heard the tree singing. She went outside to see it, and it sang and moved. She remembered her husband's warning so she did not climb in the tree, but she hit it with a great stick, one that was to become a fence post. When she hit the tree once nothing happened. When she hit the tree the second time nothing happened, but then, when she hit it a third time, it burst open.

Out of the tree flew all of the birds of paradise! All of the birds! All of the birds came out at once. The crested bird of paradise, Loria's bird of paradise, the magnificent riflebird, the twelve-wired bird of paradise, the buff-tailed sicklebill, the black sicklebill, the brown sicklebill, Princess Stephanie's astrapia, the superb bird of paradise, Carola's parotia, Lawe's parotia, the King of Saxony bird of paradise, the king bird of paradise, the magnificent bird of paradise, the blue bird of paradise, and the Raggiana bird of paradise. Some went to live near the He River. Some went to live near the Nimi River. Some went up high into the mountains. They went to the top of Bopoyana. They went the place where the salt water begins. They went all over the world.

Kabe and His Sons

I watched Kabe through the window as he approached my house in Maimafu. He walked casually up the airstrip, stopping along the way to scratch his dog's head, check the ripening progress of a bunch of bananas that he had wrapped in leaves and twine so that flying foxes would not eat them at night, and adjust something he held under his arm. When he got to the front yard he whistled—Kabe's not a knocker—and I went outside to greet him. Kabe had a Raffray's bandicoot (*Peroryctes raffrayana*) in his carefully packed bundle. He had taken banana leaves and wrapped the creature and then tied vines around the package so it was secure. He looked at the bandicoot lovingly as he told me about killing it. He had been harvesting some greens for his wife to eat (at the time she was quite ill, and he taken over the household cooking duties) when he saw it moving in the leaf litter on the edge of his garden. He said that he quietly took up a stone in one hand and his spear in another. He aimed and threw the stone at the bandicoot hitting it and stunning it. He said, "When I got it, I knew that you would want to see it!" And then he smiled and touched my face.

Kabe and I have a long history. When I am in Maimafu, I live on his land, in a house that he built, and I have been intimately incorporated into his family. Kabe lost a daughter years ago, and in the mid-1990s, when I first arrived in Maimafu, Kabe dreamed about me, a Goodfellow's tree kangaroo (*Dendrolagus goodfellowi*), and his dead daughter. Over the course of many years he has watched me closely and has come to the decision that I am also his daughter. He has ordered me within his family and within a set of social obligations, responsibilities, and rights; I am his child and the sibling to his sons, John and Rick. This process has not happened quickly, nor has it happened only with acts of social reproduction undertaken by Kabe and his wife. I have, through this relationship and others, incorporated aspects of being-in-the-Gimi-world into my being.

When Kabe arrived at my house on the day I am recounting, John and Rick were already there. Because they are my brothers I am quite free around John and Rick, and we laugh and joke and spend a great deal of time together. On the day in question they are at my house distracting me from work. I was supposed to be working my way through the big New Guinea book of mammals, using it to check my Gimi language mammal names that I had been collecting for years. I was trying to get Rick and John to help me, but they were being bad distracting brothers and luring me to talk about all manner of non-work-related things. In lieu of work, we were gossiping about a certain young man in the village who had gone to Goroka recently and failed to purchase any of the items for which his aunties and mother had given him money when he left. We speculated about what would befall him and roared with laughter when Rick mimicked the young man receiving a smack from his father's sister.

When Kabe arrived, the book was open to the pages concerning echidnas. Echidnas are monotremes, and together with the platypus, they are the only surviving members of an order of egg-laying mammals. There are two kinds of echidnas, short-beaked (*Tachyglossus aculeatus*) and long-beaked (*Zaglossus bruijni*). The short-beaked ones are distributed throughout southern and eastern New Guinea, mainland Australia, Kangaroo Island, and Tasmania; long-beaked ones occur only on New Guinea.

Kuiaru is the Gimi word that everyone has always used around me when talking about echidnas. Kabe picked up the book and I, wanting to show off a bit, said, "Oh, it's kuiaru, right?" And Kabe said, no, "*Femomo*." Rick, John, and I said, in unison, "WHAT?" Kabe said, "Kuiaru is one name, but they are also femomo." John and Rick laughed at their father and Rick and said, "Kage su Neke [Kabe is going senile]." Kabe laughed at Rick and jokingly brandished an arrow at him. I said, "Why senile?" And Rick told me that femomo is actually a plant—a type of bromeliad—that grows in high altitude forests. I asked Kabe, "Kabe, why do you say it is femomo and not kuiaru?"

Kabe told us that an echidna is kuiaru when it is alive and femomo when it is dead. Its name changes. Femomo is, indeed, the name for the bromeliad that Rick had identified. This plant is short and spiny like an echidna, and it serves as a den for ants. Kabe told us that ants use the inside of the plant as a house. Then he told us that echidnas eat ants so the inside of an echidna is the same as the inside of the bromeliad. Kabe said, "They are both full of ants. The ants live in the femomo so as to hide from the kuiaru. The kuiaru won't approach the femomo because it is the same as a dead kuiaru, so the ants are safe."

I said, but the kuiaru (living echidnas) can't climb a tree, so how would it see the femomo? Kabe told us that "the ants carry the femomo from the ground up the tree and nestle it in the branches to create a safe haven. You can tell this because the femomo plant has no roots—it just sits in the tree—something had to put it there. It was the ants."

I asked Kabe what else he knew about kuiaru-femomo, and we talked about their denning habits. He told us that that they dig dens and sleep in them but that they don't use them like permanent houses—they dig new ones all the time—and sometimes they just sleep under the leaf litter. He told us that mothers dig dens and leave their offspring there when they go out to find food. We talked about where the best place to encounter them is. He said they prefer places where the forest is not too terribly thick. Kabe told us that he thinks that they are like farmers: they dig up the soil with their beaks and that helps new plants to grow. He told us that they don't have teeth but that they have extremely dangerous sharp claws. And in addition to ants, they eat grubs and earthworms that they dig with the claws. Then he told us the best place to find them in the forests of Bopoyana, and he recounted several stories about hunting them with his father and brothers years ago.

We eventually moved on from echidnas and spent the rest of the afternoon discussing other mammals and various village events. Slowly people began to leave for the day. Kabe went home to check on his wife. John went to wash and get ready for evening services at the Seventh Day Adventist community church he attends, and it was just Rick and I left outside watching the light change as the sun dropped behind the mountaintops that stretch as far as you can see from the veranda of my house. We sat quietly for a while, and then Rick said, "The old man knows a lot about the forests." I didn't respond. I just shook my head affirmatively. And Rick said, "I don't know any of it." I didn't respond. I just shook my head affirmatively. We sat in silence a bit longer, Rick lighting a cigarette, me taking it out of his hand, taking a puff, and handing it back, and him getting up to head home. As he walked away I called out, "So you will come back with Kabe tomorrow, and we can do some more names?" And Rick, without turning around, raised his hand in the air and said, "ohoh."

For the rest of that summer Kabe, Rick, and I worked out the Unavisa Gimi system of taxonomy, and Rick and I documented animal names and collected stories from every person over forty in his father's extended family network. And every time since then that I have been back to Maimafu, Rick has worked with me, documenting his father's and his ancestor's world.

Ulysses Costings

In the early 2000s I was walking with my husband from my house at Beabaitai to Motai, the main ridgetop settlement in the larger village of Maimafu. As we rounded a corner, Sarau and Moyha rounded the corner coming the other way. We all startled each other, laughed about it, and sat down on the trail to have a rest and a chat. As we were chatting, Sarau's brother, Koma, joined us. Koma, unlike most Gimi men, moved to his wife's father's hamlet when he got married and thus lives in Kora, a village some two days' walk from Maimafu. Because of this, Koma didn't

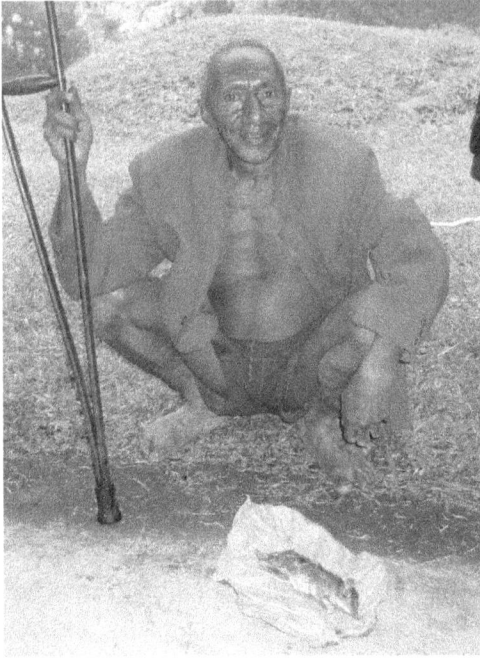

FIGURE 4.2   Kabe, Maimafu Village. Photograph courtesy of J. C. Salyer.

really know my husband and me, and he assumed that we were tourists, conservation biologists, or Peace Corps volunteers. After some general catching up on news from around the village, Koma pulled a Ulysses butterfly (*Papilio ulysses telemachus*) out of his bag. He had carefully wrapped it a scrap of an old plastic bag, and as he unwrapped it he told us about finding it. These are not rare creatures, but they are stunningly beautiful, with iridescent blue wings and inky black markings. Next Koma pulled out a bright green beetle (*Ischiopsopha hyla*)—another extraordinarily beautiful creature with a shiny green carapace that sparkles in the sunlight. He told us that he was willing to sell both of the specimens to us. We said that we were so happy to see them, that we were not really interested in collecting specimens, but that we would love to photograph him with them. Koma thought about this a bit and then suggested that since we would—in all likelihood—take the pictures, develop them, then turn them into postcards and sell them in the United States and become fabulously wealthy from this, that he would need some sort of monetary compensation from us if we were to photograph them. We tactfully declined; he packed up his specimens, and we all went on our way.

Who's Got the Monkey

The first time I heard the following story was in 1998, on one of the first nights I spent camping in the high forests of Bopoyana with a group of hunters. It was late at night, and we were all sitting around a fire. We were in a forest where no one had lived or made gardens in living Gimi memory or in the oral histories known by older Gimi. This forest is ancient. It is most certainly not "untouched" or "pristine" because Gimi move through it, altering its plant and animal communities and structure by their presence and by their collecting of vines, fungus, orchids, medicinal plants, fruits, and nuts and their hunting, but it is ancient and breathtaking. Atilla, one of the men I was with that night, who was about fifty at the time, told me the following story, and as before with Kobe's story, this is my retelling of his telling, a comingling of our voices.

For as long as people had been living on the slopes of Bopoyana, the forests had been thick with monkeys. Big ones, small ones, loud ones, quiet ones, black ones, white ones, red ones, blue ones—there had been every kind of monkey you could possibly imagine. They swung through the trees, they swam in the rivers, they ate bananas, and they engaged in charming and humorous behaviors. At night they all slept together in a big cave near the river Sera. Today, however, there are no monkeys anywhere. Why?

One day many years ago a helicopter came in the deep dark of the night. People heard it flying over the villages, but it was night so they didn't see where it landed. The next morning they woke up and all the monkeys were gone. All of them. And there has never been another monkey seen anywhere near Bopoyana since.

For years people wondered what happened to their monkeys. They knew that if the monkeys were still there they would be fabulously wealthy because thousands of tourists would come to Bopoyana to see the monkeys. Atilla told me, "Ago bana soko monkeys [White people love monkeys]." Finally, many years after the monkeys disappeared, people realized that Mal Smith, the expatriate former Eastern Highlands governor who renounced his Australian citizenship when he became a citizen of Papua New Guinea and who owns the Pacific Helicopter Company and who had spent time when he was younger exploring the slopes of Bopoyana and building a helicopter-serviced ecotourism lodge there, stole their monkeys. It was the Gimi's monkeys, you see, that had provided Mal Smith with his riches.

Gimi Theories of Possession, Dispossession, and Accumulation

The first story can be read as a Gimi study of the nature of life, values, relatedness, exchange, and connections. The man that the mother encounters in the forest is trespassing. He is, as he trespasses, taking in air, water, light, and other forms from her husband's family's land. He is reproducing himself physically with the matter of others—matter he is taking out of the cycle of reproduction that is ongoing for her husband's lineage. So the story starts with a dispossession; it begins with a taking of *kore* in multiple forms from another lineage's never-ending cycle of exchange with their ancestors. It also establishes the link between sovereignty over land and sovereignty over the human body. Gimi bodies are inextricably linked to the beings and processes and intricacies of what Euro-Australian-American science would call "the environment." For Gimi, you possess the possibility of holding rights to your self and your surroundings because of the ongoing transfer of *auna* and kore. Bodily sovereignty and sovereignty over territory is philosophically, and fundamentally, linked.

The man, after meeting the woman, also discursively takes the land— he asks her why she is on his ground, even when she knows it is her husband's. By rhetorically dispossessing her of her capacity to glean from this land, he is lessening her—making her seem as if she is out of place and out of order. With this act of violence, we learn that lying about land is a fundamental assault on space (the land and all that is on and in and of it) and on persons (as her bodily sovereignty is inextricable from the land she engages with to feed herself and her children and that, through the movement of kore back into them, brings her into the world as a placed person—the wife of a man who is part of a family).

After his lie, she follows him, concerned about finding enough food for her children, and he begins to beg for the frogs she has been collecting. In eating the frogs, he is literally eating the feminine aspects of the ongoing cycle of production and reproduction. For Gimi, frogs are associated with the feminine; they are described as smelling of women's bodies. Very particularly, they smell of the vagina, and they are damp and moist. As the man asks for the frogs she is hiding from him, he humiliates her and takes both her reproductive capacity (to feed her children and thus create them as persons) and her sovereignty over her own body. The frogs are her reproductive organs—laid bare to him. By eating them he also removes her from the possibility of transferring the auna of herself back into her husband's family's land. He pollutes her through his greedy violent taking. Finally, by killing her—as he did her husband—he takes her life and her ability to continue to produce her children through endless acts of maternal production, reproduction, and exchange.

As the man returns down the mountain wearing the mother's skin, he has literally dispossessed her of everything, and by becoming her, the trickster begins to merge his auna with that of her unknowing children. He begins to produce and reproduce them as other kinds of selves without them even knowing it. And as the story continues, his acts of dispossession go on and on. As do his acts of accumulation. He eats the frogs and drinks the water the young daughter brings him, all the while incorporating her auna and that of her father's lineage into his person, becoming more because of her actions. These acts are horrifying for Gimi. To "become" through the act of exchange is fundamental to Gimi being-in-the-world, and for someone to become based on lies and treachery is the worst of humanity.

This story gives us a philosophically based answer to the question of why Crater Mountain Wildlife Management Area (CMWMA) conservation project on Gimi lands failed (see chapter 3). It teaches us that even though land is passed patrilineally in the Gimi world, it was a woman, the daughter, who—through her actions and through her reverence for children (her dead brother) and the original releasing of the kore (her brother's spirit) by chopping the tree—originally created all the birds of paradise. Each Gimi extended family group—and these are patrilineally related men's groups—has a secret bamboo flute that is, when played, the living incarnation of one of the birds of paradise species. The lineage descends from this species and the flutes, which are sacred and unknown to women and children (although women know all about them, of course), bring forth the ancestral linage when played.[2] They do not "represent" the birds; rather, they transmogrify the men hearing the flutes when they are played into the ancestral bird.

Kabe's family has a sacred bird of paradise flute. When that flute is played Kabe becomes a bird and is, during its song, the physical incarnation of all of his ancestors. This is more than an act of reverence and religion. It is an act, based on this story, that prohibits Gimi from ever killing a bird of paradise. To kill one is to kill a man, but more than that it is to kill an entire lineage, to wipe from the earth a history of a family. It is also an act that inextricably ties men and forests together for all eternity. In the story, the reproductive capacity that gave rise to the birds, who are the ancestors of men, is attributed to women. This gives women a hold on a realm of life, the forest, that outsiders often see as the domain of men. It also creates a form of deep reverence for and respect for women's reproductive capacity.

The conservation project worked almost exclusively with men, thereby failing to understand or acknowledge women's reproductive capacity when it came to some of the species (birds of paradise) that outsiders deemed important to draw conservation-minded people to Gimi lands (West 2006:1–4). The project was, for women, an extraordinary act of ongoing dispossession: dispossession of acknowledgment, of the proper reverence, for the fact that the state of the world *is* because of the actions of women. Over the course of the life of the conservation project, women were repeatedly left out of conversations, barred from participating in planning events, and relegated to cooking and cleaning for outsiders when they visited Gimi lands. Women, initially annoyed, grew, as my Gimi teacher Anna says, "bone weary" of this and began to theorize the conservation project as a source of accumulation for Gimi men—they got to go to trainings, they got paid to go on field projects with ecologists, and they were assumed to be acquiring knowledge. And this accumulation was at the expense of women. All of these conditions focused women's attention on their dispossession—they were spending time working for the project in the background and receiving no benefits directly. They were being asked to produce handicrafts, which is time-consuming, as an "income-generation" strategy, but the handicrafts were not generating any income.

With this story we see that Gimi philosophy, as articulated in narrations of past events, crafts both *ontology*, or a set of propositions about what *is* in the world, and *epistemology*, as the story is then used by Gimi women to understand what is happening in the present. A tale some might have discounted as a "myth" is actually a clear set of propositions that help people understand and be in the worlds they create and in the worlds that they are cast into with outside interventions of all kinds.

Today, many younger Gimi can no longer tell the complex versions of stories like the one about the young girl and the birds. They might be able to narrate the highlights of the story, but the details are less finely articulated than in the versions I collected from older people in the 1990s. All of the versions I collected were narrated by women and men who had been initiated and brought into the Gimi world through secret and sacred practices in men's and women's houses.

Seventh Day Adventist missionaries have been working in the Gimi area since the 1970s, and most Gimi today identify as Christians. For older Gimi, like Kabe, that identification is fleeting. He was fully brought up as a subject in a world without Christian ideas of right and wrong and heaven and hell. All younger Gimi were brought into being as subjects in a world where Christian philosophical claims and Gimi philosophical claims share the stage in social reproduction. Christianity is one of the social forms that Gimi philosophers theorize when they discuss dispossession.

Many elderly Gimi argue that the external push to convert Gimi to Christianity was an act of dispossession akin to the acts undertaken by the murdering man in the birds of paradise story. Loma once told me that the missionaries "took our stories and told us never to tell them. They told us that they were evil and would bring Satan into our lives." She then asked me, "How could we teach our daughters how to be women without telling these stories? How could we teach our sons how to be men?" These same elderly Gimi see many of their children and grandchildren as insufficiently prepared for life, and they attribute this taking, this dispossession, of the ability to prepare their lineages as sitting squarely on the shoulders of missionaries.

For Christians, frogs become frogs and not physical manifestations of female ancestors' life forces; birds become birds, not living proof that women's powers generate both forest and humanity as powerfully as men's do. John and Rick, Kabe's sons from the second story, both grew up with the Adventist church in their village. They both went to mission school—Rick attended almost all the way through high school—and they both live in a world of new and blended ontological propositions and epistemological practices. Additionally, because they spent their childhoods in school, they did not go to the forest with their father. They did not learn the old stories, nor did they learn the things that Kabe knows about animals. This is, again, seen by older Gimi as a form of dispossession.

Kabe told us that kuiaru is a gardener, that he burrows, that he eats ants, that he aerates the soil by digging with this nose, that he disperses seeds, and that because of this, he helps the forest grow. Kabe basically told us about the behavioral ecology of echidna based on his observations of them. He uses a posteriori knowledge, knowledge gained by experience and observation, to understand the behavior of the animal. On another day Kabe told me that he believes that kuiaru, because of the way that he digs and moves things around, is responsible in part for the structure of the forest. So Kabe has a theory of ecological function for echidna.

Kabe knows all of this because he hunts, because he spends time on his lineage's ground, and because he watches and listens. Ethnobotanical work done globally has shown that activities undertaken by native populations enriches vegetation cover, helps to diversify plant species, and improves soil. Use creates structure and changes function. Use is also driven by epistemology and ontology. And use feeds back into epistemology and ontology. Because Kabe knows that kuiaru is responsible for the forest through his actions, he would only hunt and kill them when he has to—when there is an appropriate ritual time for one or when there is a physical need to reincorporate the fat of the ancestors back into the bodies of the living. Echidna are extremely fatty, and they are hunted and killed when people (sick children, women close to child birth) are thought to be in dire need of fat. In the past, before the coming of Christianity, this would have been rarely. Remember, the form of Christianity that came to Maimafu is Seventh Day Adventism, and the church prohibits the eating of pork. In the past, when people needed fat, they would usually hunt a pig. Today, the echidna is the fattiest animal that people can eat, so they eat it much more often.

Hunting and gathering are far more than economic actions, and so-called hunting trips often involve important identity work—the tying of people to each other and to the landscape, making people feel a part of something bigger—and may not always be about subsistence at all. Kabe's hunting is epistemological: it is how he knows the world and how he acquires knowledge. It is how he produces knowledge. It is also the source of his ontology—he understands what exists, what features of objects are essential, what categories things fit into (kuiaru or femomo) and what identifies objects. Hunting is another subject around which Gimi theorize dispossession. Specifically, many see the rules of conservation, known as the "conservation laws" during the era of the Crater Mountain Wildlife Management Area, as a form of dispossession (of their rights to animals on their lands) and accumulation (by conservation actors who are intent of keeping these animals so that they can examine them and study them). Some older people articulate an even deeper theory of dispossession.

One hunts on one's ancestor's lands. With this, one pulls life force of the ancestors into oneself, and into the creation and re-creation of self.

Remember, all the Gimi world is animated by the lives of the past. By tracking, killing, and eating a creature, you bring your ancestors' auna into your body, and it works to make you as their descendent. By curtailing hunting, the conservation project worked, according to Gimi, to slow the flow of past into present and into future, thereby making Gimi less Gimi than in the past. This broke down the ongoing cycle of exchange that, again for older Gimi, is key to their notion of how the social world is reproduced. Their assessment of this situation is that curtailing hunting is a taking—a dispossession of the ability to make and remake persons and creatures and landscape process and features in a way that is the proper, moral way to make them.

On the day Kabe brought me the echidna, Rick came to see the vast knowledge that his father possess in a new light. We might say that he came to value it—it became something that he assigns value to and that he inserts into his internal hierarchy of value. And this is the moment, in the stories, when value comes into play. The way Kabe sees and knows the world are not about "value" in the sense that outsiders understand value. In the past, Gimi came to be in the world and knew the world through their social relations of exchange with the natural world. It was not a case of "valuing it." It was an epistemological and ontological system by which nature and culture were one. To Gimi, the idea of humans creating a hierarchy into which they place plants, animals, and other natural things, evaluating which is more important than the other, is absurd.

But Rick, who does not share the exact same philosophical world as his father, comes to see value in Kabe's knowledge because of research. A long time ago the anthropologist Marshall Sahlins wrote about the sublime ironies of indigenous people seeing an inherent power in the knowledge that Europeans saw as worthwhile. It is somewhat troubling that my finding value in Kabe's knowledge worked to create it as valuable for his son, but it did; this co-production of value is something I return to at the end of this chapter. Rick has been brought up in a world where the Gimi are cast as poor and behind and underdeveloped. The church and the conservation organizations working on Gimi lands have produced this world of alternate values.

The conservation organizations, well-meaning people who wished to protect and conserve the extreme biological diversity on Gimi lands, attempted to conserve by introducing conservation as development projects. It was thought that through these projects Gimi would come to value and preserve biodiversity if they had businesses that were based on it—businesses like ecotourism and handicraft production. What they failed to understand was that by producing the idea of underdevelopment and by telling Gimi that they were poor and needed development in order to value and conserve their forests—they were both discounting Kabe's way of seeing and being in the world (by not attempting to understand it and by assuming that forest use was only contributing to the loss of biological diversity) and working to create the notion of "lack" among Gimi. This notion, that old ways and tradition had to be changed so that people could access cash and development, inadvertently contributed to the devaluation of Kabe's kinds of knowledge, an epistemology and ontology that has unintended conservation benefits.

The butterfly story and the monkey story are clearly Gimi theories of contemporary dispossessions and accumulations. So what is up with the monkeys? Well, first off, aside from a few primates that have been introduced by Indonesians into West Papua in the past few years (brought as pets and escaped into the vast forests there) there are no nonhuman primates on the island of New Guinea. There never have been. The ancestors of what became modern-day primates never made it to New Guinea. So how do my Gimi friends even know what a monkey is (and the story is always told in either the Gimi language or Melanesian Tok Pisin—a creole language spoken in Papua New Guinea—using the word "monkey")?

Some years ago ecologists Debra Wright and Andrew Mack built a fantastic biological research station on the slopes of Bopoyana. The Sera research station operated for almost two decades as one of the only remote research stations in the country and, in my highly biased opinion, the best one. It drew researchers from across the globe and served as a really successful national scientific capacity building project. In the early 1990s, the station manager was an American who received lots and lots of conservation-related magazines and publications from home. The station manager would read them and then put them out on the tables at the station for the Gimi men and women who worked there to read. Many of these Gimi were not literate, but they loved looking at the magazines and having people who could read, read them to them.

Their assessment was as follows: for Europeans, Australians, and Americans, knowledge about the world comes from printed materials. People acquire knowledge through printed materials, and they produce and disseminate it through printed materials. And these people, "white people" as my Gimi friends would say, have lots of knowledge about animals. Lots and lots of it. Every magazine had numerous stories about them and numerous pictures of them. And the most salient category across all of these knowledge-conveying and knowledge-producing forms was "monkeys." There were stories about monkeys in Asia, Africa, and the Americas. There were hundreds of pictures of monkeys. So, logically, monkeys must be very important and valuable. They must be important because people seem to talk about them so much in these magazines, and they must be valuable because the same people that brought and produce these magazines were telling Gimi that the biodiversity on their ancestral lands was valuable and that if they worked to protect it they would get money through handicraft and tourism businesses. So what we have here is a Gimi theory about Western philosophy and values.

Gimi were also told, repeatedly, that their forests were the most bio-logically diverse and richest on the planet and that that was one of the reasons that they should work to conserve them. Well, if there forests were so rich and diverse, then where were the monkeys? Because every story about monkeys in the magazines told about the forests they lived in, and the Gimi forests were better, so where were the monkeys? There had to be some logical explanation for where they went. Gimi made sense out of the disparity of wealth between themselves and Mal Smith—a white man who has been in and around Gimi territory since the late 1960s—by connecting him to the monkeys. They use Mal and the monkeys to formulate a Gimi theory of accumulation as tied to dispossession.

The butterfly story is similar. Late the same night we had been offered the creatures, sitting around the fire at Rick's house, we talked about what had happened with Koma and his specimens. Kabe suggested that as long as scientists had been coming to his lands that they had been taking plants, animals, birds, and bugs away with them. A group of scientists from the Wildlife Conservation Society and the University of Papua New Guinea had come en masse in 1992, before I first arrived there, and spent weeks camping in the high forests beyond Maimafu and collecting things. Kabe said, "They caught them and killed them and then with the animals and birds they dressed them for cooking but never cooked them. They just kept the outside of the animal, not the meat." He recounted that they packed all of the creatures away in big solid patrol boxes that they locked at night. The scientists had taken thousands of pictures of the animals, both in situ, when they were living, and in the camp, when they were dead.

Kabe and Koma had worked with a Biodiversity Conservation Network–funded research team in 1996, as had many other senior men who know the forests well. They had watched the leaders of that team of researchers come back to the Bopoyana area over the years. Kabe said, "John Ericho [a Papua New Guinean conservation ecologist], he was a boy, a student when they were here, and now he is rich. He is a big man. Debra Wright and Andy Mack, they were students then, and now they live in a big house in Goroka." As he continued he laid out a theory of how the visitors had taken the specimens and the photographs of things that they collected on land owned by people from Maimafu and become rich by selling them. But it is not just that they become rich from selling objects and images. In doing this, Gimi theorize, again, that they deplete the Gimi world and they take matter out of the never-ending transactive cycle that produces and reproduces the world.

People living in the Gimi world have experienced outsiders coming to their lands over and over again telling them what they should and should not be hunting, what they should and should not be valuing, and how they should be living. Indeed, conservation actors actively sought to transform Gimi modes of being throughout the life of the conservation project. One night in 2007, Kabe told me that he "didn't know he was poor" until the conservation ecologists working on his lands started doing income-generation projects in Maimafu. Kabe indicated that the ways the project casts him and his fellow Gimi as in need of help from outside were disrespectful. "Once they said we were poor, people started to listen." From there, "people started to forget all the things that we have that make us rich." This transformation in how the men and women of Kabe's generation see themselves and how young Gimi perceive themselves and others is not traceable only to the conservation-related projects on Gimi lands but also to the interactions that Gimi had with conservation-related actors. Today there is the almost constant discourse of "loss" among older Gimi and "lack" among younger Gimi.

Older Gimi value the past and argue that wider changes have caused them to lose important things. They see a connected set of losses that can be traced back initially to the late 1950s and the first exposures to the colonial government. People argue that when the first colonial agents came to Maimafu they convinced people to begin to take part in the cash economy in two ways. First, they offered young men work on coastal plantations, which opened up new avenues for male migration between Maimafu and urban areas. Second, they introduced coffee as a cash crop, which tied people to the money economy. People argue that through the initial migrations for waged labor on plantations, "young men began to see other places and began to feel like our place was not good enough."

Kabe and his generation, who were the first generation to migrate for labor, talk about feeling like they were "nothing" and "nobody" when they were working in far-flung places. They felt detached from their social networks and began, over time, to feel less than human because the intimate exchange relations that they perceive as bringing them into the world as Gimi were not taking place. All of these men, aside from two who were "adopted" by others and who eventually ended up in Port Moresby in school, returned to Maimafu after a few years. Today they argue that this initial migration set up a route that has led to the social dislocation of their young people, especially young men. Today men normally leave Maimafu at some point during their late teens or early twenties. They go to Goroka or other Highland regional centers to try and find work. When they are gone, they, according to older Gimi, become less Gimi. The social relations and exchanges that are crucial to being Gimi dissipate over time if people do not participate in them, Kabe says. "They become someone else."

This is an astute analysis of the sorts of transformations that happen when young men and women leave their natal villages. Although they have been brought up Gimi, the kinds of social processes that keep them deeply connected to their lands and their extended families do lessen. The bonds of kinship and exchange are strong, and they do not fade quickly or totally, but over time, and with extended stays way from natal villages, young men, and less often young women, come to be persons that are composed of social relations and transactions that are not fully Gimi. They meet and connect to people from other places; they meet and exchange with people from other places; they come into the world through new social processes. These processes are deeply Melanesian, but they are not specifically Gimi. This, according to Kabe and his age-mates, causes a loss of knowledge about appropriate social behavior and about the Gimi landscapes and the plants and animals that in exchange with living Gimi and the ancestors, bring that landscape into being.

These older people also see tying the local ways of making a living to the coffee economy as detrimental to Gimi society. Women and men of Kabe's age, but mostly women, argue that once coffee became a part of daily life, "everything changed." They perceive themselves in a constant state of overwork because of their commitment to their coffee gardens. And they perceive their connection to the cash economy as exhausting. Soba, a woman of Kabe's generation, says, "We have to grow coffee to get money because we have to have money to buy medicine and school fees. So now our whole life is tied to coffee." This is perceived as a loss of autonomy—the ability to control and govern one's own time—and control.

Younger Gimi, especially young men, have a marked lack of respect for the past, and they blame their elders for the state of "underdevelopment" they feel they live in. This blame is tied, in part, to the older men's decision in the 1980s and 1990s to take part in the conservation-as-development project. Gilbert, a long-time friend of mine, about my age, says, "If I had been a big man when [the first conservation-related actor] came here I would have told him to go to hell. What have they brought us? Nothing. And they have kept companies from coming and giving us jobs." Some of these young men have, in part because of their parents' coffee businesses, been sent to Goroka for school. These men have traveled widely across Papua New Guinea. They take part in networks of migration tied to social connections they make while living in Goroka and going to the Seventh Day Adventist high school there. The school has students from across the country. The young men who attend the school make friends and travel with them to their homes in Lae, Hagen, Madang, Port Moresby (occasionally if the friend is wealthy and their parents can pay), and elsewhere. These young people see a world that appeals to them tremendously. In this process of traveling and connecting, they become, in the eyes of their parents and grandparents, less Gimi.

For young Gimi, being fully Gimi is not enough. Fulfilling the rights and responsibilities that make Kabe and his generation feel whole does not make Gilbert and his generation feel whole at all. They crave more—more money, more opportunities, more social relations external to their family and lineage, more travel, more adventure. While Kabe and his generation lament the "lack of development" in terms of schools, medical care, access to markets, and the like, Gilbert and his generation lament their rural lifestyle altogether. They feel trapped by their villages, families, and forests, and they would do almost anything to access the opportunities they see as inaccessible to them. Yet they see the conservation actors who have benefited from their engagement with Gimi lands as having accumulated great wealth and power.

Shadow Dialogues and Gimi Subjectivity

In theorizing the role of anthropologists in the production of textual knowledge, Vincent Crapanzano (1992) argued that anthropological dialogues are never simply dialogic. He saw them as multiply dialogic, full of what he called shadow dialogues: multiple engagements that the ethnographer has before, during, and after an encounter but that she brings to her final analysis and textual production. Those engagements may be with texts, with music, with other anthropologists—really, with anything. Drawing on work from psychoanalysis, we can expand this notion of shadow dialogues to better understand the kind of intersubjectivity that emerges during ethnographic encounters and that, in addition to the prior textual or discursive engagements of the ethnographer, works to produce ethnographic understandings and articulations (see West 2005a). Thomas Ogden argues that psychoanalytic encounters produce an "analytic third," or a subjectivity present in the coproduction that happens during analysis (Ogden 1999:462). This third is neither the psychoanalyst nor the patient but rather a new coproduction of the past, the present, and the future (Ogden 1999:471). Combine this idea with Crapanzano's sense of the constant ongoing dialogues we are always already having and we can begin to see a novel way to reconsider the ethnographic production of texts.

Within the Gimi theory of subjectivity, stories, narrations, persons, and all such assemblages are agent-objects having subjectivity. Recall that Gimi philosophers pose that the life forces of auna and kore animate, transform, and reanimate all being. When people die, their auna leaves their bodies and transforms into the force that animates creatures and features on and of their ancestral lands. When a hunter or a gatherer takes and ingests plants, animals, water, wind, or anything else animated by auna (and as everything is so animated, this means all the world) there is a coproduction of the entire Gimi world in that transaction. The subject comes to be because of this exchange with the past. This is also the philosophical underpinning of Gimi ideas about exchange between persons: to give and to receive don't just tie you to another; in that exchange you become in coproduction with the other. There are not two but one, and that one is made between those exchanging.

Conceptualizing these stories as being brought forth by multiple forms of coproduction is a first step. But consider the actual encounters that produced my ability to tell these stories using Gimi philosophy. Kobe sat with me for hours and hours telling and talking about the birds of paradise story. Prior to our conversations, she had recounted the story before, but in our engagement she recounted it for a different purpose. It was to be recorded and told to others; it was to be memorialized in a book (and she knew this and was proud of the fact that we spent so much time talking about it for the book). In our discussions she thought about the story in ways she had not considered it before. She turned it over and over in her mind (to paraphrase her description of the process the last time I saw her alive). She and I brought this story forth from her memory and philosophical trainings and my ethnographic training. We rubbed it against the work of Gillian Gillison, who as I said above, wrote about and analyzed it in her first book. We worried it with questions about violence and questions about social reproduction. We troubled it with conversations about inequality and death. My point is this, and it holds for all of the stories I have recounted above: as philosophical propositions or narrations of philosophy or ethnographic vignettes that illustrate philosophical principles, all of these forms *come to be* through encounter.

What if we took Gimi philosophical propositions about how the world works and read the story of that first European-captured tree kangaroo through it? What if we failed to privilege Euro-American-Australian forms of narrating history in a liner fashion? What if we rubbed what we know about some things that happened (perhaps?) against Gimi recountings of life, death, and life force? Finally, what if we used a narrative form that is not comfortable for us? In what follows I attempt to do just that. This is, in part, a thought experiment and, in part, an argument for allowing indigenous philosophical theory to have the same explanatory power as other forms of theoretical abstraction.

Discovery and Death: Retellings

Eta, the little tree kangaroo, felt exhausted, afraid, and alone. She had never been away from her mother and her father before, and she had been calling out for them for such a long time now. Eta only knew the world through her parents; every moment of every day of her life had been spent with them. Indeed, Eta didn't really know that she existed outside of the mutual recognition of her family until quite recently. The last thing Eta could remember from before was foraging with her parents at the base of a big tree on the south side of her mountain home when they heard the singing of dogs coming from the valley below. The dogs sounded far away so they slowly, without worry, began climbing up, up, up the tree back to their treetop home. Suddenly, Eta felt something grab her tail, and she fell down, down, down[3] to the base of the tree. She smelled strange smells and heard strange sounds and then the world went black.

When Eta awoke, the first thing she did was sniff for her parents. She sniffed and sniffed and sniffed as hard as she could, but she couldn't smell them anywhere. Her mother had taught her to sniff the air for family, food, and danger, and she knew her forest home by its smells. When she didn't smell her parents, or anything else she understood, she began to call out for her parents. She called and called and called, but nobody answered. Eta listened for any sounds she was familiar with and heard nothing. There were no calls of birds of paradise late in the day from their lek near Eta's treetop home, no click click click of frogs calling for rain at dusk, no mingled voices of humans walking through the forest to their gardens on the north side of the mountain.

Eta could feel cold air on her nose and ears, so she thought that she might be at the top of a very tall tree, but she couldn't see branches or leaves or light. Maybe she was inside a hollow or den. She slowly hopped toward the place where the cold air was coming from and found what looked like tree limbs, all straight and slick lined up along the face of the hollow. She licked the walls of the hollow and knew it was a tree she was in, but it tasted wrong. It didn't taste like the damp-mossy-warm taste of her treetop. It tasted cold and slick and empty. When Eta licked the wall of the hollow where she lived with her parents, she tasted her mother's fur, the grubs her father found and brought home, and the musk of her family comingled with the stories her parents told her about her grandparents and great-grandparents and so on and so on and so on. She tasted life. Here, in this strange hollow, she tasted nothing familiar or comforting.

As Eta was contemplating her strange surroundings, she heard a noise. She pricked up her ears and listened as hard as she could. The noise came closer, and she realized it was human voices. They didn't sound like the humans who sometimes walked underneath her treetop home but they had the unmistakable tin of humanity. Eta wasn't exactly afraid of humans, but she was very cautious about them. Her father taught her that, like everything else in their forest, they were connected to the humans who walked there and who sometimes camped underneath their tree. Her father taught her that just like she ate grubs he brought her that the humans ate things the gathered in the forests. And just as the grubs became part of Eta, whatever the humans ate became part of them. This was all part of the never-ending cycle of exchange that her father was teaching her about.

As best as she understood it, nothing had a beginning or end. Everything simply changed form over time. She knew that she was made up of flesh and spirit and that someday her spirit would leave her flesh and fly out into the forest. Her family had lived in this forest for as long as anyone could remember, so her spirit would find places in the forest to stop and lodge while it transformed and become part of every living part of the forest. And after that, as tree kangaroo parents ate plants and animals from that forest, she would become part of them and their families.

As Eta thought about these things, and about her parents, the strange human voices grew closer. Suddenly she felt the hollow she was in shake, and she saw the strange slick branches open and light flood into her dark space. She was scared but curious, so she slowly hopped toward the light. When her eyes adjusted she didn't understand what she was seeing. Everything looked like tree, but it was different. Instead of the knobby barky epiphyte-covered world she knew, like the sides of the strange hollow, the tree world in front of her was slick and gleaming. Eta was confused, so she hopped out of the hollow and up to a higher point. Perhaps if she got high enough in the tops of the trees, she would understand where she was and find a way back to her mountaintop. She hopped from slick branch to slick branch and suddenly she heard the human voices yell out. She didn't understand them, but they seemed to be coming toward her so she went higher and higher and higher, to the top of the tallest tree. It seemed that she was on a flat tree surrounded by inky blackness below. Eta was terribly confused. At night, from her home tree, she and her mother would look up into the sky and tell stories about the stars above. The stars lived in inky blackness above, but the tree she was on seemed to be floating in inky blackness below. Eta could hear the humans shouting and see them jumping toward her the way that she had seen dogs at the base of trees sometimes. They jumped and made noise. Eta was terrified.

All of a sudden, Eta felt a wind come from nowhere. The tree she was in swayed and swayed and swayed, and the humans yelled and yelled and yelled then Eta lost her grip. She fell down down down into the inky blackness. Eta couldn't breathe. The black was the coldest thing she had ever felt. She couldn't move her body and couldn't stop falling. She tried sniffing to make sense of the black and something rushed into her nose. She tried calling and something rushed into her mouth. She felt so cold and she couldn't sniff or call or hear. And then, just like before, the world went black.

When Eta woke up she felt strange. She felt stranger than she had ever felt before. She couldn't feel her body touching anything. Normally, Eta could feel the tiny pink pads on the bottom of her feet against her tree or the ground. She could feel her long tail as it swished behind her. She could feel the heels of her hind legs as they dug in right before she hopped. She could feel her fur as she snuggled next to her parents as they slept. Now, she couldn't feel any of this. Eta looked down to try and find her tail, to get a sense of her whereabouts, and she saw that she seemed to be floating in the cold inky blackness.

Just as Eta was trying to understand her predicament she heard a noise. Suddenly, and startlingly, she heard something calling to her out of the cold inky blackness.

"Hey, hey, hey. Whatcha doing? Whatcha doing? Whatcha doing? Huh? Huh? Huh?"

Eta looked and there, to her surprise, was a creature. It was darting around Eta, moving with great ease and with great rapidity.

"Who are you? Who are you? Who are you?"

Eta opened her mouth to call to the creature but it went on without waiting.

"I'm Pfiesteria. Pfiesteria Heterotrophic Dinoflagellate.[4] But you can call me Feisty. If I had friends or family, that's what they would call me. But I don't have those things. But if I did, they would call me that. Feisty. Because Pfiesteria Heterotrophic Dinoflagellate, that is too much. Don'tcha think? Don'tcha think? Don'tcha think? I had them, I mean I think I did, I mean I had other things like me, lots and lots and lots of them. But I got lost. Now I have me. But even with just me, Pfiesteria Heterotrophic Dinoflagellate, that's too much. So Feisty, call me Feisty. Okay? Okay? Okay?"

Eta wasn't sure what to do. She wanted to know where she was and how to find her way home, but she wasn't sure about this creature. As it darted about it seemed to shift form. At one angle it seemed to be flat, the color of berries. At a different angle it seemed to be thick, the color of a river rock. When it darted below her, it flashed like lightning against the night sky. When it darted above her, it left streaks the color of the tail of a bird of paradise. As the creature continued with its darting and its mono-logue, Eta assessed her situation. She was lost. She was scared. She was alone. And these three states of being were states she had not understood could exist until the strange men took her from her home and her family. They were not a part of her world until recently. Eta thought about it. She could try to make her way back to the bizarre tree she had jumped from, she could try to find her way home to her mountaintop on her own, or she could try to calm the strange creature down and enlist its help.

Eta reached her paw out slowly toward the creature and rested it on what she thought was the thing's body. As her paw touched it, it stopped vocalizing and it stopped moving. It seemed to float in front of Eta, looking at her with huge eyes. Eta held her paw on it, and the longer she touched it the more form the creature seemed to take. It seemed to become solid right before Eta's eyes. It grew a tail—not, of course, such a fine tail as Eta's, but a tail nonetheless. It grew ears—not the tiny pointy ears of Eta's kind but ears on its head that looked like hollows. It grew a solid body that was brightly colored like birds' feathers and orchids. And it grew eyelashes that fluttered like palm fronds as it blinked its eyes. Finally, it grew two small protrusions that seemed to wiggle behind it. The longer Eta touched it, the more it seemed to come into the world of permanence.

After a long while, Eta called out to the thing: "My name is Eta and I'm pleased to meet you Feisty. I'm lost and confused. I don't know where I am or really even, what sort of world this is. Can you help me?"

Feisty, replied, "Of course I will help you!"

And then Feisty told her story: "I'm here alone. I was once part of a bigger something, an aggregate of things like me, but then we all went in separate directions. Before that, we all lived together in a group and sometimes we would all meet up and form a bigger group to eat. But I got lost. When we disaggregated I went toward the east while everyone else went west. Then I got caught up in the pull of the ocean. That is where we are now, in the ocean."

Eta interrupted, comforting the strange creature as best as she could with her wet paw and said, "I'm glad we are in this together."

Afterword

Birdsongs: In Memory of Neil Smith (1954–2012)

Neil Smith, one of my mentors and teachers, died unexpect-
edly one year before I delivered the Leonard Hastings Schoff Memorial
Lectures at Columbia University. This book is, as mentioned in the introduction, based on those lectures. I was asked to give the lectures—an
extraordinary honor—in the spring of 2012, a few months before Neil's
death on September 29. Since his death I have thought quite a bit about
what sorts of networks and paths bring us to our intellectual or scholarly
homes. My work is infused by Neil's brilliant work on nature, uneven
development, and the frontier ideology. If we are to take seriously the idea
of assemblage and network in contemporary anthropology, and I think
we should, it is fair to say that this book is partly due to Neil's scholarly
legacy. If we are to take seriously Gimi ideas about assembled persons
and the trace of ourselves that we leave with others when we leave this
world, and I think we should, then Neil is still here. Forms of coproduction have been central to everything I have discussed in these pages,
and I want to end with some thoughts about how we come, as scholars, to hold particular kinds of analytics dear. I have been writing around
dispossession and accumulation for my entire career as an anthropologist. I analyze the world through these forms and feel, to some extent,
that this is in part because of Neil's influence on me. In what follows

I trace that influence to honor his memory, not as a scholar but as a producer of students.

Exactly thirteen days after Neil died, I met Laurie Lewis and Tom Rozum, two extraordinary bluegrass musicians. For lots of New Yorkers meeting them would have been an interesting sort of social curio, something to be put away only to be pulled out and dusted off at some future cocktail party where another guest brought up Bill Monroe: "Yes, Monroe *was* so important. You know, I once met Laurie Lewis and Tom Rozum. Oh, *you* don't know who *they* are . . . ?" to show a kind of cultural superiority that we New Yorkers love to demonstrate. For me it was something quite different. Lewis's 2002 CD, *Birdsong*, is among my top three or four favorite albums of all time. Laurie Lewis is a star to me, a famous person I have always wanted to meet.

London Calling, Murmur, Substance, and *Birdsong*: one of these things is not like the others. The music of the Clash, REM, and New Order does not, in any form or fashion, resemble the hauntingly beautiful bluegrass music on *Birdsong*.

One of the songs on the album, "The Blackest Crow," is an ancient Appalachian lament.[1] It has a tune with a pentatonic scale, something that means that it is older than old, perhaps making its way over to the Americas with the Presbyterian Scotch-Irish dissenters who came from Ulster in the eighteenth century and then migrated down the eastern seaboard as they tried to escape the New England Quakers who thought of them as savages. It was probably played and sung as they moved down the mountain chains and dispossessed, displaced, killed, and raped the descendants of the Coosa paramount chiefdom, one of the Muskogean-speaking chiefdoms that De Soto and Juan Pardo started down the road to dispossession in the sixteenth century. It may have been played and sung much earlier, when the Scottish and English ancestors of the Scotch-Irish colonized Ulster in Ireland in order to dispossess the Irish of their land and put it under the control of James VI of Scotland (who was also King James I of England). It may have even been the tune being hummed by the Scottish clans that so intrigued Karl Marx, as they were violently dispossessed of their land by the English at the dawn of capitalism.

The song, the way I hear it, tells of impending, inevitable loss and the knowledge that the singer has of the heartbreak to come. It speaks of the choice that we make in being wiling to truly love someone given that we know that the connections we make with other humans in this world are tenuous; people leave, they move on physically and psychologically. And people die. The song reminds me that in choosing to love, we open ourselves to joy and pain equally. And the song speaks of how, when someone leaves, we feel that they are still with us and that they have written themselves, and we have written them, into our hearts and minds.

Laurie Lewis's version of the song is heart-wrenchingly, otherworldly beautiful, as are all the other songs on *Birdsong*, an album made up entirely of songs about birds (all the proceeds went to benefit the Audubon society in northern California). Because of this, I gave Neil, an avid "birder," a copy of the CD as a birthday gift right after it was released. So instead of mustering up my too-cool New Yorker persona when I met Laurie Lewis thirteen days after Neil died, I was left speechless. I could not find words yet to narrate Neil or my grief over his passing. When I could speak, all I could say to this extraordinary person was that her music was one of the many connections that I had to another extraordinary person.

Bird-Watching in New Jersey

My first memory of Neil is of meeting him at a party at Dorothy Hodgson's house in 1995 when I was a first-year PhD student in anthropology at Rutgers University, where Neil was a professor from 1986 to 2000. All fall semester as we worked together to develop my thinking about my proposed research. Dorothy (my PhD coadviser and mentor) had been telling me I needed to meet her friend and neighbor, a geographer who spent a great deal of time thinking about space and nature. I finally met him as I stood next to a bowl of olive dip at Dorothy's holiday party. Physically, Neil was a cross between an entrenched bulldog guarding a juicy bone and a friendly cartoon walrus. He was compact and brimming with energy and had a fuzzy, out-of-control mustache and expressive and utterly unruly eyebrows. Although I do not actually remember this to be fact, I suspect that when introduced to me for the first time he gave me what would come to be known by everyone in my graduate-student house as "the dreaded double kiss."

Neil was a kisser. He would lean in and envelop you with his huge capacity for love and joy and kiss you on both cheeks. I am from Appalachia, a descendent of strict Presbyterian Scotch-Irish settlers. We do not hug or kiss easily. We do not kiss our family in greeting. We do not kiss our friends in greeting. We most certainly do not kiss strangers. My graduate student housemates dubbed Neil's kiss as "the dreaded double kiss" because, initially, it made me enormously uncomfortable. It made me feel my noncosmopolitan hillbilly background acutely.

The night we met, Neil and I only talked briefly. We agreed that at the beginning of the next semester, I would make the long trip from Douglas Campus to his office on Livingston Campus to begin a real conversation about work. I am sure that my description of my proposed PhD project was so unsophisticated at that point as to be ridiculous, but Neil told me that he thought it was a great project and that he thought someone doing an ethnography of how Euro-American ideas about nature and culture and indigenous ideas about nature and culture come into contact during an environmental conservation effort was a brilliant idea.

It was in this brief exchange that I got my first glimpse of Neil's fierce engagement with students and his ability to hear their ideas, no matter how unformed or ill thought out, and take them seriously. I had not forgotten about this exactly but was reminded of it after he died when I started receiving e-mails from my former students. I received about thirty e-mails from former PhD, MA, and undergraduate students who were first introduced to Neil's work through my teaching and mentoring. The e-mail that most made me think of Neil's work with students was from Danielle DiNovelli-Lang, who, in the mid 2000s after she and I read some of Neil's work together, went to CUNY, where Neil was a professor from 2000 until his death, to take a graduate seminar with him. Her e-mail offered her condolences, but more importantly, in it she remembered how intellectually generous Neil had been to her, how he had taken her, and all the other students, seriously, and made them feel like their ideas *really mattered*. At that point in his career, Neil had been teaching graduate seminars about space and nature for about twenty-five years, yet he still found the teaching and the student's thoughts on space and nature compelling.

I read Neil's first book, *Uneven Development: Nature, Capital, and the Production of Space*, over the winter holiday break the January after meeting him and it changed my world. My whole life, I had been, like almost everyone else I knew, thinking about space and nature as having strictly geometrical and biological meanings. It had never occurred to me that space and nature were not given, that they were in any way brought into being through human action and not simply the backdrop for, and receivers of, human action. That they were conceived, perceived, and lived in ways that brought them into the world was an astounding revelation to me. It sounds so naive to say this now, after so many years of being thought of as one of the people in anthropology who thinks about the production of space as nature, but when I read *Uneven Development*, it blew my mind. In that first reading, the fact of space and nature as physical, mental, and social, and the possibility of the radical shattering of space and nature by capitalism, colonialism, and the like and the reformation or production of new forms of space and nature, came to be real for me.

I had been struggling since my junior year in college to understand how, where, and when Marx's ideas about dispossession—ideas that I, because of my young reading of *Capital* in Dr. Gerald Ginocchio's sociology theory seminar when I was twenty, associated only with the emergence of capitalism and the working class in Britain—connected to the places in the world I was interested in. Places like Papua New Guinea, which seemed to me, at the time, far from the reaches of markets and capital. In that first reading of *Uneven Development*, I began to put together the pieces of what would become the conceptual and analytic focus of all of my research since.

The first time Neil and I talked about *Uneven Development* was in the early spring of 1996 standing in an oak forest in Herrontown Woods near Princeton, New Jersey, while looking for birds. Herrontown Woods is one of the best places in the state to see migratory birds during the fall and spring, and Neil was on the lookout for warblers. We hiked, looked for and at tiny brown birds, and talked about everything from *Capital* to first and second nature to why I was interested in New Guinea to our shared, yet very different, Scottish ancestry to how someone like Neil who seemed so focused on and interested in nature could be publishing a new book on gentrification and New York City. It was during that first day talking that I realized what a far-reaching intellect Neil's was.

Uneven Development was essentially Neil's PhD thesis. He graduated from St. Andrews, in Scotland, in 1977 with a BS and then from Johns Hopkins in 1982 with a PhD in geography. He was twenty-eight years old when he earned his PhD and started his first teaching job at Columbia University. He was only thirty when *Uneven Development* was published, in 1984. Neil's second single-author book, published in 1996, was *The New Urban Frontier: Gentrification and the Revanchist City*.

Uneven Development and *The New Urban Frontier* ask the reader, among other things, to look at something that we take for granted as the outcomes of specific kinds of natural processes (biophysical, evolutionary in the case of nature, in the former, and historic, steady, and driven by human social needs and desires in the case of cities, in the latter) and then allow Neil to show us that they, as highly social forms, are actually produced by economic processes connected to the needs of capital and not to the needs of plants, animals, or people. Both of the books demonstrate how capitalism produces landscapes that are crucial for its own survival. Neil shows how the logics of capitalism emerged and how those logics necessitate particular kinds of natures and cities and how those kinds of natures and cities then feed back into the growth of capital and survival of the system. In other words, they both show that space and its productions are the key to the survival of capitalism.

Lots of scholars focus on the multiple kinds of degradations under capitalism that Neil demonstrates in these two works. However, one of the things that I took away from them early on was that because capitalism is productive of natural and urban space, and because we can track these productions and understand how, when, and why they happen the way that they do, we can also imagine how other forms of social relations can be productive of natural and urban space. This became one of the driving questions of my PhD work, and it still focuses some of my academic work today. More importantly, it focuses all of my activism.

Chicks, Grue, and Birds

During the 1996–1997 academic year, Neil was the acting director of the Center the Critical Analysis of Contemporary Culture at Rutgers. In 1994, he, Sue Gal, and Bruce Robbins had written a proposal to the Rockefeller Foundation for funding for a three-year seminar on culture and environments in the public sphere. During Neil's year as acting director I was a graduate student fellow at the center as well as his paid graduate research assistant. As a graduate fellow at the center, I was meant to participate in the weekly seminar, present my own work at the seminar, and interact around questions of nature and culture with the Rutgers faculty fellows and graduate fellows as well as the visiting faculty fellows and visiting post-docs. As Neil's RA I was expected to help with the research for the book he was working on, assist with some of the minor editorial duties he undertook for the journal *Environment and Planning D: Society and Space*, and basically do whatever he needed me to do to help run that year's seminar smoothly.

That year was also when I learned that no matter how hard I work, no matter how clear and focused my writing and thinking become, and no matter how kind and generous I try to be to other scholars, there are academics out there who will treat me like nothing more than a hillbilly kid from Georgia who, because of her looks, accent, and class background, must have achieved what she has achieved because she is sleeping with some man in power.

That year, one of the other Rutgers graduate student fellows and her postdoc boyfriend started a rumor that I was sleeping with Neil. I was not, and I never had been, and never did, sleep with Neil. But the rumor flew around the center, especially among the postdocs and graduate students. It was thought that sex was the only way I could have earned the financially secure position as an RA and the intellectually secure position as a fellow. Neil heard the rumor before I did and tried to shield me from it. He was not successful, and when I finally heard it, I was devastated. I was not naïve, exactly, but I did believe that I had escaped the extraordinary sexism and misogyny that I had grown up with and faced daily in both my undergraduate years in South Carolina and my M.A. program at the University of Georgia. I thought that elite academic circles in the Northeast would be places where sexism and misogyny were dissected, understood, and countered through scholarship and activism. Not being able to shield me from the rumor or my own inability to quickly come to terms with the reality of the sexism and misogyny among seemingly left-leaning elite academics, Neil got mad on my behalf. From then on, he protected me. That might seem like an infantilizing thing to say, but he did. And it is worth saying that Neil was indeed a horrible womanizer, but that was not the form through which he related to me. Throughout our friendship he tried to soften the blows when my naïve and optimistic ideals about the academy were shattered. And they have been shattered over and over again.

Fast-forward to the spring of 2001 when I was on the academic job market for the first time. I was lucky. I had six on-campus interviews that spring and felt reasonably secure that I would land some position. Part of this security was based on my dissertation defense the previous spring when my wonderful committee (Dorothy Hodgson, George E. B. Morren, Bonnie J. McCay, and Neil) had passed my dissertation with no revisions and nominated it for a national award. Part of my security was based on Neil's description, at that meeting, of sitting down to read my dissertation. He said that he had put it off until the last minute. According to him, the Saturday afternoon before the defense he sat down to read it and realized a few pages in that it was not what he expected. He had not read any drafts of chapters and, I think, expected the kind of writing that he had seen from me during my year at the Center the Critical Analysis of Contemporary Culture. What he got, he recounted, was a book-style work that forced him to open a bottle of wine, sit back, and read the whole thing in one sitting. At my defense he said that it was one of the most pleasant experiences he had ever had as an academic. That, and the fact that Dorothy had been pleased with it (finally, after what seemed like a million drafts, all of which she read carefully), made me feel like I was well placed to enter faculty life.

One of my interviews that spring was at Hunter College, one of the many colleges of the City University of New York. Neil had been at CUNY almost a year and was, I suspect, my biggest supporter in the Hunter search. The interview went poorly and the culmination of a bad day came at the end of my professional talk (part of the ritual of academic hiring is for prospective employees to give an hour-long lecture about their research). After the talk, a truly angry member of the faculty stood up, yelled at me, and stormed out of the room. My work and my critical analysis of the ways environmental conservation in some cases dispossesses people living in highly biologically diverse areas of land, labor, and rights struck a nerve with him. It also, I found out later, struck a nerve that Neil was one of my supporters. I managed to maintain my composure during the berating and through the rest of the interview process, but on the way home, standing on the subway platform, I fell apart. I called Neil in his office at CUNY and met him to debrief. After listening to me, and agreeing that "Yes, that faculty member is a total asshole" and "Yes, he is mad about your work because you are right," and "Yes, it was totally unprofessional and inappropriate," Neil stopped me and gave me a serious lecture about the structural position I was about to enter into in the U.S. university system. He was clear and brilliant, and I will never forget his teaching me, in that moment, that I am and will always be labor. That my university will not love me. That my colleagues may become friends. But that in the end, those in power will position us against each other, and we will position ourselves against each other to compete over limited resources. I had to stop imagining the university as a place where everyone would have good politics.

Flight

I am a runner. Not a marathoner or even a serious six-miles-six-times-a-week runner. I'm a stress runner. I tend to run to clear my mind and detoxify my body of the stress of academic life. My longest runs ever were in the two years prior to my earning tenure at Columbia University in April 2009. Some of my most vivid memories of Neil are of him during those two years. When running didn't work, and when I could catch him in town, I would talk to him about the awfulness of the tenure process for me. He would listen lovingly and then, in very strong terms, tell me honestly what he thought. He would also, again in very strong terms, make clear to me when I was being justifiably paranoid and when I was being obnoxiously narcissistic—a tendency one finds among many, many academics.

During the year I worked for Neil at Rutgers, he was also writing *American Empire: Roosevelt's Geographer and the Prelude to Globalization,* which was published in 2003. I think he was also collecting materials that, post-9/11, would contribute to his thinking for his 2005 book *The Endgame of Globalization.* As his RA, some of my waged labor that year was to collect documents for his growing file on geographer Isaiah Bowman. In reconstructing the biography of Bowman, *American Empire* also gives us the biography of geography as an academic discipline and the biography of American imperialism between World War I and the beginning of the Cold War. Bowman was all about frontiers, so-called expedition and discovery, conquests, environmental determinism, power through territorial control, and the emerging liberal justification for all of these in postwar America. Neil's analysis of Bowman is a brilliant construction of how American neoliberal imperial ideology came to be, and what it meant for the globe. In *The Endgame of Globalization* Neil drew on this analysis to show that America's entry into the Iraq war was not simply about U.S. oil interests, the Bush administration, or Washington, D.C., neoconservatives. It was directly connected to this history of imperial ideology, an ideology that was economic as well as political and cultural.

Neil was well known before *American Empire* and *The Endgame of Globalization,* but their publication pulled him into a kind of academic fame that few scholars will ever experience. From reading his CV, it looks like Neil gave eighty-four invited lectures and twenty-seven keynote lectures between when I met him in 1995 and when he died. He organized eight conferences and gave talks in Ireland, Croatia, Argentina, Sweden, Hong Kong, Spain, Scotland, Britain, South Korea, Brazil, South Africa, the Canary Islands, Turkey, India, Germany, Norway, Japan, Bolivia, Australia, and Mexico. He became a global academic celebrity.

Neil's admonishing me for my own narcissistic tendencies during the years I was undergoing tenure review was striking because even with his extreme academic fame, he never became full of himself or self-focused in a way that precluded him from paying attention to students or scholars who wanted his time at conferences or people who wanted him to come and speak or activists who wanted to strategize with him about politics or the CUNY administrators who wanted to use his brilliance to create new spaces of scholarship or colleagues who wanted to be near him and his fame. I think Neil gave of himself to all of these people. But I also think that as his fame grew and as more and more people wanted a piece of him, he lost some of the moorings that keep us all grounded in this world.

On days that I can't run, I go to my gym in central Harlem. I've been a member since 2007 and have made more friends there than at any other social site in the city. Some of my friends from the gym have become go-to people for going out, playing sports, and other social outlets. Some of my friends from the gym have a subtler role in keeping me in this world.

Every Tuesday and Thursday I go to a noon class at the gym. My routine does not vary. I arrive five minutes before the class, deposit my jacket and bag in the locker room, then stop by the weight machine wherever my friend Mike is lifting. He and I exchange a hello, and then I go to class. After class, we meet at the water fountain and talk for a few minutes. I don't know his last name. He is about twenty years older than I and is from the neighborhood. He has two children, one of whom works and one of whom is in college. She is the first person in her family to go to college. Mike and I discuss things of no importance, the weather, and things of great importance, the Yankees and politics.

The point is this: Mike, and the other people I interact with every day in my life, keep me in this world. I look forward to seeing Mike. If I miss a day at the gym because of academic travel, he asks after me. If he misses a day because of going to visit his daughter at school, I ask after him. I tell him when I'm going to be in away for long periods of time for research. He tells me when he is going to be on vacation. In this small way we moor each other to the world. I think that as Neil became more and more famous, as more and more people wanted a piece of him, he somehow lost his ability to moor himself and others in this world.

Birds of Paradise

For all of my career I have worked with people from the island of New Guinea. Some of these people are urban-dwelling academics, activists, and businesspeople. Some of them are rural-dwelling farmers and hunters who live in places without power, roads, schools, and hospitals. Some have extraordinary, ancient, stories about birds of paradise—forty species of spectacularly plumed birds found only on New Guinea, its outlying islands, the Moluccas, and far northeastern Australia. The Gimi bird stories are a small part of their coproductive practice, or the process by which the come to know, understand, and experience the world.

The story of where the birds came from, which I recount in chapter 4, was one that Neil loved. We talked about it over and over again during our many discussions about space, place, and nature in New Guinea. It is one of the stories I would remind him of when I bugged him to visit me in New Guinea, where I go every North American academic summer.

One of the last, actual in-person, not via e-mail, conversations I had with Neil before he died was about this story. I had been revisiting it, and my analysis of it, to think more carefully about ontology, epistemology, and indigenous theories of dispossession and accumulation—revisiting it for what has ultimately become the chapter in this book. I was doing this, in part, because some of my Pacific Islander colleagues have been pushing me to think much more carefully and critically about the notions that I bring with me to my research, analysis, and writing that may foreclose deep and complex understandings of indigenous ontology and epistemic practices. The other part of my revisiting the story was to rethink some of my early arguments about Gimi and the production of space and nature.

I wrote a short piece about this as part of a longer essay about the production of scale, space, and nature, all things that I learned about, initially, from Neil. He read the essay, and it irritated him. Or at least that is my reading of his response to me about it. He thought that in my essay I got scale "slightly wrong" and that the current "ontological-turn" in anthropology is a kind of sleight of hand that simply, among other wrongs, brings the fraught concept of "culture" back into the discipline.

FIGURE A.1   Backflips on Ela Beach, Port Moresby. Photograph courtesy of J. C. Salyer.

After reading my essay, Neil made me promise to read Ian Hacking's *Historical Ontology* and to reread both Sallie Marston's and his own early work on scale. Then we made a date to meet and have dinner at Red Rooster, a new hot spot on a gentrifying block of Frederick Douglass Boulevard, to discuss scale, our lives, and our (additional and ongoing) disagreement about the nature of gentrification in Harlem. He died before we ever had that dinner.

Notes

Introduction

1. Melanesia comprises the countries of Fiji, New Caledonia, Papua New Guinea, the Solomon Islands, and Vanuatu, as well as the Indonesian colony of West Papua.

2. There are forty-one species of birds of paradise (family Paradisaeidae). They are found only on New Guinea, its associated islands, the Maluku Islands of Indonesia, and northeastern Australia. They are known for their spectacular feathers and extraordinary male courtship behaviors during mating.

3. See Stella 2007, as well as Douglas 1998, 1999; Kulick and Willson 1992; and Lipset 2015. Also see Jahoda 1999 for a brilliant and extensive discussion of the image of the savage globally and throughout Western thought.

4. I foreground Stella's work here because he was Melanesian (see also Kabutaulaka 1997). Anthropology, as a discipline, tends to privilege the work of European, American, and Australian scholars when examining images tied to the colonial in New Guinea. Many others have written about the intertwining of colonial representations and ideas about the Pacific. See, for example, Dixon 2011; Landman 2006; Landman and Ballard 2010; Quanchi 2007; and Specht and Fields 1984. Additionally, Martin Slama and Jenny Munro (2015) have just edited a book concerned with how these forms are articulated today in West Papua, and David Lipset has examined how filmic representations of Pacific Islanders more generally pose particular ideas about their moral personhood in comparison to settler society, the environment, and the viewers of film (Lipset 2015:105).

5. Webb Keane (2003, 2007) argues along similar lines in his work on semiotic ideology. He focuses on "the dynamic interconnections among different modes of signification at play within a particular historical and social formation" and shows that people use language in ways that reflect "certain underlying assumptions about the world and the beings that inhabit it" (Keane 2003:410). For him, semiotic ideology is both "a reflection upon, and an attempt to organize, people's experiences of the semiotics of the materiality of semiotic form" that encompasses languages alongside visual imagery, food, architecture, and other social forms (Keane 2007:21).

6. Sir Michael Somare served as prime minister three times: from 1975 to 1980, from 1982 to 1985, and from 2002 to 2011.

7. See Morris 2016 for a brilliant reconsideration of the term "primitive" versus the term "original" in Marx's work.

8. "One thing, however, is clear: nature does not produce on the one hand owners of money or commodities, and on the other hand men possessing nothing but their own labor-power. This relation has no basis in natural history, nor does it have a social basis common to all periods of human history. It is clearly the result of a past historical development, the product of many economic revolutions, of the extinction of a whole series of older formations of social production" (Marx 1975: 237).

9. Harvey 2005:128. "The discovery of gold and silver in America, the extirpation, enslavement and entombment in mines of the aboriginal population, the beginning of the conquest and looting of the East Indies, the turning of Africa into a warren for the commercial hunting of black-skins, signalized the rosy dawn of the era of capitalist production. These idyllic proceedings are the chief momenta of primitive accumulation. On their heels treads the commercial war of the European nations, with the globe for a theatre. It begins with the revolt of the Netherlands from Spain, assumes giant dimensions in England's Anti-Jacobin War, and is still going on in the opium wars against China, Etc." (Marx 1975: 915).

10. Marx saw privatization as the pivotal point in the primitive accumulation he theorized and David Harvey argues that privatization, financialization, management and manipulation of crises, and state redistributions guide neoliberal accumulation by dispossession today. Harvey also, again drawing heavily on Rosa Luxemburg and also on Neil Smith, connects accumulation by dispossession to uneven development: "Access to cheaper inputs is, therefore, just as important as access to widening markets in keeping profitable opportunities open. The implication is that non-capitalist territories should be forced open not only to trade (which could be helpful) but also to permit capital to invest in profitable ventures using cheaper labour power, raw materials, low-cost land, and the like. The general thrust of any capitalist logic of power is not that territories should be held back from capitalist development, but that they should be continuously opened up" (Harvey 2005:139).

Accumulation by dispossession also allows capital to address and stabilize the ever-present threat of crisis of over accumulation since accumulation by dispossession makes natural resources less expensive for the capitalist, allowing him

more profit (Harvey 2005). This process of accumulation takes from people situated in one geographical area and gives to people situated in a different one, thereby
producing both wealth and capital (for capitalist) and poverty and oppression (for
workers). But the process also gives rise to the actual geography of the areas. To
illustrate this principle, Marx uses the Highland clearances, in which agricultural
populations in Scotland were cleared off of the land by the British so that the
crown initially could profit by installing sheep farms and then, once it was clear
that higher rents and revenues for the land could be found in other ways, by es-
tablishing hunting preserves for deer (Marx 1975:728–731). With this example we
see how accumulation by dispossession gives rise to uneven development that is
both social (in terms of the lot in life left for the displaced agricultural clans) and
geographic (in terms of the spatial production of the Highlands as a forested, wild
hunting Mecca).

Uneven development is one of the contradictions of capitalism because it simultaneously creates wealth for some and poverty for others (the capitalists and
the workers respectively). This is the uneven development of capital on the scale
of the individual. Uneven development with regard to geography is the similar
contradiction whereby the growth and prosperity of one area of the globe is always, in capitalist development, dependent on the impoverishment of a different
area of the globe. Marxist geographers like Neil Smith have focused on uneven
development as "the hallmark of the geography of capitalism" insofar as it is "the
systematic geographic expression of the contradictions inherent in the very constitution and structure of capital" (Smith 1984:xi). This focus has led to questions
about uneven development both as geographical ("what characterizes the specific
geography of capitalism?") and as political ("how does the geographical configura-
tion of the landscape contribute to the survival of capitalism?").

11. There is a large literature on both culture change and capitalism in New
Guinea. Most of it is configured around questions of the production and alteration of traditional inequality. For classic work, see M. Strathern 1988; R. Kelly
1993; Godelier 1986; and A. Strathern 1982.

This last work, *Inequality in New Guinea Highlands Societies*, was based on fieldwork done in the 1950s, 1960s, and early 1970s and took it as axiomatic that the
societies discussed had been "pre-capitalist" just prior to and even during some
of this research. Focused on the Highlands region of Papua New Guinea, the
scholars contributing to the volume wished to discuss how societies changed over
long periods of time and used the temporal glosses of "pre-colonial" and "post-
independence" throughout their writing. They also wished to use a comparative
method to try and describe larger regional changes and not simply single society
histories of change. The essays in the book are artifacts of their time, taking the
then-current topics in Highland ethnography (kinship, gender relations, the big-
man versus great-man political forms, horticultural production systems, exchange
relations) and theorizing the production of inequality using them as markers. As
a whole they give a picture of the forms of social hierarchies that might have existed prior to colonialism, although reconstituting social forms after the shock of
colonization is much harder than the authors seemed to think. The essays then

trace how these hierarchies have been altered, enhanced, or erased by the integra-
tions of these societies into cash economies, state-focused political formations,
and colonial-era logics of social relations. Much of the anthropology that followed
this volume was focused on change and inequality as an emergent phenomena.
This is in part because of the genius of the papers in the volume. It is also in part
because of the anthropological obsession with Highland New Guinea as a laboratory that shows the movement from prehistoric to the present. This is because
social forms that were precapitalist did endure in New Guinea longer than in
other places and because there was less global capital pouring into the island as
compared with other colonial areas.

For recent work on inequality and its emergence and endurance in Papua New
Guinea, see Allen et al. 2005; Andersen 2014; Bainton 2008; Connell 2005; Cox
2014; Foster 2002; Gilberthorpe 2007; Golub 2014; Jacka 2015; Kirsch 2006; Macintyre 2003; Wardlow 2004; Robbins and Wardlow 2005.

12. Katz defines social reproduction as "the broad material social practices and
forces associated with sustaining production and social life in all its variations.
It is the stuff of everyday life as well as the structuring forces that constitute
any social formation. Its temporality is at once daily, generational, and the *longue
duree*. Its spatiality is similarly varied; it has no single scale such as the household
or the community, but rather is everywhere bound dialectically to production. It
is not reducible to consumption, ideology, or the making of a labor force, but
embraces all of these and more in a fluid congeries of material social practices
with three aspects—political economic, cultural, and environmental—that are
accomplished by social actors in multiple social contexts associated with the state,
the workplace, the household, and civil society" (Katz 2008:18).

13. The classic text that helped solidify the frontier myth is Frederick Jackson
Turner's *The Frontier in American History* (1920). It has been reread and decon-
structed widely. See Cronon 1987; Cronon et al. 1992; Slotkin 1973; Steiner 1995;
and White and Limerick 1995.

14. See West 2006: chap. 7 for an extensive discussion of Papua New Guinean
theories of failures to reciprocate and the consequence of these failures for both the
creation of persons and the success of things like environmental conservation projects.

15. See Jacka 2015 for the most sophisticated analysis of dispossession where
there are no possessions in Papua New Guinea.

16. Malinowski 1922; see also Young 2004. Malinowski was, of course, not the
first anthropologist in this area. There had been a phase of British anthropology
prior to the publication of *Argonauts of the Western Pacific*. This time period was
characterized by the work of A. C. Haddon and C. G. Seligman and the Torres
Straits expedition (Haddon 1895, 1920; Haddon and Hornell 1936–1938; Seligman
1910). For analysis of the era, see J. Bell 2009b and Herle and Rouse 1998.

17. This happened at the 1996 Annual Meeting of the American Anthropological
Association, prior to my actually going to Papua New Guinea—it was still a proposed research site. See also Lederman 1998:429.

18. My work as an anthropologist in Papua New Guinea has been focused
on the ethnographic description and sociological examination of sites (material,

discursive, historic, contemporary) where indigenous philosophical propositions about the world come into contact with European philosophical propositions about the world.

1. "Such a Site for Play, This Edge"

The title of this chapter is drawn from Taussig 2000.

1. New Ireland Province is a marine province made up of the big islands of New Ireland, New Hanover, and Mussau, as well as the Saint Matthias group, the Tabar group, the Tanga group, the Feni islands, and many other smaller islands. Its nearly 150,000 residents speak twenty languages with forty-five different dialects.

2. Between February 2007 and August 2011 I conducted twenty-four months of ethnographic work on surf-related tourism in New Ireland, Papua New Guinea. During the 2007–2008 surf season, the Kavieng Surf Club sponsored a visitor survey in order to better understand the people coming to Kavieng to surf. Of the 239 surveyed, four were from the United States, two were from New Zealand, one was from the UK, and one was from Taiwan. The rest (231) were from Australia. Eight respondents were female; the rest, 231, were male. Twenty were between the ages of ten and nineteen, 20 were between twenty and twenty-nine, 65 were between thirty and thirty-nine, 74 were between forty and forty-nine, 52 were between fifty and fifty-nine, and 6 were over sixty. Two hundred seventeen of those surveyed stayed at the Nusa Island Retreat. Of the 219 people who answered the question "Is this your first time surfing in Papua New Guinea?" 42 were return customers and 177 were new customers. Of the 176 people who answered the question "How did you find out about Kavieng surf?" 21 visited on the recommendation of friends and family, 10 came because of the recommendation of travel agents, 87 visited because of a combination of media and "word of mouth," and 62 visited Kavieng specifically because of media (including print, Internet, and television).

Between 2008 and 2012 I conducted e-mail interviews with forty-five people who had been to Papua New Guinea to surf. My sample was based on snowball sampling—asking people I met in Papua New Guinea to connect me with friends who had visited the country, as well purposeful sampling through my frequenting of chat rooms dedicated to surfing. When people mentioned Papua New Guinea in a chat room, I contacted them and asked if they had been there. If they had, I asked if I could interview them via e-mail or through a live chat mechanism (iChat or Facebook). Additionally, I am in e-mail contact with twenty-four of the surfers whom I met in Papua New Guinea during my fieldwork.

All direct quotations in this chapter are drawn from interviews conducted during fieldwork in Papua New Guinea or conducted via e-mail and live chat mechanisms. All of the names are pseudonyms.

3. Diaz 2011; Hau'ofa 1994. Indeed, for Moana peoples the sea is even much more than a network or a site for movement; it is a form of living knowledge about time and space, ecology, navigation, and such (Diaz 2011). It is alive with

metaphoric meaning. Diaz distinguishes between "surface" meanings of the sea and "deep metaphoric meanings and argues that they cannot adequately be (nor should they be) considered separately" (Diaz 2011:24). Since this chapter focuses on expatriate visitor notions about earth and sea, I do not cover the indigenous meanings of the sea for New Ireland's residents here, although those meanings are part of a larger project.

4. In 1960, *Surfer* magazine (the oldest magazine dedicated to the sport) had a circulation of 5,000; by 1970 that had increased to about 100,000 (Reed 1999).

5. There is a large literature on tourism within anthropology. A review of that literature is beyond the scope, and page limit, of this chapter, but see West and Carrier 2004 and West et al. 2006 for extensive reviews of the tourism literature with special attention paid to ecotourism.

6. See Bakhtin 1981. For the first use of Bakhtin's ideas about chronotopes and the dialogic in the case of New Guinea, see Lipset 1997, 2004, and 2007.

7. See Warshaw 2010 for the most complete written history of surfing.

8. See Trask 1993 and Nendel 2009. The U.S. government helped to overthrow the Queen Liliuokalani of Hawai'i in 1893, and by 1898 it had established itself as the colonial power. In 1959, it was established as the fiftieth state (see Kauanui 2008 and Tengan 2008).

9. Australia's surf culture was in sharp contrast to the image of surfers that was filtering out of Hawai'i, and Waikiki in particular, during and after World War II. As the tourism industry began to grow in Hawai'i, stories of the Waikiki beachboys filtered out to other places (Walker 2008). The beachboys were native Hawaiian men who taught *haloa* tourists, especially women, how to surf. They were imagined as virile and savage and highly sexualized. Contrary to this image and its perpetuation, the beachboys were, in fact, a group of men empowered in the face of colonialism to defy colonial ideas about Hawaiian masculinity (Walker 2008).

10. In interviews with Australian surfers in the their sixties today, most of them mention these early "alternative" films, film and music festivals, and the sites in Adelaide and Sydney where they were screened.

11. See http://www.surfresearch.com.au/rm.html for images from the first issues of *Surfing World*.

12. Harvey 1990:38. See Booth 2002 for a compelling and much more complete analysis of the political economy of surfing and beach culture in Australia.

13. Booth 2005; Stedman 1997; Wheaton 2005. Booth (2005) argues that some of the anxiety about image came from surfers who had begun the industry working in small-scale shops and on underground magazines. He argues that their alienation increased as they watched the industry grow and the merging of commodity and media, causing the divide between the athletic surfers and the soul surfers.

14. Buckley 2006:194. In a study that surveyed 430 surfers who had traveled with the Sydney-based Surf Travel Company, 41.5 percent of respondents identified as being intermediate surfers and 45 percent identified as advanced. Sixty percent preferred waves between six and four feet and 47.5 percent traveled with

one to four other surfers on dedicated surf trips. Between 90 and 98 percent of the surfers surveyed were male. Ten percent of the respondents preferred destinations in Indonesia, 24 percent preferred destinations in Central, South, or North America and Hawaiʻi, 8 percent preferred to go to either Indonesia or Australia, 16 percent preferred to stay in Australia, 25 percent only surf on holiday on the Queensland and New South Wales coasts of Australia, and 17 percent reported that they would travel anywhere on the globe to surf and that they undertake international surf holidays at least twice a year. Of this 17 percent, 59 percent reported that finding new destinations and new breaks was a key to their destination decision making (Dolnicar and Fluker 2004).

15. See Lazarow 2009 and 2007 for an analysis of the economic impacts of surfing in Australia today. See Lazarow et al. 2008 for an analysis of the social values of surfing in Australia.

16. At the time Patterson was the editor of *Water*. Previously he had been editor of *Surf* magazine, editor of TransWorld's *Skate* magazine, and a freelance journalist.

17. Booth 2002:7. Note here that Booth is not analyzing what surfers say; he is saying that this is what happens during surfing. He argues that among surfers there is a "common experience" of this "moment of transcendence."

18. Booth 2002 quotes Bernard "Midget" Farrelly from his *This Surfing Life* (1965).

19. The word "modernity" was used repeatedly by surfers I talked with at Nusa and with whom I interacted with on-line and in e-mail interviews. It appears 232 times in my interview transcripts and in my e-mail interviews. I do not use it or bring it up in any of these interviews. It is, in every instance used, tied to a lament about what has been lost in Australia, the United States, and Europe and what is still to be found in places like Papua New Guinea.

20. The phrase "Stone Age" appears 409 times in my surfer-generated interview data set.

2. "We Are Here to Build Your Capacity"

1. Papua New Guinea is a country with approximately 839 living indigenous languages, representing 839 distinct ethnic groups. The country also has large expatriate communities from Australia, New Zealand, the United States, Fiji, India, Bangladesh, China, Malaysia, Indonesia, and the Philippines, as well as other expatriates from places like Belgium, Denmark, England, Finland, France, Germany, Hong Kong, Ireland, Italy, Japan, the Netherlands, New Caledonia, Portugal, Russia, Samoa, Scotland, Singapore, the Solomon Islands, South Africa, South Korea, Spain, Sweden, Tahiti, Taiwan, and Tunisia. One could argue, therefore, that Port Moresby is, in fact, the most ethnically diverse city in the world.

2. The ethnographic data presented in this chapter was collected between 2011 and 2015. It was collected using participant observation in New Ireland Province, the Eastern Highlands Province, and in Port Moresby. The ethnographic vignettes

I use to introduce my analysis of larger processes and structures represent a much larger sample of ethnographic data. I present these particular narrative examples because they contain many of the elements that have come up over and over again since I began conducting field research in Papua New Guinea in 1997.

3. At the time, the minimum wage in Papua New Guinea (what everyone who works in nonmanagement roles at the Airways Hotel makes) was 2.29 kina per hour—about US$1.15. The average annual income for a full-time hourly waged employee in the country was 2,520 kina, or about US$1,260.

4. This focus on technology connects all development to anthropologically inspired notions of social evolution that posit a directional progression of a suite of cultural characteristics which move societies from "primitive" to "modern" (see chap. 2). These include technology, agriculture, social organization, and political organization. These theories assume a one-to-one correlation between level of technology and level of cultural evolution.

5. The two pre-1970 references to capacity building come from the Far East and Australasia report by the UNDP for 1969 and from the personal papers of Brian Herbert Roberts, an Australian urban planner who lived abroad working for the Australian government in the 1940s.

6. Australia is the largest source of aid money for Papua New Guinea with a 2015–2016 estimate of AU$553.6 million. See http://dfat.gov.au/geo/papua-new -guinea/development-assistance/pages/papua-new-guinea.aspx accessed September 19, 2015.

7. Senate Foreign Affairs, Defense and Trade Legislation Committee, Budget Estimates, 2010–2011, Answers to Questions on Notice from AusAID, June 2010, pp. 10–11, http://www.aph.gov.au/senate/committee/fadt_ctte/estimates /bud_1011/dfat/Ans-AusAID-Jun10.pdf accessed November 12, 2014.

8. Review of the PNG-Australia Development Cooperation Treaty (1999), April 19, 2010, p. 3, http://www.ausaid.gov.au/publications/pdf/PNGAustralianAidReview .pdf accessed November 12, 2014.

9. T. Anderson 2006a. While Anderson's estimates focus on Madang and Oro Province, these numbers fit with my understanding of household income equivalences in the Eastern Highlands and New Ireland. By "household income equivalences" I mean the measure of what a household would have to spend on subsistence if buying in local stores and markets if there were no productive landscapes or seascapes available to them.

3. Discovering the Already Known

1. The number of species of tree kangaroos has been a point of debate among scientists. Currently the accepted scientific classification holds that there are four-teen species, with two living in far north Queensland and twelve living on the island of New Guinea.

2. Conservation scientists and activists in Papua New Guinea are strangely silent about logging, mining, and palm oil although these are the three major

threats to the islands, plants, animals, and rural peoples' ability to subsist. In my research on the politics and ecology of conservation in the country it was always explained to me that conservation must work on the local level, the small scale, the individual's behavior, and the cultural practices of use—that conservation scientists cannot take on large-scale resource-extraction projects (West 2006). On-the-ground conservation actors argue that large-scale processes (like climate change) and economic-political issues (like the government of Papua New Guinea focusing on resource extraction as the most viable source for economic development for the country) should be addressed by other people and that they must spend their valuable time saving species "before it is too late."

3. I have conducted research in the Gimi-speaking world since 1997. This research has included multiple methodologies. I have lived in Maimafu Village for long periods of time (e.g., fourteen months in 1997–1998), short periods of time (e.g., three weeks in 2013), and everything in between. While there I have practiced some research methods repeatedly, including participant observation, life history interviews, structured interviews, and semistructured interviews. I have also helped to compile a Gimi-language dictionary. Additionally, over the course of this long time period I have done small, question-specific projects employing a range of qualitative and quantitative ethnographic methods. The data on tree kangaroos presented in this chapter—in particular the data from the Lagrot family's visit to the Gimi world—I collected as part of a larger project on how Gimi and others see the worth of animals. As with all my Gimi-related work, I draw on the history of ethnography in their world. The anthropologist Gillian Gillison worked with Gimi speakers in the 1970s and 1980s. Len Glick worked with them in the 1960s and 1970s. And today Enock Kale and Ben Ruli, both trained in environmental anthropology as well as in conservation ecology, and both native Gimi-speakers, work with their own communities to document the past and the present.

4. This is a dialect of the Gimi language, a non-Austronesian, trans–New Guinea language with about 34,000 speakers.

5. Women come into the world through a different set of reproductive and productive capacities. See West 2012:101–131 for a detailed discussion of women's role in the cycle of auna and kore.

6. The early history of European identification has been covered beautifully in Flannery et al. 1996. The first part of this section is based on their work translating texts in French and Dutch. I collected and read English- and German-language texts, but I rely on Flannery et al. for texts in Dutch and French.

7. These phrases come from interviews I performed with Conservation International staff in Washington, DC, in May 2006 and in Port Moresby, in June and July 2004.

8. Gimi do, in fact, have the notion that certain songs, poetic recitations, and the like can affect the social relations between the living and the dead, the relations between women and gardens, and other important exchange relations, but these are not single words and they are certainly not names of animals (kama) or Melanesian Pidgin words (kapul).

9. Lagrot 2003:48. It cannot be stressed strongly enough here that dogs in Maimafu, and elsewhere in Papua New Guinea, are bred and trained to hunt tree kangaroos. Once dogs catch a scent, it is impossible to call them off of it.

4. Indigenous Theories of Accumulation, Dispossession, Possession, and Sovereignty

1. As mentioned in the previous chapter, I have conducted research in the Gimi-speaking world since 1997. This research has included multiple methodologies. I have lived in Maimafu Village on and off for long periods of time (e.g., fourteen months in 1997–1998) and short periods of time (e.g., three weeks in 2013). While there I have practiced some research methods repeatedly, including participant observation, life history interviews, structured interviews, and semi-structured interviews. I have also helped to compile a Gimi language dictionary. Additionally, over the course of this long time period I pursued small, question-specific projects employing a range of qualitative and quantitative ethnographic methods.

2. See Gillian Gillison's brilliant *Between Culture and Fantasy* (1993) for a masterful argument about the conversation between men's stories and women's stories.

3. Gimi storytelling uses the convention of repeating verbs three times. I've replicated this here.

4. See Schrader (2010). I chose *Pfiesteria piscicida* here because of an engagement that I had with the author of this paper during an American Anthropological Association meeting. This dinoflagellate is not a creature scientists have known before, and Schrader uses it to theorize indeterminacy.

Afterword

1.   "The Blackest Crow" (trad.)
      The time draws near, my dearest dear
      When you and I must part
      And no one knows the inner grieves
      Of my poor aching heart
      It's what I suffer for your sake
      The one I love most dear
      I wish that I could go with you
      Or you might tarry here
      I wish my breast was made of glass
      Wherein you might behold
      Oh, there you'd find your name lies writ
      In letters made of gold
      Oh, there you'd find your name lies writ

Believe in what I say
You are the only one I love
Until my dying day
My dear old father's hard to leave
My mother's on my mind
But for your sake, I'd go with you
I'd leave them both behind
But for your sake, I'd go with you
Oh, Mother, fare thee well
For fear I'll never see you no more
While here on earth we dwell
And when you're in some foreign land
Think on your absent friend
And when the wind blows cold and clear
A line or two please send
And when the wind blows cold and clear
Please send it home to me
That I may know by your hand writ
How things have gone with thee
The blackest crow that ever flew
Will surely turn to white
If ever I prove false to you
Bright day will turn to night
Bright day will turn to night, my love
The elements will mourn
If ever I prove false to you
The seas will rage and burn

Bibliography

Abel, Andrew C., and Danny O'Brien
2015 Negotiating Communities [sic]: Sustainable Cultural Surf Tourism. *In* Sustainable Stoke: Transitions to Sustainability in the Surfing World. G. Borne and J. Ponting, eds. Pp. 154–165. Plymouth, UK: University of Plymouth Press.

ACFID (Australian Council for International Development)
2010 ACFID Analysis: Aid Budget 2010. https://acfid.asn.au/sites/site.acfid/files /resource_document/ACFID-annual-report-2010%E2%80%9311.pdf accessed November 12, 2014.

Agamben, Giorgio
1998 Homo Sacer: Sovereign Power and Bare Life. Daniel Heller-Roazen, trans. Stanford: Stanford University Press.

Allen, Bryant, R. Michael Bourke, and John Gibson
2005 Poor Rural Places in Papua New Guinea. Asia Pacific Viewpoint 46(2):201–217.

Al-Mohammad, Hayder
2010 Towards an Ethics of Being-With: Intertwinements of Life in Post-Invasion Basra. Ethnos 75(4):425–446.

Althusser, Louis
2001 Lenin and Philosophy and Other Essays. Ben Brewster, trans. New York: Monthly Review Press.

Andersen, Barbara

2014 Our People Are Still Out There: Nursing Education and Dilemmas of Development in Papua New Guinea. PhD Dissertation, Department of Anthropology, New York University.

Anderson, Tim

2006a On the Economic Value of Customary Land in Papua New Guinea. Pacific Economic Bulletin 21(1):138–152. http://peb.anu.edu.au/pdf/PEB21-1Anderson -focus.pdf accessed September 22, 2015.

2006b Oil Palm and Small Farmers in Papua New Guinea. Port Moresby and Sydney: Report for the Centre for Environmental Law and Community Rights.

2010 Land Registration, Land Markets, and Livelihoods in Papua New Guinea. In In Defence of Melanesian Customary Land. Tim Anderson and Gary Lee, eds. Pp. 11–20. Sydney: AID/WATCH. http://www.aidwatch.org.au/wp-content /uploads/2014/06/In-Defence-of-Melanesian-Customary-Land.pdf accessed September 22, 2015.

Anderson, Warwick

2006a The Cultivation of Whiteness: Science, Health, and Racial Destiny in Australia. Durham: Duke University Press.

2006b Colonial Pathologies: American Tropical Medicine, Race, and Hygiene in the Philippines. Durham: Duke University Press.

Asad, Talal

1973 Anthropology and the Colonial Encounter. Amherst, NY: Humanity Books.

AusAID

2000 Improving Access to Land and Enhancing the Security of Land Rights: A Review of Land Titling and Land Administration Projects. Quality Assurance Series No. 20. Canberra: AusAID, Canberra.

Bachelard, Gaston

1986 The Formation of the Scientific Mind: A Contribution to a Psychoanalysis of Objective Knowledge. Mary McAllester Jones, trans. Boston: Beacon Press.

Bainton, Nicholas A.

2008 Men of Kastom and the Customs of Men: Status, Legitimacy, and Persistent Values in Lihir, Papua New Guinea. Australian Journal of Anthropology 19(2):194–212.

Bakhtin, M. M.

1981 The Dialogic Imagination: Four Essays by M. M. Bakhtin. Caryl Emerson and Michael Holquist, trans. Austin: University of Texas Press.

Barker, Joanne, ed.

2005 Sovereignty Matters: Locations of Contestation and Possibility in Indigenous Struggles for Self-Determination. Lincoln: University of Nebraska Press.

Baser, Heather, and Peter Morgan

2008 Capacity, Change, and Performance: Study Report. Discussion paper no. 59b. European Centre for Development Policy Management, Maastricht, Netherlands.

Baugh, Daniel
1990 Sea Power and Science: The Motives for Pacific Exploration. *In* Background to Discovery: Pacific Exploration from Dampier to Cook. Derek Howse, ed. Pp. 1–55. Berkeley: University of California Press.

Bell, Harry L.
1975 Mount Bosavi as an Ecological Island. New Guinea Bird Society Newsletter 110:178–182.

Bell, Joshua A.
2006 Marijuana, Guns, Crocodiles, and Radios: Economies of Desire in the Purari Delta. Oceania 76(3): 220–234.
2009a Documenting Discontent: Struggles for Recognition in the Purari Delta of Papua New Guinea. Australian Journal of Anthropology 20(1):28–47.
2009b "For Scientific Purposes a Stand Camera Is Essential": Salvaging Photographic Histories in Papua. *In* Photography, Anthropology, and History: Expanding the Frame. C. Morton and E. Edwards, eds. Surrey: Ashgate.

Bettie, K.
2001 Sick, Filthy and Delirious: Surf Film and Video and the Documentary Mode. Journal of Media and Cultural Studies 15(3):333–348.

Biersack, Aletta
1991 Thinking Difference. Review of The Gender of the Gift. Oceania 62(2): 147–154.

Billings, Dorothy K.
1969 The Johnson Cult of New Hanover. Oceania 40(1):13–19.

Booth, Douglas
2002 Australian Beach Cultures: The History of Sun, Sand, and Surf. London: Frank Cass.
2005 Paradoxes of Material Culture: The Political Economy of Surfing. *In* The Political Economy of Sport. J. Naughright and K. S. Schimmel, eds. Pp. 104–123. New York: Palgrave.

Boulding, Harriett
2015 Capacity Building as Instrument and Empowerment: Training Health Workers for Community-based Roles in Ghana. Paper presented at Hope and Insufficiency: Capacity Building in Ethnographic Comparison, Copenhagen, Denmark, May 20–22.

Bourdieu, Pierre
1986 The Forms of Capital. In Handbook of Theory and Research for the Sociology of Education. J. Richardson, ed. Pp. 241–258. New York: Greenwood.

Bourke, R. Michael
2009 History of Agriculture in Papua New Guinea in Food and Agriculture in Papua New Guinea. Canberra: Australian National University Press.

Bourke, R. Michael, and V. Vlassak
2004 Estimates of Food Crop Production in Papua New Guinea. Canberra: Australian National University.

Brockington Dan, and Jim Igoe
2006 Eviction for Conservation: A Global Overview. Conservation and Society 4(3):424–470.

BSP (Biodiversity Support Program)
1996 Biodiversity Conservation Network 1996 Annual Report: Stories from the Field and Lessons Learned. Washington, DC.
1997 Biodiversity Conservation Network 1997 Annual Report: Getting Down to Business. Washington DC.

Buckley, Ralf
2003 Adventure Tourism and the Clothing, Fashion, and Entertainment Industries. Journal of Ecotourism 2(2):126–134.
2006 Adventure Tourism. Cambridge, MA: CAB International.

Büscher, B., and W. Dressler
2007 Linking Neoprotectionism and Environmental Governance: On the Rapidly Increasing Tensions Between Actors in the Environment-Development Nexus. Conservation and Society 5(4):586–611.

Büscher, Bram, Conrad Steenkamp, and William Wolmer
2007 The Politics of Engagement Between Biodiversity Conservation and the Social Sciences. Special section of Conservation and Society 5(1):1–114.

Buschmann, Ranier
2009 Anthropology's Global Histories: The Ethnographic Frontier in German New Guinea, 1870–1935. Honolulu: University of Hawai'i Press.

Castree, Noel
2010 Neoliberalism and the Biophysical Environment: A Synthesis and Evaluation of the Research. Environment and Society: Advances in Research 1(1):5–45.

Caton, Kellee, and Carla Almeida Santos
2008 Closing the Hermeneutic Circle? Photographic Encounters with the Other. Annals of Tourism Research 35(1):7–26.

CBD (Convention on Biological Diversity)
2005 Business and the 2010 Biodiversity Challenge: Exploring Private Sector Engagement in the Convention on Biological Diversity. Montreal. http://www.cbd.int/doc/meetings/biodiv/b2010– 01/official/b2010–01-02-en.pdf accessed September 10, 2015.

Cepek, Michael L.
2012 A Future for Amazonia: Randy Borman and Cofán Environmental Politics. Austin: University of Texas Press.

Champion, Ivan
1940a The Bamu-Purari Patrol, 1936. Geographical Journal 96(3):190–206.
1940b The Bamu-Purari Patrol, 1936 (Continued). Geographical Journal 96(4):243–257.

Chandler, Jo

2013a It's 2013, and They're Burning Witches. Global Mail. February 15.

2013b Plagued: TB and Me. Global Mail. June 13.

2014a Manus Detention Centre Bears Blame for PNG Pair's Deaths, Families Say. Guardian. December 14.

2014b Welcome to Manus, The Island That Has Been Changed Forever by Australian Asylum-Seeker Policy. Guardian. December 15.

Clancy-Smith, Julia, and Frances Gouda, eds.

1998 Domesticating the Empire: Race, Gender, and Family Life in French and Dutch Colonialism. Charlottesville: University Press of Virginia.

Clarke, Matthew

2010 Reimagining Capacity Building When Participation Is Constrained: Illegal Burmese Migrants in Thailand. *In* Challenging Capacity Building: Comparative Perspectives. Sue Kenny and Matthew Clarke, eds. New York: Palgrave, Macmillan.

Clifford, James

1997 Routes: Travel and Translation in the Late Twentieth Century. Cambridge, MA: Harvard University Press.

Clinton, Hillary

2011 America's Pacific Century. Foreign Policy. October 11.

Connell, John

2005 Papua New Guinea: The Struggle for Development. London: Routledge.

Cooke, Bill, and Uma Kothari

2001 Participation: The New Tyranny? London: Zed Books.

Coulthard, Glen Sean

2014 Red Skin, White Masks: Rejecting the Colonial Politics of Recognition. Minneapolis: University of Minnesota Press.

Cox, John

2014 "Grassroots," "Elites," and the New "Working Class" of Papua New Guinea. SSGM in Brief No. 6. Canberra: State, Society, and Governance in Melanesia Institute, Australian National University.

Crapanzano, Vincent

1992 Hermes' Dilemma and Hamlet's Desire: On the Epistemology of Interpretation. Cambridge, MA: Harvard University Press.

2004 Imaginative Horizons: An Essay in Literary-Philosophical Anthropology. Chicago: University of Chicago Press.

Creator

2014 Elizabeth Wurtzel's "Creatocracy": An Excerpt in 20 Quotes. December 11. https://creator.wework.com/think/elizabeth-wurtzels-creatocracy-excerpt -20-quotes/ accessed January 15, 2016.

Cronon, William

1987 Revisiting the Vanishing Frontier: The Legacy of Frederick Jackson Turner. Western Historical Quarterly 18(2):157–176.

Cronon, William, George Miles, and Jay Gitlin, eds.
1992 Under an Open Sky: Rethinking America's Western Past. New York: Norton.

Croy, Glen, Warwick Frost, and Sue Beeton
2009 Introduction: Tourism and Media. Tourism Analysis 14(2):153–154.

Cruikshank, Julie
2005 Do Glaciers Listen? Local Knowledge, Colonial Encounters, and Social Imagination. Toronto: University of Toronto Press.

Davidov, Veronica
2013 Amazonia as Pharmacopia. Critique of Anthropology 33(3):241–260.

Deleuze, Gilles, and Félix Guattari
1987 A Thousand Plateaus: Capitalism and Schizophrenia. Brian Massumi, trans. Minneapolis: University of Minnesota Press.

Deloria, Philip J.
1998 Playing Indian. New Haven: Yale University Press.

Descola, Philippe
1994 In the Society of Nature: A Native Ecology in Amazonia. Cambridge Studies in Social and Cultural Anthropology 93. Nora Scott, trans. Cambridge: Cambridge University Press.
1996 The Spears of Twilight: Life and Death in the Amazon Jungle. Janet Lloyd, trans. New York: New Press.
2013 Beyond Nature and Culture. Janet Lloyd, trans. Chicago: University of Chicago Press.

Diamond, Jared
2008 Vengeance Is Ours: What Can Tribal Societies Tell Us About Our Need to Get Even? New Yorker. April 21.

Diaz, Vicente M.
2011 Voyaging for Anti-Colonial Recovery: Austronesian Seafaring, Archipelagic Rethinking, and the Re-mapping of Indigeneity. Asia Pacific Inquiry 2(1):21–32.

Diaz, Vicente M., and J. Kehaulani Kauanui
2001 Native Pacific Cultural Studies on the Edge. Contemporary Pacific 13(2):315–342.

DiNovelli-Lang, D.
2010 Nature, Value and Territory in Alaskan Subsistence Politics: The View from Brown Bear Bay. PhD Dissertation, Department of Anthropology, Columbia University.

Dixon, Robert
1995 Writing the Colonial Adventure: Race, Gender, and Nation in Anglo-Australian Popular Fiction, 1875–1914. Cambridge: Cambridge University Press.
2011 Photography, Early Cinema, and Colonial Modernity: Frank Hurley's Synchronized Lecture Entertainments. London: Anthem Press.

Doane, Molly

2001 A Distant Jaguar: The Civil Society Project in Chimalapas. Critique of Anthropology 21(4):361–382.

2005 The Resilience of Nationalism in a Global Era: Megaprojects in Mexico's South. *In* Social Movements: An Anthropological Reader. J. Nash, ed. Vol. 7. Pp. 187–202. New York: Blackwell.

2007 The Political Economy of the Ecological Native. American Anthropologist 109(3):452–462.

2010 Relationship Coffees: Structure and Agency in the Fair Trade System. *In* Fair Trade and Social Justice: Global Ethnographies. S. Lyonand M. Moberg, eds. Pp. 229–257. New York: NYU Press.

2012 Stealing Shining Rivers: Agrarian Conflict, Market Logic, and Conservation in a Mexican Forest. Tucson: University of Arizona Press.

2014 From Community Conservation to Lone (Forest) Ranger: Accumulation by Conservation in a Mexican Forest. Conservation and Society 12(3): 233–244.

Dolnicar, Sara, and M. Fluker

2004 The Symptomatic Nature of Past Destination Choice Among Surf Tourists. University of Wollongong, Research Online. http://ro.uow.edu.au/commpapers /247 accessed January 18, 2016.

Douglas, Bronwen

1998 Science and the Art of Representing "Savages": Reading "Race" in Text and Image in South Seas Voyage Literature. History and Anthropology 11(2–3):157–201.

1999 Science and the Art of Representing "Savages": Reading "Race" in Text and Image in South Seas Voyage Literature. History and Anthropology 11(2–3):157–201.

Douglas, Bronwen, and Chris Ballard

2008 Foreign Bodies: Oceania and the Science of Race, 1750–1940. Canberra: Australian National University E-Press.

Douglas, Ngaire

1997 They Came for Savages: 100 Years of Tourism in Melanesia. Manoa: University of Hawaiʻi Press.

Dowie, M.

2009 Conservation Refugees: The Hundred-Year Conflict Between Global Conservation and Native Peoples. Cambridge, MA: MIT Press.

D'Urville, Jules-Sébastien-César

2003 On the Islands of the Great Ocean. Isabel Ollivier, Antoine de Biran, and Geoffrey Clark, trans. Journal of Pacific History 38(2):163–174.

Eade, Deborah

2007 Capacity Building: Who Builds Whose Capacity? Development in Practice 17(4):630–639.

Ellis, Susan
2015 Corrective Capabilities: From Unruly Politics to Democratic Capacitación. Presented at Hope and Insufficiency: Capacity Building in Ethnographic Comparison, Copenhagen, Denmark, May 20–22.

Ellison, Susan
2013 Mediating Democracy in El Alto: The Politics of Conflict Resolution in Bolivia. PhD Dissertation, Department of Anthropology, Brown University.

Errington, Frederick, and Deborah Gewertz
2001 On the Generification of Culture: From Blow Fish to Melanesian. Journal of the Royal Anthropological Institute 8(7):509– 525.

Fabian, Johannes
1983 Time and the Other: How Anthropology Makes Its Object. New York: Columbia University Press.

Filer, C.
2012 The Commission of Inquiry into Special Agricultural and Business Lease in Papua New Guinea: Fresh Details for the Portrait of a Process of Expropriation. Crawford School of Public Policy, Australian National University, Canberra. Paper presented to the second international academic workshop on Global Land Grabbing, Cornell University, Ithaca, NY, October 17–19.

Finney, Ben
1996 Colonizing an Island World. Transactions of the American Philosophical Society, New Series, 86(5):71–116.

Flannery T. F., R. Martin, and A. Szalay
1996 Tree Kangaroos: A Curious Natural History. Port Melbourne, Australia: Reed Books.

Foale, Simon J., and Martha A. Macintyre
2005. Green Fantasies: Photographic Representations of Biodiversity and Ecotourism in the Western Pacific. Journal of Political Ecology 12(1):1–22.

Ford, N., and D. Brown
2006 Surfing and Social Theory: Experience, Embodiment, and Narrative of the Dream Glide. London: Routledge.

Foster, Robert
1999 Melanesianist Anthropology in the Era of Globalization. Contemporary Pacific 11(1):140–159.
2002 Materalizing the Nation: Commodities, Consumption, and Media in Papua New Guinea. Bloomington: Indiana University Press.

Foucault, Michel
1970 The Order of Things. New York: Pantheon Books.
1975 Discipline and Punish: The Birth of the Prison. Alan Sheridan, trans. New York: Random House.

1980 Truth and Power. *In* Power/Knowledge: Selected Interviews and Other Writings by Michel Foucault, 1972–1977. Colin Gordon, ed. Pp. 109–133. Brighton: Harvester Wheatsheaf.

Frodin, D. G.
2007 Biological Exploration of New Guinea. *In* The Ecology of Papua, Part One. A. J. Marshall and B. M. Beehler, eds. Pp. 14–107. Hong Kong: Periplus.

Fukuyama, Francis
2007 Governance Reform in Papua New Guinea. Unpublished paper accessed at http://www.sals-jhu.edu/ accessed February 15, 2011.

Gegeo, David Welchman, and Karen Ann Watson-Gegeo
2001 "How We Know": Kwara'ae Rural Villages Doing Indigenous Epistemology. Contemporary Pacific 13(1):55–88.

Geschiere, Peter
2009 The Perils of Belonging: Autochthony, Citizenship, and Exclusion in Africa and Europe. Chicago: University of Chicago Press.

Gilberthorpe, Emma
2007 Fasu Solidarity: A Case Study of Kin Networks, Land Tenure, and Oil Extraction in Kutubu, Papua New Guinea. American Anthropologist, New Series 109(1):101–112.

Gillison, Gillian
1993 Between Culture and Fantasy: A New Guinea Highlands Mythology. Chicago: University of Chicago Press.

Godelier, Maurice
1986 The Making of Great Men: Male Domination and Power Among the New Guinea Baruya. Cambridge: Cambridge University Press.

Golub, Alex
2014 Leviathans at the Gold Mine: Creating Indigenous and Corporate Actors in Papua New Guinea. Durham: Duke University Press.

Gosarevski, Steven, Helen Hughes, and Susan Windybank
2004 Is Papua New Guinea Viable? Pacific Economic Bulletin 19(1):133–136.

Grandia, L.
2012 Enclosed: Conservation, Cattle, and Commerce Among the Q'eqchi' Maya Lowlanders. Seattle: University of Washington Press.

Haddon, A. C.
1895 Evolution in Art: As Illustrated by the Life-Histories of Designs. London: Walter Scott.
1920 The Migrations of Cultures in British New Guinea. Journal of the Royal Anthropological Institute 50:234–280.

Haddon, A. C., and J. Hornell
1936–1938 Canoes of Oceania. Bernice P. Bishop Museum Special Publication 27–29. Honolulu: Bernice P. Bishop Museum.

Hall, Stuart
1997 The Work of Representation, Cultural Representations, and Signifying Practices. London: Sage.

Halvaksz, Jamon
2003 Singing About the Land Among the Biangai. Oceania 7(3):153–169.
2006a Becoming "Local Tourists": Travel, Landscapes, and Identity in Papua New Guinea. Tourist Studies 6(2):99–117.
2006b Cannibalistic Imaginaries: Mining the Natural and Social Body in Papua New Guinea. In Melanesian Mining Modernities. P. West and M. Macintyre, eds. Special issue of Contemporary Pacific: A Journal of Island Affairs 18(2):335–359.
2008 Whose Closure?: Appearances, Temporality and Mineral Extraction Along the Upper Bulolo River, Papua New Guinea. Journal of the Royal Anthropological Institute 14(1):21–37

Halvaksz, Jamon A., and Heather Young-Leslie
2008 Thinking Ecographically: Places, Ecographers, and Environmentalism. Nature+Culture 3(2):183–205.

Haraway, Donna
2008 When Species Meet. Minneapolis: University of Minnesota Press.

Harvey, David
1990 The Condition of Postmodernity: An Enquiry Into the Origins of Cultural Change. Cambridge, MA: Blackwell.
2005 A Brief History of Neoliberalism. Oxford: Oxford University Press.
2006 Spaces of Global Capitalism: A Theory of Uneven Development. London: Verso.

Hau'ofa, Epeli
1994 Our Sea of Islands. Contemporary Pacific. 6(1):147–161.

Heal, Geoffrey
2000 Nature and the Marketplace. Washington, DC: Island Press.

Heidegger, Martin
1962 Being and Time. John Macquarrie and Edward Robinson, trans. Oxford: Basil Blackwell.
1982 The Basic Problems of Phenomenology. Albert Hofstadter, trans. Bloomington: Indiana University Press.

Helmrich, Stefan
2007 Blue-Green Capital, Biotechnological Circulation, and an Oceanic Imaginary: A Critique of Biopolitical Economy. BioSocieties 2:287–302.
2009 Alien Ocean: Anthropological Voyages in Microbial Seas. Berkeley: University of California Press.

Henare, Amiria, Martin Holbraad, and Sari Wastell, eds.
2006 Thinking Through Things: Theorising Artefacts Ethnographically. New York: Routledge.

Henderson, Margaret
1999 Some Tales of Two Mags: Sports Magazines as Glossy Reservoirs of Male Fantasy. Journal of Australian Studies 23(62):64–80.

Hereniko, Vilsoni
1994 Representations of Cultural Identities. In Tides of History: The Pacific Islands in the Twentieth Century. K. R. Howe, Robert C. Kiste, and Brij V. Lal, eds. Pp. 406–436. St. Leonards, UK: Allen and Unwin.

Herle, A., and S. Rouse, eds.
1998 Cambridge and the Torres Strait: Centenary Essays on the 1898 Anthropological Expedition. Cambridge: Cambridge University Press.

Hewlett, Christopher
2014 History, Kinship, and Comunidad: Learning to Live Together Amongst Amahuaca People in the Peruvian Amazon. PhD Thesis, Department of Social Anthropology, University of St. Andrews.
2015 Community Capacity Building in Peruvian Amazonia: Transforming Amerindian Bodies and Minds in Peruvian Amazonia. Paper presented at Hope and Insufficiency: Capacity Building in Ethnographic Comparison, Copenhagen, Denmark, May 20–22.

Hodgson, Dorothy L.
2011 Being Maasai, Becoming Indigenous: Postcolonial Politics in a Neoliberal World. Bloomington: Indiana University Press.

Holbraad, Martin
2012 Truth in Motion. Chicago: University of Chicago Press.

Hughes, Helen
2004 The Pacific Is Viable! Issue Analysis No. 53. Report for the Centre for Independent Studies, Sydney. http://www.cis.org. au/issue_analysis/IA53 /IA53.pdf accessed September 22, 2015.

Husson, A. M., and F. W. Rappard
1958 Note on the Taxonomy and the Habitats of Dendrolagus Ursinus Temminck and D. leucogenys Matschie (Mammalia: Marsupialia). Nova Guinea, New Series 9:9–14.

IFC (International Financial Corporation of the World Bank Group)
2012 Performance Standard 6: Biodiversity Conservation and Sustainable Management of Living Natural Resources. January 1. http://www.ifc.org /wps/wcm/connect/bff0a28049a790d6b835faa8c6a8312a/PS6_English_2012. pdf?MOD=AJPERES accessed September 19, 2015.

ITS Global
2009 The Economic Benefits of Land-Use in Papua New Guinea. http://fiapng
.com/PDF_files/PNG%20Land%20Use%20Report%20Final4%20Nov%20
2009.pdf accessed September 22, 2015.

Jacka, Jerry K.
2009 "Global Averages, Local Extremes: The Subtleties and Complexities of
Climate Change in Papua New Guinea." *In* Anthropology and Climate Change:
From Encounters to Actions. S. Crate and M. Nuttall, eds. Pp. 197–208. Walnut
Grove, CA: Left Coast Press.
2010 The Spirits of Conservation: Ecology, Christianity, and Resource Management
in Highlands Papua New Guinea. Journal for the Study of Religion, Nature,
and Culture 4(1):24–47.
2015 Alchemy in the Rain Forest: Politics, Ecology, and Resilience in a New
Guinea Mining Area. Durham: Duke University Press.

Jackson, Michael D.
1998 Minima Ethnographica: Intersubjectivity and the Anthropological Project.
Chicago: University of Chicago Press.
2005 Existential Anthropology: Events, Exigencies, and Effects. New York: Berghahn.

Jahoda, Gustav
1999 Images of Savages: Ancient Roots of Modern Prejudice in Western Culture.
New York: Routledge.

Jenkins, Olivia H.
2003 Photography and Travel Brochures: The Circle of Representation. Tourism
Geographies 5(3):305–328.

Johnson, R. Wally
2013 Fire Mountains of the Islands: A History of Volcanic Eruptions and Disaster
Management in Papua New Guinea and the Solomon Islands. Canberra:
Australian National University E-Press.

Kabutaulaka, Tarcisius
1997 I Am Not a Stupid Native: Decolonising Images and Imagination in Solomon
Islands. *In* Emerging from Empire? Decolonisation in the Pacific. Donald
Denoon, ed. Pp. 165–171. Canberra: Division of Pacific and Asian History,
Research School of Pacific and Asian Studies, Australia National University.

Kahn, Miriam
2011 Tahiti, Beyond the Postcard: Power, Place, and Everyday life. Seattle:
University of Washington Press.

Kamakau, S. M.
1991 The Works of the People of Old: Na Hana a Ka Po'e Kahiko. Bernice
P. Bishop Museum Special Publication 61. Honolulu, HI: Bishop Museum
Press. Originally published 1865.

Kampion, Drew
2003 Stoked!: A History of Surf Culture. Salt Lake City, UT: Gibbs Smith.

Katz, Cindi

1998 Whose Nature, Whose Culture? Private Productions of Space and the "Preservation" of Nature. *In* Remaking Reality: Nature at the Millennium. Bruce Braun and Noel Castree, eds. Pp. 45–59. London: Routledge.

2002 Vagabond Capitalism and the Necessity of Social Reproduction. Antipode 33(4):709–728.

2004 Growing Up Global: Economic Restructuring and Children's Everyday Lives. University of Minnesota Press.

2008 Bad Elements: Katrina and the Scoured Landscape of Social Reproduction. In Gender, Place, and Culture: A Journal of Feminist Geography 15(1):15–29.

Kauanui, Kēhaulani J.

2008 Hawaiian Blood: Colonialism and the Politics of Sovereignty and Indigeneity. Durham: Duke University Press.

Keane, Webb

2007 Christian Moderns: Freedom and Fetish in the Mission Encounter. Berkley: University of California Press.

2003 Semiotics and the Social Analysis of Material Things. Language and Communication 23(2003):409–425.

Kelly, Alice B.

2011 Conservation Practice as Primitive Accumulation. Journal of Peasant Studies 38(4):683–701.

Kelly, John D.

1992 Fiji Indians and "Commoditization of Labor." American Ethnologist 19(1):97–120.

Kelly, Raymond

1993 Constructing Inequality: The Fabrication of a Hierarchy of Virtue Among the Etoro. Ann Arbor: University of Michigan Press.

Kenny, Sue, and Matthew Clarke

2010 Challenging Capacity Building: Comparative Perspectives. New York: Palgrave Macmillan.

Kirksey, Eben

2012 Freedom in Entangled Worlds: West Papua and the Architecture of Global Power. Durham: Duke University Press.

Kirksey, Eben S., and Stefan Helmreich

2010 The Emergency of Multispecies Ethnography. Cultural Anthropology 25(4):545–576.

Kirsch, Stuart

2006a Kutubu, Papua New Guinea. American Anthropologist 109(1):101–112.

2006b Reverse Anthropology: Indigenous Analysis of Social and Environmental Relations in New Guinea. Stanford: Stanford University Press.

Knauft, Bruce
1999 From Primitive to Postcolonial in Melanesia and Anthropology. Ann Arbor: University of Michigan Press.

Kuklick, Henrika, ed.
2008 A New History of Anthropology. Malden, MA: Blackwell.

Kulick, Don and Margaret Willson
1992 Echoing Images: The Construction of Savagery Among Papua New Guinean Villagers. Visual Anthropology 5:143–152.

Lagrot, Jean-François
2003 Kangaroos in the Tops of Trees. Asian Geographic. March–April:42–53.

LaHatte, Kristin
2015 Professionalizing Persons and Foretelling Futures: Building Capacity in Post-Earthquake Haiti. Paper presented at Hope and Insufficiency: Capacity Building in Ethnographic Comparison, Copenhagen, Denmark, May 20–22.

Lanagan, David
2002 Surfing in the Third Millenium: Commodifying the Visual Argot. Australian Journal of Anthropology 13(3):283–291.

Landman, Jane
2006 "The Tread of a White Man's Foot": Australian Pacific Colonialism and the Cinema, 1925–1962. Canberra: Australian National University Press.

Landman, Jane, and Ballard, Chris
2010 An Ocean of Images. Journal of Pacific History 45(1):1–20.

Langmore, Diane
1989 Missionary Lives: Papua, 1874–1914. Pacific Islands Monograph Series No. 6. Honolulu: University of Hawai'i Press.

Latour, Bruno
1993 We Have Never Been Modern. Cambridge, MA: Harvard University Press.
2004 Politics of Nature: How to Bring the Sciences Into Democracy. Cambridge, MA: Harvard University Press.

Lazarow, N.
2007 The Value of Coastal Recreational Resources: A Case Study Approach to Examine the Value of Recreational Surfing to Specific Locales. Journal of Coastal Research 50(SI):12–20.
2009 Using Observed Market Expenditure to Estimate the Economic Impact of Recreational Surfing to the Gold Coast, Australia. Journal of Coastal Research. 56(SI):1130–1134.

Lazarow, N., M. L. Miller, and B. Blackwell
2008 The Value of Recreational Surfing to Society. Tourism in Marine Environments 5(2–3):145–158.

Lea, David
2004 Customary Land Tenure in Papua New Guinea: What Does It Really Mean? NRI Special Publication No. 35. Port Moresby: National Research Institute.

Lederman, Rena
1998 Globalization and the Future of Culture Areas: Melanesianist Anthropology in Transition. Annual Review of Anthropology 27:427–449.

Lefebvre, Henri
1991 The Production of Space. D. Nicholson-Smith, trans. Oxford: Blackwell.

Lipset, David M.
1997 Mangrove Man: Dialogics of Culture in the Sepik Estuary (Papua New Guinea). Cambridge: Cambridge University Press.
2004 Modernity Without Romance? Masculinity and Desire in Courtship Stories Told by Young Papua New Guinean Men. American Ethnologist 31:205–224.
2007 Women Without Qualities: More Courtship Stories Told by Papua New Guinea Youth. Ethnology 46:93–111.
2011 The Tides: Masculinity and Climate Change in Coastal Papua New Guinea. Journal of the Royal Anthropological Institute 17(1):20–43.
2013 The New State of Nature: Rising Sea-Levels, Climate Justice, and Community-Based Adaptation in Papua New Guinea. Conservation and Society 11(2):144–158.
2015 Hero, Savage, or Equal? Representations of the Moral Personhood of Pacific Islanders in Hollywood Movies. Pacific Studies 38(1–2):103–135.

LiPuma, Edward
2000 Encompassing Others: The Magic of Modernity in Melanesia. Ann Arbor: University of Michigan Press.

Luxemburg, Rosa
2003 The Accumulation of Capital. Agnes Schwarzschild, trans. London: Routledge Classics. Originally published 1913.

Lyons, Scott Richard
2000 Rhetorical Sovereignty: What Do American Indians Want from Writing? College Composition and Communication 51(3):447–468.

MacCannell, Dean
1976 The Tourist: A New Theory of the Leisure Class. New York: Schocken.

Macintyre, Martha
1995 Violent Bodies and Vicious Exchanges: Personification and Objectification in the Massim. Social Analysis 37:29–43.
2003 Petztorme Women: Responding to Change in Lihir, Papua New Guinea. Oceania 74(1–2):120–133.

Malinowski, Bronislaw
1922 Argonauts of the Western Pacific: An Account of Native Enterprise and Adventure in the Archipelagoes of Melanesian New Guinea. London: Routledge and Kegan Paul.

Marx, Karl
1975 Capital. Ben Fowkes, trans. Vol. 1. New York: Penguin. Originally published 1867.

Marx, Karl, and Frederick Engels
2001 The German Ideology, Part One, with Selections from Parts Two and Three, Together with Marx's "Introduction to a Critique of Political Economy." C. J. Arthur, trans. New York: International Publishers.

McDonald, Kenneth
2010 The Devil Is in the (Bio) Diversity: Private Sector "Engagement" and the Restructuring of Biodiversity Conservation. Antipode 42(3):512–549.

McGavin, George
2009 Report: 2009 Scientific Expedition to Mount Bosavi: Southern Highlands, Papua New Guinea. Report for British Broadcasting Corporation, September 1. http://downloads.bbc.co.uk/springwatch/llotv_finalreport_20090907.pdf accessed January 26, 2016.

Mihesuah, Devon Abbott, and Angela Cavender Wilson
2004 Indigenizing the Academy: Transforming Scholarship and Empowering Communities. Lincoln: University of Nebraska Press.

Mirzoeff, N.
2011 The Right to Look: A Counterhistory of Visuality. Duke University Press.

Moore, Clive
2003 New Guinea: Crossing Boundaries and History. Honolulu: University of Hawai'i Press.

Moretti, Franco, and Dominique Pestre
2015 BankSpeak: The Language of World Bank Reports. New Left Review 92:75–99.

Morris, Rosalind C.
2016 Ursprüngliche Akkumulation: The Secret of an Originary Mistranslation. Boundary 2. Nergis Ertürk and Ozge Serin, eds. Forthcoming.

Mosko, Mark
2008 Partible Penitents: Dividual Personhood and Christian Practice in Melanesia and the West. Journal of the Royal Anthropological Institute 16(2), 215–240.

Muecke, Stephen
2004 Ancient and Modern: Time, Culture, and Indigenous Philosophy. Sydney: University of New South Wales Press.
2011 Australian Indigenous Philosophy. CLCWeb: Comparative Literature and Culture 13(2). http://dx.doi.org/10.7771/1481-4374.1741 accessed February 19, 2016.

Müller, Salomon
1858 Contributions to the Knowledge of New Guinea. Journal of Royal Geographical Society 28:264–272.

Murray Li, Tania

2000 Articulating Indigenous Identity in Indonesia: Resource Politics and the Tribal Slot. Comparative Study of Society and History 42(1):149–179.

Narokobi, Bernard

1999 Concept of Ownership in Melanesia. Occasional Paper No. 6. Second Printing. Melanesian Institute, Goroka. Originally published 1988.

National Geographic

2006 "Lost World" of New Species Found in Indonesia. http://news.nationalgeographic .com/news/2006/02/photogalleries/newguinea/ accessed January 25, 2016.

Nendel, Jim

2009 Surfing in Early Twentieth-Century Hawai'i: The Appropriation of a Transcendent Experience to Competitive American Sport. International Journal of the History of Sport 26(16):2432–2446.

Neves-Graca, Katja

2002 A Whale of a Thing: Transformations from Whale Hunting to Whale Watching in Lajes do Pico, Azores. PhD Dissertation, Department of Social Anthropology, York University.

2010 Cashing in on Cetourism: A Critical Engagement with Dominant E-NGO Discourses on Whaling, Cetacean Conservation, and Whale Watching. Antipode 42(3):719–741.

Oakland Institute

2013 On Our Land: Modern Land Grabs Reversing Independence in Papua New Guinea. http://pang.org.fj/wp-content/uploads/2013/11/OaklandInstitute_PNG _report_web-1.pdf accessed September 22, 2015.

O'Brien, Danny, and Jess Ponting

2013 Sustainable Surf Tourism: A Community-Centered Approach in Papua New Guinea. Journal of Sports Management 27:158–172.

Ogden, Thomas H.

1999 The Analytic Third: Working with Intersubjective Clinical Facts. In Relational Psychoanalysis: The Emergence of a Tradition. S. A. Mitchell and L. Aron, eds. Pp. 459–492. Hillsdale, NJ: Analytic Press.

Ormond, J.

2005 Endless Summer (1964): Consuming Waves and Surfing the Frontier. Film and History 35(1):39–51.

Patterson, Joel

2008 The Next Mentawais? Surfline's Water 26(Summer):56–71.

Pearson, K.

1979 Surfing Subcultures of Australia and New Zealand. St. Lucia: University of Queensland Press.

Peluso, N.

1996 Reserving Value: Conservation Ideology and State Protection of Resources. *In* Creating the Countryside. E. M. DuPuis and P. Vandergeest, eds. Pp. 135–165. Philadelphia: Temple University Press.

Penny, H. Glenn

2002 Objects of Culture: Ethnology and Ethnographic Museums in Imperial Germany. Chapel Hill: University of North Carolina Press.

Perelman, Michael

2000 The Invention of Capitalism: Classical Political Economy and the Secret History of Primitive Accumulation. Durham: Duke University Press.

Petri, Peter A., Michael G. Plummer, and Fan Zhai

2012 The Trans-Pacific Partnership and Asia-Pacific Integration: A Quantitative Assessment. Policy Analysis in International Economics 98. Washington, DC: Peterson Institute for International Economics.

Ploeg, Anton

2002 "De Papoea": What's in a Name? Asia Pacific Journal of Anthropology 3(1):75–101.

Ponting, Jess

2009 Projecting Paradise: The Surf Media and the Hermeneutic Circle in Surfing Tourism. Tourism Analysis 14(2):175–185.

Poole, R.

2005 An Excess of Description: Ethnography, Race, and Visual Technologies. Annual Review of Anthropology 34:159–179.

Povinelli, Elizabeth A.

2002 The Cunning of Recognition: Indigenous Alterities and the Making of Australian Multiculturalism. Durham: Duke University Press.

2011 Economies of Abandonment: Social Belonging and Endurance in Late Liberalism. Durham: Duke University Press.

Powdermaker, Hortense

1933 Life in Lesu: The Study of Melanesian Society in New Ireland. New York: Norton.

Preston-Whyte, Robert

2002 Constructions of Surfing Space at Durban, South Africa. Tourism Geographies 4(3):307–328.

Quanchi, Max

2007 Photographing Papua: Representation, Colonial Encounters, and Imaging in the Public Domain. Newcastle: Cambridge Scholars.

Raheja, Michelle H.

2013 Reservation Reelism: Redfacing, Visual Sovereignty, and Representations of Native Americans in Film. Lincoln: University of Nebraska Press.

Reed, Michael Alan
1999 Waves of Commodification: A Critical Investigation into Surfing Subculture. M.A. Thesis, Department of Geography, San Diego State University.

Reid, L., and N. Smith
1993 John Wayne Meets Donald Trump: The Lower East Side as Wild Wild West. *In* Selling Places: The City as Cultural Capital, Past and Present. G. Kearns and C. Phillo, eds. Pp. 193–209. Oxford: Pergamon.

Reinhold Forster, Johann
1996 Observations Made During a Voyage Round the World. Nicholas Thomas et al., eds. Honolulu: University of Hawai'i Press. Originally published 1778.

RGS (Royal Geographical Society)
1858 On "Contributions to the Knowledge of New Guinea," by Dr. Salomon Müller, Ninth Meeting, Monday, March 22nd, 1858. Proceedings of the Royal Geographical Society of London 2(3):181-185.

Robbins, Joel, and Holly Wardlow, eds.
2005 The Making of Global and Local Modernities in Melanesia: Humiliation, Transformation, and the Nature of Cultural Change. London: Ashgate.

Robinson, John G.
2012 Common and Conflicting Interests in the Engagements Between Conservation Organizations and Corporations. Conservation Biology 26(6):967–977.

Rutsky, R. L.
1999 Surfing the Other: Surf Films from the 1950s, 1960s and How Teenagers Responded. Film Quarterly 52(4):12–23.

Sahlins, Marshall
1985 Islands of History. Chicago: University of Chicago Press.
1989 Cosmologies of Capitalism: The Trans-Pacific Sector of "the World System." Proceedings of the British Academy 74:1–51.
2005 The Economics of Develop-Man in the Pacific. *In* The Making of Glogal and Local Modernities in Melanesia: Humiliation, Transformation, and the Nature of Culture Change. Joel Robbins and Holly Wardlow, eds. Pp. 23–42. Burlington, VT: Ashgate.

Said, Edward
1978 Orientalism. New York: Vintage Books.

SAPNG
n.d. Surf Management Program. http://www.sapng.com accessed November 28, 2015.

Schrader, Astrid
2010 Responding to Pfiesteria Piscicida (the Fish Killer): Phantomatic Ontologies, Indeterminacy, and Responsibility in Toxic Microbiology. Social Studies of Science 40 (2):275–306.

Schultze-Westrum, Thomas

1972 Neu Guinea: Papua-Urwelt im Aufbruch. Bern: Kuemmerly & Frey Geographischer Verlag.

Scott, Paul

2003 "We Shall Fight on the Seas and the Oceans . . . We Shall": Commodification, Localism, and Violence. M/C: A Journal of Media and Culture 6(1):61–90.

Seligman, C. G.

1910 The Melanesians of British New Guinea. Cambridge: Cambridge University Press.

Sillitoe, Paul

1998 An Introduction to the Anthropology of Melanesia. New York: Cambridge University Press.

Simpson, Audra

2014 Mohawk Interruptus: Political Life Across the Borders of Settler States. Durham: Duke University Press.

Slama, Martin, and Jenny Munro, eds.

2015 From "Stone-Age" to "Real-Time": Exploring Papuan Temporalities, Mobilities, and Religiosities. Canberra: Australian National University E-Press.

Slotkin, Richard

1973 Regeneration Through Violence: The Mythology of the American Frontier, 1600–1800. Middletown, CT: Wesleyan University Press.

Smith, Neil

1979 Gentrification and Capital: Theory, Practice, and Ideology in Society Hill. Antipode 11(3):24–35.

1984 Uneven Development: Nature, Capital, and the Production of Space. London: Basil Blackwell.

1987 Gentrification and the Rent Gap. Annals of the Association of American Geographers 77(3):462–465.

1992 New City, New Frontier: The Lower East Side as Wild, Wild West. In Variations on a Theme Park: The New American City and the End of Public Space. Michael Sorkin, ed. Pp. 61–93. New York: Hill and Wang.

1996 The New Urban Frontier: Gentrification and the Revanchist City. London: Routledge.

2002 American Empire: Roosevelt's Geographer and the Prelude to Globalization. Berkeley: University of California Press.

2007 Nature as an Accumulation Strategy. Socialist Register 43:16–36.

2008 Uneven Development: Nature, Capital, and the Production of Space. Athens: University of Georgia Press.

Soukup, Martin

2010 Anthropology in Papua New Guinea: History and Continuities. Anthropologia Integra 1(1):45–54.

Specht, Jim, and John Fields
1984 Frank Hurley in Papua: Photographs of the 1920–1923 Expeditions. Bathurst, NSW: R. Brown and Associates in Association with the Australian Museum Trust.

Stasch, Rupert
2011 Textual Iconicity and the Primitivist Cosmos: Chronotopes of Desire in Travel Writing About Korowai of West Papua. Journal of Linguistic Anthropology 21(1):1–21.

Stedman, Leanne
1997 From Gidget to Gonad Man: Surfers, Feminists, and Postmodernism. Australia and New Zealand Journal of Sport 33(1):75–90.

Steiner, Michael C.
1995 From Frontier to Region: Frederick Jackson Turner and the New Western History. Pacific Historical Review 64 November:479–501.

Stella, Regis Tove
2007 Imagining the Other: The Representation of the Papua New Guinean Subject. Honolulu: University of Hawai'i Press.

Strathern, Andrew, ed.
1982 Inequality in New Guinea Highlands Societies. Cambridge: Cambridge University Press.

Strathern, Marilyn
1988 The Gender of the Gift: Problems with Women and Problems with Society in Melanesia. Berkley: University of California Press.

Sullivan, Sian
2013 Banking Nature? The Spectacular Financialisation of Environmental Conservation. Antipode 45(1):198–217.

Swadling, Pamela
1996 Plumes of Paradise: Trade Cycles in Outer Southeast Asia and Their Impact on New Guinea and Nearby Islands Until 1920. Port Moresby: Papua New Guinea National Library.

Taussig, Michael
2000 The Beach (A Fantasy). Critical Inquiry 26(2):248–278.

Taylor, Monique M.
2002 Harlem: Between Heaven and Hell. Minneapolis: University of Minnesota Press.

Tcherkezoff, Serge
2003 A Long and Unfortunate Voyage Toward the Invention of the Melanesia-Polynesia Distinction, 1595–1832. Journal of Pacific History 38(2):175–196.

Teaiwa, Teresia K.
2006 Rethinking the Pacific in a Global Context. Contemporary Pacific 18(1):71–87.

Tengan, Ty P. Kāwika
2008 Native Men Remade: Gender and Nation in Contemporary Hawai'i. Durham: Duke University Press.

Tengan, Ty P. Kāwika, Tēvita O. Ka'ili, and Rochelle Tuitagava'a Fonoti, eds.
2010 Genealogies: Articulating Indigenous Anthropology in/of Oceania. Special issue of Pacific Studies 33(2–3).

Trask, Haunani-Kay
1987 The Birth of the Modern Hawaiian Movement: Kalama Valley, O'ahu. Hawaiian Journal of History 21:126–153.
1993 From a Native Daughter: Colonialism and Sovereignty in Hawai'i. Honolulu: University of Hawai'i Press.
1994 Kupa'a 'Aina: Native Hawaiian Nationalism in Hawai'i. In Hawai'i: Return to Nationhood. Ulla Hasager and Jonathan Friedman, eds. Pp. 243–260. Copenhagen: International Work Group for Indigenous Affairs.
1999 From a Native Daughter: Colonialism and Sovereignty in Hawai'i. Honolulu: University of Hawai'i Press.

Trouillot Michel-Rolph
1991 Anthropology and the Savage Slot. In Recapturing Anthropology: Working in the Present. Pp. 17–44. Santa Fe, NM: SAR.

Tsing, Anna
2004 Friction: An Ethnography of Global Connection. Princeton: Princeton University Press.

Tuhiwai Smith, Linda
1999 Decolonizing Methodologies: Research and Indigenous Peoples. London: Zed.

Tumarkin, D. D.
1993 Miklouho-Maclay and the Perception of the Peoples of New Guinea in Russia. Pacific Studies 16(1):33–42.

Turner, Dale
2006a This Is Not a Peace Pipe: Towards a Critical Indigenous Philosophy. Toronto: University of Toronto Press.
2007 What Is Native American Philosophy?: Towards a Critical Indigenous Philosophy. In Philosophy in Multiple Voices. G. Yancy, ed. Pp. 197–217. Lanham, MD: Rowman and Littlefield.

UNDP (UN Development Program)
2009 Capacity Development: A UNDP Primer. New York: UNDP.

UNWTO (UN World Tourism Organization)
2011 2010 International Tourism Results and Prospects for 2011. http://mkt.unwto .org/sites/all/files/pdf/unwto_hq_fitur11_jk_1pp.pdf accessed January 25, 2016.

Urry, J.
2002 The Tourist Gaze. 2nd Ed. London: Sage.

Verity, Fiona
2007 Community Capacity Building: A Review of the Literature. Report for the South Australian Department of Health, Flinders University of South Australia.

Viveiros de Castro, Eduardo
2003 And: After-Dinner Speech Given at Anthropology and Science, the 5th Decennial Conference of the Association of Social Anthropologists of the UK and Commonwealth, 2003. Manchester Papers in Social Anthropology, University of Manchester.
2004a Exchanging Perspectives: The Transformation of Objects Into Subjects in Amerindian Ontologies. Common Knowledge 1(3):463–484.
2004b Perspectival Anthropology and the Method of Controlled Equivocation in Tipití. Journal of the Society for the Anthropology of Lowland South America 2(1):3–22.
2014 Cannibal Metaphysics. Minneapolis, MN: Univocal Publishing.

Waiko, John Dademo
2007 A Short History of Papua New Guinea. Oxford: Oxford University Press.

Walker, Isaiah Helekunihi
2008 Hui Nalu, Beachboys, and the Surfing Boarder-lands of Hawai'i. Contemporary Pacific 20(1):89–113.

Wallace, Alfred R.
1880 Island Life. London: Macmillan.

Wardlow, Holly
2004 Anger, Economy, and Female Agency: Problematizing "Prostitution" and "Sex Work" Among the Huli of Papua New Guinea. Signs 29(4):1017–1040.

Warrior, Robert Allen
1992 Intellectual Sovereignty and the Struggle for an American Indian Future. Wicazo Sa Review 8(1):1–20.
1994 Tribal Secrets: Recovering American Indian Intellectual Traditions. Minnesota: University of Minnesota Press.

Warshaw, Matt
2004 The Encyclopedia of Surfing. Camberwell, VIC: Viking Penguin.
2010 The History of Surfing. San Francisco: Chronicle Books.

Weedon, Chris
1987 Feminist Practice and Poststructuralist Theory. Oxford: Basil Blackwell.

Weiss, Gabriele
2012 From the Pacific: A Passionate Collector—F. H. Otto Finsch (1839–1917). Vienna: Museum of Ethnology.

West, Paige
2005a Holding the Story Forever: The Aesthetics of Ethnographic Labor. Anthropological Forum 15(3):267–275.

2005b Translation, Value, and Space: Theorizing an Ethnographic and Engaged Environmental Anthropology. American Anthropologist 107(4):632–642.

2006 Conservation Is Our Government Now: The Politics of Ecology in Papua New Guinea. Durham: Duke University Press.

2008 Scientific Tourism: Imagining, Experiencing, and Portraying Environment and Society in Papua New Guinea. Current Anthropology 49(4):597–626.

2012 From Modern Production to Imagined Primitive: The World of Coffee from Papua New Guinea. Durham: Duke University Press.

West, Paige, Daniel Brockington, and James Igoe
2006 Parks and Peoples: The Social Effects of Protected Areas. Annual Review of Anthropology 20(3):609–616.

West, Paige, and James G. Carrier
2004 Getting Away from It All? Ecotourism and Authenticity. Current Anthropology 45(4):483–498.

2010 Surroundings, Selves, and Others: The Political Economy of Environment and Identity. Landscape Research 34(2):157–170.

West, Paige, and Enock Kale
2015 The Fate of Crater Mountain: Forest Conservation in the Eastern Highlands of Papua New Guinea. *In* Forests of Oceania: Environmental Histories, Present Concerns, and Future Possibilities. J. Bell, P. West, and C. Filer, eds. Canberra: Australian National University Press.

Wheaton, Belinda
2005 Selling Out? The Commercialization and Globalization of Lifestyle Sport. *In* The Global Politics of Sport: The Role of Global Institutions in Sport. Lincoln Allison, ed. Pp. 140–161. London: Routledge.

White, Richard, and Patricia Nelson Limerick
1995 The Frontier in American Culture. Berkeley: University of California Press.

Wills, John E.
2007 Journeys Mostly to the West: Chinese Perspectives on Travel Writing. Huntington Library Quarterly 70(1):191–201.

Wurtzel, Elizabeth
1999 Bitch: In Praise of Difficult Women. New York: First Anchor Books.

2001 Radical Sanity. New York: Random House.

2013 My One Night Stand of a Life. New York Magazine. January 14.

Young, Michael W.
2004 Malinowski: Odyssey of an Anthropologist, 1884–1920. New Haven: Yale University Press.

Index

GPSR Authorized Representative: Easy Access System Europe, Mustamäe tee
50, 10621 Tallinn, Estonia, gpsr.requests@easproject.com